CONTENTS

The Great
Wine Swindle

Malcolm Gluck

gibson square
London

This is book is dedicated to CVV,
who was it progenitor.

This edition first published in by

Gibson Square

UK Tel: +44 (0)20 7096 1100
       Fax: +44 (0)20 7993 2214

US Tel: +1 646 216 9813
       Fax: +1 646 216 9488

Eire Tel: +353 (0)1 657 1057

info@gibsonsquare.com
www.gibsonsquare.com

ISBN 9781906142360

THE GREAT WINE SWINDLE

The world of wine is populated by liars, scroungers and cheats. It is administered by mountebanks. It runs on misrepresentation and ritualised fraud. Wine drinkers are duped by wine producers, wine merchants, wine waiters, and wine writers.

How did the essentially pastoral pastime of turning grapes into alcohol become corrupted like this? The reasons are simple, six stand out, and they are incorrigible.

1. Wine, unlike all other products, is not uniform. It is unstable. It is badly packaged. Wine is a different product each vintage, it changes in the bottle over time, and if that bottle is sealed with a cork no guarantee can be given of the state of the contents.

2. Wine is easily manipulated into a status symbol. This allows many producers, merchants and restaurateurs spectacularly to overcharge for their products and myths to be created with no substance. These myths are nurtured by many wine writers. This situation also creates a fervent breeding ground for the pest known as The Wine Educator or Expert who wishes only to bamboozle the laity by peddling the jargon of his/her perceived expertise. Wine is the only everyday product which most of its users believe so complex that one must pass an advanced driving test in order to steer one's way through it. Yet who knows more about wine, who understands anything more vital, than the ordinary consumer who can honestly say, in defiance of any self-serving expert's pomposity, that 'I know what you do not; I know what I like'?

3. Wine, unsurpassed by any other consumer product, is surrounded by legal and administrative blather which dupes the drinker. It is akin to religious heresy, for example, to deny the divinity of certain vineyards in Europe which have the full force of

regulations to protect their reputations whatever the quality of the wines they produce.

4. Wine writers and wine producers are twin cheeks of the same backside. This elegant posterior is not only seen in countries where wine is produced (Australia, South Africa, New Zealand, and in Europe) it is also the case in Britain where the lackey-culture abounds. The truly independent wine writer is a myth, a fantasy, an impossible creation. S(he) does not exist. Unsophisticated people posing as wine writers morph into being servants of the corporate wine culture and become no better than public relation executives. We wine writers have to make a living or starve. We could drive buses or tube trains for a living but we are bribed to keep drinking. We pretend, as we swig our free samples, that all is for the best in this best of all possible worlds.

5. It is assumed, without thinking (by wine drinkers), that everyone involved with the production of wine and its marketing, and importantly, its publicity by wine writers, is graced with an immaculate palate. This is untrue. Some people involved with wine can barely discern chalk from cheese. Some cannot even tell white wine from red.

6. The world-wide wine industry, obsessed with succeeding in the UK where the bargain culture abounds, is forced to cut corners to meet supermarket and wine chain profit margins. The only forces that can reckon with such retail colossi, and dictate something like their own terms, are major wine conglomerates like Constellation and E&J Gallo. Just as retail choice has shrunk in the UK because of the disappearance of so many wine shops and chains (and supermarkets like Safeway), so the wine producers have been forced to amalgamate and lose their individuality. Some wine makers who have built up a reputation as mavericks, like Bruce Jack in South Africa, now lend personality to large company brands. Others, like Brent Marris in New Zealand, sell out a family business for a fortune in order – their spell of corporate bondage over – to start up afresh as a personal entity. Thus, what was once a cottage industry

is now an international corporate force, with unfriendly accounting methods predicated on shareholder income, and this has further eroded quality, quirkiness and choice. This force is not interested in good wine only wine which can be manufactured at a certain cost, it is not devoted to sustainable viticulture or organics, and it encourages uniformity and blandness.

There are many other things which make the world of wine irresistibly exploitable for those who enjoy power, money and the trappings of superficial celebrity, and we will, dear reader, uncover them all as we journey together through these pages. My intention is not to spoil what can be a sublime experience. For wine is, at the level of an everyday beverage conferring health and well-being, a delightful adjunct to a civilised, thoughtful, relevant existence.

My intention is to empower. It seems a strange, not to say perverse, thing to say but after I had written my first wine columns nearly twenty years ago in the *Guardian* newspaper, to the shock and horror of other wine critics who seethed at the impiety of my appointment (more of these arrogant snobs later), and readers flocked in their tens of thousands to plunder the shelves of my recommendations, I felt a profound sense of unease. I dislike power, abhor competitiveness, mistrust the expert.

This book is an expiation of those initial misgivings as they have ripened with mature reflection. One day I was a sceptical wine drinker, with a vast number of wines under his belt. The next day I was a wine writer with a vast number of readers in his parish. Until now, I have held my tongue. It is now time to loosen it; for the skeletons to be uncupboarded, the worms in the bud to be fumigated, the dubieties of the wine world to be shown up. Nothing manures vines likes bullshit. As we uncover the latter, the fragrance will, I promise you, be highly entertaining.

1

OUT AND OUT WINE CHEATS

Is that a chardonnay? Or is it just a müller-thurgau
that's been mucked about with?

At Waiheke Island ferry terminal there to meet me is local winemaker Chester Nichols. This was some years ago now (and Chester's gone to work elsewhere in New Zealand) but I've never forgotten the meeting. Chester's red for the Obsidian label, from cabernet sauvignon, merlot, cabernet franc and malbec grapes was, for one vintage at least (in my limited experience), not your average pretentious gargle of Waiheke gunge.

On the short drive from the ferry terminal to the vineyard we discuss the scandal of a few years back when a well-known Kiwi wine maker, Kim Crawford, was rumbled turning müller-thurgau grapes into chardonnay when he worked for the winery Cooper's Creek (whose family owner, the Hendrys, have a share in Obsidian). Chester, his myriad freckles seeming to dance on his features as he drives in the UV-saturated sunlight, is most eloquent on the matter.

'What that winemaker did other wineries in New Zealand have done many times. Anyone can add müller-thurgau to chardonnay and get away with it. A bit of malolactic [fermentation] on a müller-thurgau and you've got a nice little chardonnay. Better than clone 5 or 6 chardonnay any day. That winemaker made a better wine than he could have done using chardonnay alone in that vintage.'

We clatter down a slope to the vineyard.

'Okay, the public was being misled but not being cheated,' he adds.

Interesting, very refreshing, point. The chardonnay grape is a somebody: fashionable, expensive, and so trendy that it's become an international brand grape in its own right to the extent that drinkers ask for it by name. Müller-thurgau (also known as rivaner) is a nobody grape variety: no-one outside of wine nerds have heard of it and no-one, its growers apart, knows, or cares, that it is a grape grown in Germany, Luxembourg, England, Switzerland, Italy and, yes, New Zealand (where only as recently as 1992 did it lose its 'widely-planted' designation).

If only new world producers didn't make such a song and dance about the grape variety on the label, and labelled their wines as they do in Europe, there would be no malpractice. True, certain European wine laws permit only specified varieties to be added, but labels (until recently) rarely made any reference to grapes, with the exception of Alsace, preferring to emphasise the vineyard or some other conceit of the producer.

The winery referred to above, Cooper's Creek (which has made some of the pleasantest Kiwi wines I've ever tasted) was, for a short time, notorious for mislabelling and blending malpractices. An investigation carried out under the auspices of management consultants Ernst and Young showed that certain wines from the 1995 and 1996 vintages, though labelled Cabernet Sauvignon, Chardonnay and Sauvignon Blanc did not contain the 85% minimum (of each stated variety) required by law for export bottles. Sauvignon contained too much of other varieties: semillon, chardonnay unacceptable levels of chenin blanc (which also contained wine from a previous vintage in spite of being labelled as single vintage 1995). What was the New Zealand wine industry's reaction to Cooper's Creek owner's misdemeanours?

Since Mr Andrew Hendry, the owner in question, was vice-chairman of the Exporter's Association it was in an embarrassing position (and perhaps took a lenient view because, and I speculate, a number of other members had done exactly the same thing as Cooper's Creek). Mr Hendry was required to resign from the Association, Cooper's Creek winemaker Kim Crawford left (and took an unfair share of the blame), and wine regulations were changed. Kiwi producers now have to make statutory declarations that all export wines contain the legal levels of grape varieties stated on the label (which can itself be a lie, as we will see later). This is, however, self-regulation and guarantees nothing.

Doctoring can do wonders for a wine

Never forget that in Europe it is still legal to add sugar to increase alcohol levels though the EU has made loud noises in a pretence to outlaw it. I have long believed that all such chaptalised wines – as sugar-added wines are called – should have to declare the fact on their labels as they must, by law, state sulphuring. For decades the French have yelled from the rooftops about *terroir* – unique geographic origin, in short – and how it is sacred, yet adding sugar, derived from beet, not only destroys typicity but can wreck style and turn origin topsy-turvy. Andrew Barr, erstwhile 1990s wine correspondent, in his book *Wine Snobbery* (1988) wrote: 'I have identified wines from their beetrooty smell as burgundies which have turned out to be heavily chaptalised clarets... I remember being one of a tasting group where we all unhesitatingly identified a 1968 claret, Domaine de Chevalier, as burgundy.' Pamela Vandyke Price, in her book *Enjoying Wine* (1982), reports of tasting Château Palmer 1958, a heartily chaptalised wine, with its part-owner Allan Sichel and the latter crying out 'Can't you smell it – can't you smell the beet?'

The practice of falsifying the origin, or the type, of the grapes in a wine, however, is out-and-out fraud and it is not always so easily detected by even the most experienced of noses.

Vins de médecin, as they are called in France, were wines from Algeria (and when that source of beefy reds dried up, it was the Rhône and Languedoc) added to bordeaux and burgundy to provide colour, weight, and alcohol. Until France lost Algeria in 1962 it was said that many burgundies were as much the Algerian variety carignan (also grown widely in France) as they were local pinot noir. Much more recently, Spanish and Midi reds, and in some cases whites, were being smuggled into some of the most famous area names of Burgundy.

This is wholly against French wine laws and when, as happened now and then, perpetrators were caught they were jailed. But most of the time a blind eye was turned to it. The climates in Bordeaux and Burgundy were, until global warming got into the act, only rarely of a sunny disposition at the right time. In poor vintages sugar had to be added to the fermenting wine to bolster the alcohol. But some crooked producers went further and doctored the wine with wines from outside the region in flagrant disregard of the laws of Appellation d'Origine Contrôlée (AOC) that guarantee the provenance and composition of all French wines made under AOC rules.

This practice to a great extent went into decline, or perhaps failed to be detected, by the mid-1970s. There were some Bordeaux growers in 1970 who were discovered to have added reds from the hot Mediterranean littoral to give their feeble ferments more backbone but hardly any scandal. The big deterrent to the *vins de médecin* vat-side manner arrived in 1973 in the shape of the Henri Cruse company, one of the oldest and most highly-regarded wine shippers in Bordeaux, which was found to have given wines claiming wholly to be local a surreptitious boost of Spanish reds from the Rioja region. The company was caught, convicted, and rather than slapped on the wrist it was fined so swingeingly it went bankrupt.

One other way to doctor a wine, to beef it up, is of course via its barrels or, if this is considered too expensive, then with the use of oak chips or oak staves or even, disgusting though it sounds, oak powder. The three latter practices are widespread in winemaking circles, not only because oak aging is very expensive but also time consuming. To properly barrel-age a wine in new oak, let us say 4000 cases of red wine, costs approximately £100,000 or 50p a bottle. Using oak chips costs 0.020p a bottle and bunging in oak dust runs up a bill of a mere 0.0036p a bottle. (I have been unable to work out a figure for oak staves but it is likely to be marginally more expensive than chips.) The argument, then, for bypassing proper barrel aging and taking short cuts, to any financial manager or economy-minded winemaker, is compelling. Not for nothing has French new barrel output, from French oak forests, fallen by over 20% since 2002 when the use of oak additives became so popular in Europe after having been pioneered in the new world.

As Francisco Baettig, chief winemaker at prominent Chilean producer Errazuriz, said in October 2007: 'Everyone's using chips and staves for cheaper wines but they don't want to talk about it – producers are afraid of what journalists and consumer think...' (*Harpers Magazine*).

Can I claim the Vat back on my anti-freeze, please?

Modern wine adulteration scandals got off to a dizzily comic start with the Austrian affair of 1985. A handful of unscrupulous producers used diethylene glycol, more commonly known as anti-freeze, to sweeten their wines so as to bring them into a higher price bracket than they could attain naturally. They were only rumbled when one of the hapless gang, one Siegfried Tschida, had the chutzpah, and stupidity, to declare, for tax purposes, his purchase of the glycol. An alert revenue inspector, perhaps a wine lover, wondered what does a wine maker want with that chemical? The bunch ended up in jail, some five million litres of adulterated wine went down the drain, and the Austrian wine industry was damaged for two decades. Even today I still find the odd long-memoried person, when I offer her a glass of sublime grüner-veltliner (the native white grape of Austria), responding with 'Oh! Is it safe to drink?' I suspect that had not the really stupid producer, Herr Tschida, perhaps been forced to flee the country after his release to escape the wrath of his fellows or maybe to change his name and go into hiding, that he could, knowing the Austrian sense of humour, have managed a career as a stand-up comedian. Not that such humour crosses the immediate border, as Germans were unamused subsequently to find, following the Austrian scandal, that some German wines were tainted with the illegal additive thus exposing the hitherto obscured fact that Austrian wine was blended with German but labelled as the latter.[1]

The US Bureau of Alcohol, Tobacco and Firearms reported that one Austrian import had a very worrying level of an illegal substance and was toxic. The wine was Golden Castle Frauenkirchner Burgenland-Rust-Neusiedlersee Beerenauslese 1983, shipped by Gold-Kastell Weinkellereiges of Schermbeck in Rhine/Westphalia (Germany).

The Bureau analysed over imported 800 wines, and discovered that 58 had been sweetened with diethylene glycol. As well as those from Austria and Germany, eight originated from Italy. A little anti-freeze goes a long way. It even reached the UK. In September 1986, a wine distributor in Leamington Spa (a subsidiary of the now defunct Safeway supermarket group) was fined £500 for offering two glycol-contaminated wines for sale.

There is an element of the situation-comedy about such scandals. But there is none with the Italian debacle of 1987 when 23 people died after drinking wine containing another anti-freeze component methyl, or methanol, an alcohol derived from wood. The Italian scandal led to a dramatic drop in Italian wine and vermouth exports in 1986, falling nearly 36% in one year. In 1988 there was the Muscadet scandal when the Martin-Jarry company was alleged to have used wine from Bordeaux to help fake the local product and sell it as genuine Appellation Muscadet Côntrolée. But then, as the famous Châteauneuf-du-Pape producer, Louise Reynaud remarked, 'appellation côntrolée is a guarantee of mediocrity.' (For which I am grateful to author Andrew Barr, quoted above, for bringing to my attention.)

The Germans went in for wine fraud in a big way in the early 1980s when, following a change in 1971 to wine laws banning the outright use of sugar additions to wine, some 2500 producers were found to be breaking the law and were prosecuted. The most prominent law-breaker was the former president of the Viticultural Association, Werner Tyrell.

The most expensive English wine ever made (or faked)

There was even a small English wine scandal in the mid 1990s. The owner of Porthallow Vineyard near Helston in Cornwall, Edward Jeffries, used a home wine kit to knock up some wines which he passed off as genuine vineyard red and white. The Falmouth magistrate took a dim view of the deception and demanded from Mr Jeffries £6000 in fines and costs. A minor incident perhaps but at least you now know the answer to the question who made the most expensive English wine ever?

The Italians are dab hands at wine frauds. Fake Chianti one year, vintage 2000, to the later scandal involving exporting cheap stuff dressed up as something pricier. The liquid came from the south of Italy but it was bottled in Tuscany. Using renowned producers names as well as inventing non-existent wineries, the famous names faked were Chianti and Brunello di Montalcino in Tuscany as well as Barolo, Barbera and Amarone in the north. Poggio San Paolo and Bricco dell'Uccellone were two highly regarded producers whose names were used and passed off as genuine.

According to Inspector De Filippi from an Italian police unit responsible for forgeries: 'The wine was sold outside Italy because it was more difficult for foreigners to know if a certain winery existed or not.' It involved 10,000 cases of wine and the scam only came to light when an Italian tourist in Holland saw a bottle of Barolo, where he came from himself, and did not recognise the name of the producer. That was in 2004. It took two years to unravel the scam because the labelling was managed out of Italy and such being the level of bureaucratic deception involved (including not only the labels but fake government seals authenticating the origin of the wines) it made things very complex and difficult to police. To date, two wine estates have been sequestered by the authorities along with 128,000 gallons of wine and seven people await trial at time of writing.

Such being the level of attempted wine fraud in Italy (the world's biggest exporter of wine let us not forget), and extent of the traffic in fake Italian wine, that in 2007 twenty five police in the national *Carabinieri* undertook sommelier courses, at an academy in Rome. They qualified, in other words, as wine waiters. These special cops, working for the relevant Italian government ministry, will also liaise with the anti-fraud officials at the European Commission.

They are, without doubt, traffic cops with long noses. Not that those organs of smell need to be super-sensitive. The difference between a fake Bricco dell'Uccellone wine and the real thing would be, I imagine, considerable but we are not discussing taste here but appearance. Colonel Pasquale Muggeo, of this cop shop of wine, was reported as saying that his men's training quickly bore fruit, unmasking fake Brunello and Barbaresco on sale in Germany and Denmark.

According to the website decanter.com another Italian agricultural police force, the Corpo Forestale dello Stato, in early 2007 investigated 'wineries in the provinces of Ravenna and Bologna, as well as in the Piedmont, Veneto and Friuli Venezia Giulia regions.' They uncovered fake pinot grigio, prosecco and pinot nero (pinot noir).

In October 2005, rather less spectacularly but interesting as typical of the Italian attitude to fakery, the Italian fraud police impounded well over nine million bottles (70,000 hectolitres) of wine claiming to be Chianti Classico at the Constellation Brands-owned winery, Ruffino, in Tuscany. The supplier of the wine, one Piero Conticelli, was alleged to have used grapes not grown in official Chianti Classico vineyards to create fake Classico wine. Hardly an earth-shattering fraud you may say, and indeed the wine might well have been good to drink. You might also point out that scandals like this only highlight the idiocy of regional differentiation which can stand in the way of a superior product being produced. But wine is an agricultural product, not Coca-Cola, and provenance, whatever its idiocies (and especially if it is trumpeted as meaningful), stands for something. If the rules are flouted, and better wines emerge, then that is evidence for the stupidity of the rules. However, applying the letter of the law, it is also fraud.

In 2000, someone in Tuscany (you just can't leave the Italians out of any wine fraud can you?) found a cache of sixteen hundred cases of wine purporting to be Sassicaia 1995. This is a so-called Super-Tuscan, once wonderful but now a pretentious luxury rarity, and faking the stuff was an employee of the producer, flogging it not quite off the back off a lorry but certainly from the back hatch of his company Peugeot. Maybe the suckers who got done thought the fact they were dealing with a Sassicaia representative was proof against fraud. I suspect, though, that the thought never entered their heads. (Perhaps not even after they tasted the wine.) The 1995 vintage of Sassicaia will cost you around £86 a bottle in a posh London wine merchant's.

The accident of the van in the night
Wine fraud is rife and often only comes to light by accident (as with the Barolo tourist above). A few years back I recall a French wine person, swearing me never to reveal his name, telling me of the incident when a truck was stopped by a gendarme on a motorbike for speeding and found to have a cargo of wine emanating from Bergerac, in the Perigord region, but which claimed to be from Bordeaux. Or as it the other way round? Alas, I cannot now recall the details of this as I was not allowed to make notes and the French wine person and I were engaged in activities not conducive to recall. I assume the speed cop was not the one who uncovered the dark side of the truck driver's employer's activities.

In 1990s, Château Giscours, a second brand from a prestigious Margaux vineyard, was ratted on by an employee with a grudge. The company was up to all sorts of dubious practices including using wood chips instead of genuine barrel aging, adding far more sugar than was legally allowed, and blending into its mid-label brand, La

Sirène de Giscours, wine from an adjacent but ineligible vineyard (Haut-Medoc). Not that any taster had spotted these irregularities at any tasting. The wine tasted as good, or as bad, as it was expected to be. But for the existence of an individual who felt hard done by, and revealed the truth, the wine would, one assumes, still be on sale. Château Giscours was found guilty of fraud in court. Sympathetic, and perhaps echoing the sentiments of many people in the UK wine industry, the UK wine trade magazine *Harpers* commented, that: 'Many of the 'wicked' things that cellar staff at Château Giscours are alleged to have perpetrated are no more than good, acceptable practices in other parts of the world.' That may be true, but a swindle is a swindle and the magazine's *laissez faire* attitude – doubtless echoed by many European winemakers – is hardly discouragement to the latter to indulge in exactly the same fraud.

In 2002, French police mounted a huge campaign against fakers of bordeaux and raided more than ten chateaux in the region. Another scandal around the same time related to the activities of a Belgian-owned business with vineyards in Languedoc. It was using wine from these vineyards and exporting it as Margaux and Pétrus, highly prized Bordeaux chateaux whose products sell for hundreds of pounds a bottle. There is, in fact, no end to such wine fraud and some experts – whatever that means – estimate that around 5% of so-called 'fine' wine on sale in export markets, especially the far East, may be fake.

The Languedoc is the major source of inspiration for the modern French con artist. The most prominent of recent cases was that concerning Jacques Hemmer, a wine merchant who falsified Bordeaux 1997 and 1998 using wine from the Languedoc-Roussillon. The Institut National des Appellations d'Origine (INAO), the body overseeing French wine laws, and five Bordeaux wine dealers (CVBG, aka Dourthe, Kressman and Delor, Cordier/Mestrézat, Dulong, Ginestet and GVG) brought a case against Monsieur Hemmer for fraud. 400,000 bottles of fake wine were involved all of which had been sold to these dealers as genuine claret. In May 2002, the case came to trial and Jacques Hemmer was sentenced to 18 months in jail and fined several hundred thousand Euros.

In the case of Bernard Grivelet, a Burgundy shipper who in 2001 sold as local produce magnums (2 bottles in 1) and Jeroboams (4 bottles in 1) of burgundy into which wine from elsewhere had been insinuated, I have been unable to discover exactly where 'elsewhere' was. Does it matter? What he sold, however, was not burgundy. It was a regional blend.

Some burgundy malpractices pass as hardly worth noting, it seems. The Hospices de Beaune label, for example, once admitted to adding both sugar, to increase alcohol, and acid, for balance, to some 1997 vintage burgundies. It is only legal to add one or the other, not both. The Hospices, one of the greatest names in Burgundy, broke the law. The fraudsters are duping those who enjoy paying through the nose for liquid they do not possess the ability to assess as genuine.

Just taste that premier cru *glue on the label*

The easiest folk to diddle are those who drink labels rather than liquids. In 2002, some crafty beggar steamed off labels of bottles of Château Lafite from the much less-well-regarded (and consequently much cheaper) vintage of 1991 and stuck on 1982 labels and put the wine on sale in China. The 1982 goes for between £5000 to £6000 a case. The 1991 goes for a fifth of this. How many buyers knew the difference on the palate rather than in the pocket?

I myself unearthed a wine-label-steaming-off-scandal in 1979 when at an official celebratory dinner at the Café Royal in London at which I was a guest my host flamboyantly asked me to order something pricey from the restaurant's legendary list. I asked the waiter for two bottles of – and my memory here is not precise – something like 1955 Château Margaux. The bottles arrived suitably attired but examining both corks I was suspicious and smelling and tasting the wine it was obviously a much younger bordeaux from a lesser vintage and considerably less well-endowed vineyard. In vain, did I tell the management (the business had recently changed hands if I recall correctly) that someone had steamed off the labels of the '55 and affixed them to bottles of ordinary bordeaux and probably flogged the real stuff to someone in the know. My host, to avoid further embarrassment to the restaurant manager who was devastated by my assertions, paid for the wines and drank them.

As recently as the middle '90s, when visiting a large co-op near Brindisi in the heel of Italy, I was proudly informed by someone from the winemaking team (until he was hushed up by someone who belatedly realised that this was a journalist they were talking to, and not a wine buyer) that once a month a tanker arrived from Macon and filled up with red made from primitivo and negro amaro grapes. It crossed my mind that here was a scoop but no-one at the *Guardian* was interested in funding the acquisition of the evidence. (And I was not keen to camp outside the winery, disguised as an olive tree, waiting for the monthly visit of the French wine tanker which I would then follow all the way to its destination in burgundy.)

In 2005, allegations of wine fraud hit beaujolais. Who, you may ask, would bother to fake so largely foppish and spineless a wine? It involved the local wine hero, Georges Duboeuf, who, though claiming that it was a winemaker's error, was in July 2006 found guilty and had to pay the French authorities, a fine of somewhere around 25,000 Euros. It was, I suspect, no worse than sloppy winery management where *vins ordinaires* were simply getting mixed up with supposedly better stuff (i.e. from one of the so-called Cru Beaujolais areas like Brouilly or Morgon). Monsieur Duboeuf pointed out that the 200,000 bottles involved never even made it on sale but were winery stock. (The wine was eventually sold in bulk as Beaujolais-Villages.)

Not all scandals are French or Italian. In 1993, the Bronco wine company of California pleaded guilty to the charge of passing off as Zinfandel and Cabernet Sauvignon, grapes of less repute. The company was fined $2.5 million and its president, personally fined $500,000, had to resign. This company has subsequently been involved in labelling disputes regarding the use of the magic word Napa on a wine label when the grapes in the bottle have not originated from this region but have merely been bottled there.

In 2004, there was the KWV wine scandal in South Africa where two of this vast wine company's winemakers were rumbled trying to copy New Zealand sauvignon blanc by adding flavourants to the local product. The company fired the men responsible, Gideon Theron and Ian Nieuwoudt. Mr Theron was responsible for the Laborie Sauvignon Blanc (enhanced with a smidgen of green pepper extract) label and Mr Nieuwoudt for KWV Reserve Sauvignon (uplifted with a pinch of an aromatic compound called pyrazine). Sixty thousand litres of wine was involved and it was, though doubtless highly drinkable and quite capable of finding an overseas buyer, put down (literally dumped in a trench thus making a visible public gesture of contrition and regret).

This scandal was the first tangible evidence supporting the claim of local wine consultant and wine judge, Michael Fridjhon, that the addition of flavourants to South African sauvignon blanc was widespread. He has also said that blackcurrant flavouring is used in Cape cabernet sauvignon and butterscotch in Cape chardonnay. Wine correspondent of *Business Day*, South Africa's leading business paper, Mr Fridjhon wrote in November 2003 that '… some of SA's best-known winery supply companies openly offer for sale ranges of fake flavourant to give cabernet that more concentrated cassis aroma, or chardonnay that creamy butterscotch taste. No one in authority does anything meaningful to stop these mountebanks.'

Who is to know when a wine is not what it says on its label? It is not always apparent to any wine critic or taster. None of us is suf-ficiently talented, or experienced, to tell every single time. Only those who are steeped in the wines of a region know when something is not right. Or a lab carries out tests. In the instance of Michael Fridjhon we have an individual apparently able to suss the obvious. As he went on further to say in his 2003 *Business Week* article:

> ... this year... an extraordinary number of cellarmasters have managed to produce sumptuously tropical wines, redolent of gooseberries, pineapples and melon fruit salad... commentators wonder at the precision, richness and finesse... They point out that, compared with Sancerre in the Loire and Marlborough in New Zealand, our sauvignons are exposed to a shorter, hotter ripening season. They suggest that it is unlikely that these more opulent fruit flavours could be obtained naturally under such circumstances. Sauvignon blanc is particularly sensitive to the effect of heat during the few weeks prior to harvest. It should come as no surprise to discover that the world's finest sauvignons come from vineyards... where the grapes are harvested four to six weeks after the equinox. SA's recently acquired reputation for sauvignon so they contend arises either from astute vinification of substantially underripe fruit or from use of illegal flavourants, which more than compensate for whatever natural sauvignon character is scorched off in our short ripening season.

In the spring of 2007 I was the recipient of several emails from a source who wishes to remain unidentified. It accused Moldavan pinot grigio of being something else altogether. Pinot grigio, as a grape variety, is going the way of chardonnay. It is being asked for in wine bars and restaurants by name. The shape of the syllables as formed by female lips makes an elegant rather than a disdainful moue and the sound suggests the exotic. But how many pinot grigio drinkers are drinking something else altogether? In the instance of the Moldavan wine, it was suggested that sauvignon and traminer grapes were standing in for genuine pinot grigio.

This latter grape is, it seems, being accused of being faked all over the place. In July 2007, *Off-Licence News*, a UK drinks trade publication, quoting Trading Standards Institute estimates, reported that 'fake pinot-grigio could account for as much as 30% of wines in the retail sector.' The magazine went on to say that 'It is widely believed that some cheaper Italian pinot grigio is cut with less commercially acceptable varieties, and that some of the wines does not originate from Italy at all.'

Apparently, a certain supplier of pinot grigio remarked that 'there is more pinot grigio in the market that is produced, so something is a bit screwy somewhere.'

A UK wine merchant said to me that there is 'five times more pinot grigio in the UK said to be from the [Italian] Veneto than the region can produce.' He went on to make a further allegation: 'It surprises me that the supermarkets don't know this as it's possible for their labs, which monitor own-label products, to analyse a wine and discover its true origins.'

But why stop at pinot grigio? What about chardonnay (as touched on above)? Sauvignon blanc? Shiraz? Riesling? Cabernet sauvignon? Pinot noir? Nothing, no grape, is sacred to the forger.

'There have been wine scams for a long time and occasionally people get taken to court and put out of business,' said John Corbet-Milward, head of technical and international affairs at the UK's Wine & Spirit Trade Association in 2007. To which one can only retort indeed yes but that appearances in court are woefully few and far between.

One UK wine merchant said to me that 'Large companies are already shipping between sites.' In other words, certain people in the UK wine industry's supply chain are ignoring true origin, and no doubt true grape variety, in order to keep product coming through. If you manufacture a soft drink or a shampoo it is easy to fulfil orders, but wine is sold, at a hefty premium, on origin, vintage, and grape variety. All three, it seems, are very easy to fake.

Perhaps the biggest wine fraud of all, because of these pressures, is about to happen (or is taking place as I write) as a result of climate change. How will Australian major brand producers, like Yellow Tail, Hardys, Rosemount, and Penfolds, cope with the crippling drought which has seen the annual Aussie harvest fall from nearly 2-million tonnes to close to 1-million tonnes? They cannot underwrite the irrigation which would enable all the growers to grow the required tonnage to meet their needs for there is not enough water to go around and they cannot simply buy all the available Aussie grapes and let everyone else go out of business. They have to buy the grapes, or most likely the juice, elsewhere.

South American wine has been shipped into Australia for some time for reprocessing into cheap Aussie wines and, appropriately labelled with country of origin, has gone on totally legal sale in Australia only. Such imported wines might, however, be used for export wines. It would be illegal but what a temptation! If such skulduggery is not undertaken how will the big brands survive as major exports? Massive shareholder interests, bank loans, and capital investment in wineries is at stake. What would you do in the same circumstances? What would I do? We'd break the law and declare the law is an ass. If the wine is still fine to drink and priced humanely who is the loser? The answer is, of course, that the loser is the drinker and any integrity the wine trade may lay claim to is destroyed. The drinker, and any ignorant retailer who buys the stuff, is being comprehensively conned.

What I have just written is speculation, but I do know that during the Apartheid era South African grape juice was shipped to Eastern Europe and then sold on as Bulgarian red and white. Who needs to grow your own grapes at a cost of so many hundred or indeed thousand dollars a tonne when you can have it shipped thousands of miles by refrigerated tankers, the liquid kept fresh under a blanket of nitrogen gas, and pay a fraction of the cost for the same?

I have no doubt that major international wine conglomerates like Constellation, if they could legitimately do this, would already be doing it. The business logic of the transaction is as plain as the outsourcing of manufacture now routinely done by UK retailers and hardware companies (like Dyson etc). Who stops to wonder where her vacuum cleaner comes from? Who cares? But when it comes to wine we are bedevilled by country of origin.

The EU bureaucrats have already sanctioned the idea of cross border wines, why not cross world ones? Pinot grigio can be made anywhere. As long as it is pinot grigio, or tastes like it, most drinkers won't care – as long they don't have to pay more than a fiver a bottle.

Aussie shiraz *est mort*! *Vive le shiraz romanien ou bulgarien ou brazilien*. As long as it says Australian Shiraz on the label I can assure you it will be retailed, bought and drunk, and enjoyed.

One way to end one small crime

The solution is that the fakery should be taken out of the equation where grape varieties are concerned. No wine should be allowed to call itself by any single varietal name but one which, taking into account the producer's tastes, reflects the vineyard or anything else that satisfies that producer's interests. What is important is in the glass and if a wine is better for being cross-border blended, or even having stuff added (like resin with retsina, the Greek wine), then let it be openly declared on the label and we, the consumers, can make up our own minds. Do I mind if an Afrikaaner winemaker adds natural extract of green pepper to a sauvignon blanc? Not if the liquid is gorgeous. And not if it is clearly stated on the label and I pay very little for the bottle. But if a winemaker wants to impress us consumers with stellar flavours – and charge a premium – he should, like any Olympic athlete, avoid the chemicals that beef up what he can't achieve otherwise.

The wine industry is in a terrible muddle about this because it wants its cake and eat it. It wants, on one hand, always to pretend a wine is an artisanal product created from perfect varieties of grapes from a demarcated area. But when nature does not co-operate to the extent of allowing a vineyard to produce those grapes so that a typical or even acceptable wine is consistently produced, it wants to maintain the purity in name only and so is forced to be underhand and, in some cases, to go to criminal lengths.

The laws, then, need to be changed. But the laws won't. The world-wide wine industry is indolent, greedy, uncaring and unable to stop rogue winemakers and wine dealers, crooked wine merchants and wine exporters, from benefitting from the susceptibilities of the easiest duped fool on the planet: the consumer who does not know what s(he) is buying. And where wine is concerned, that consumer represents over 99% of the market. Wine is easily faked and not difficult to mislabel. It is a nightmare to police and the fact is that it is mainly accidents which bring the truth to light.

In my forty years of studious wine drinking I have, I reckon, happily guzzled a good few fake wines, proclaiming them marvellous, without being one wit the wiser or sorrier. If a wine tastes terrific, as Cooper's Creek for example always did, and the price is right, the drinker's pleasure is heightened not lessened. Perhaps if the UK's major supermarkets, who apply so much pressure to their suppliers to meet often absurdly low price points, stood in the dock alongside the winemaker who could only fulfil a re-order for chardonnay at its rock-bottom wholesale price by sneaking in an overdose of chenin or semillon grapes, then we might see the rules changed.

However, when an industry is dominated by bureaucratically entrenched dinosaurs change is always slow in coming and, most times, never arrives. It seems, then, that wine fraud, in all its myriad forms, will always be with us.

2

CROOKED WINE

Why that Cabernet Sauvignon isn't quite what it is says it is.

Earlier I quoted John Corbet-Milward, head of technical and international affairs at the UK's Wine & Spirit Trade Association. This was to do with fake pinot grigio. However, what Mr Corbet-Milward said further in this regard (as reported in *Off-Licence News*) is also applicable to the subject under review here: what is on the label is not what is in the wine.

But we are not discussing fakes here. We are talking in this chapter about wines which have the blessing of the authorities. Wines which say Three-Legged Dog Creek Cabernet Sauvignon on the label but which, as fully admitted on the back label (but rarely scrutinised by any but the most meticulous drinker), contains 2% shiraz, 4% merlot and 5% cabernet franc or whatever.

'The principle of the labelling regulation is that what's on the label has to reflect what's in the bottle,' said the worthy gentleman from the W&STA. 'The law enforcement people would certainly not turn a blind eye.'

Now it is true he is speaking here of fake wine, wine made not wholly from the grape variety stated on the label and as such illegal, but can he explain the difference between that and my fictitious Three Legged-Dog Creek Cabernet Sauvignon which, wholly within its region's wine laws and local wine trade and any importing regulations, is not cabernet sauvignon but only partially so?

If the principle of a labelling regulation — entirely logically and laudably — is to ensure what is on the label reflects what is in the bottle how can the state of affairs where anything goes be tolerated?

The shocking and utterly confusing truth is this: a wine

produced within the European Community can legally be labelled with one particular variety and yet contain up to 15% of other varieties (where these are permitted to be grown in the wine's region).

In some wine regions of Europe, the laws are far stricter. A red burgundy must be 100% pinot noir (unless it comes from the Irancy region where 5% of the grape called césar may be added) and only recently have the authorities permitted some lower-end burgundy producers to put the grape variety on the label. (Nonetheless, for years, in defiance of this law, much burgundy was anything but 100% pinot noir as mentioned in the previous chapter.)

Alsace has long had a tradition of putting a grape variety on each label – uniquely in France – but it was strictly understood that this implied 100% of the variety. A blend of varieties had to call itself something else (yesteryear it was 'Edelzwicker', nowadays it can be called 'Gentil d'Alsace'). In Germany, a 'Riesling' has to be 100% riesling to be so labelled. In Italy, a Barolo has to be exclusively from the nebbiolo grape.

But in Tuscany there was a change in 1984 to allow cabernet sauvignon, merlot and syrah to be blended with the local sangiovese grape and the wine still be allowed to call itself Chianti Classico. Such a wine to call itself thus must be a minimum of 75% sangiovese (and can include white varieties as well as the famous international red grapes). Rioja, in Spain, allows seven varieties of which the most famous, with the reds, is tempranillo. And so on.

Now all this is fine. We, the drinkers, know what we are getting (leaving aside the fraudsters who, though the wine may be deliciously drinkable, add unauthorised varieties undetectable to anyone or throw in wine imported from outside the region altogether). These wines' grape recipes, by not being specified on the label, can, if we are interested, only be found on the back label or, if not there, by reference to the merchants' list or the website of the producer.

It is in the New World that the problem of varietal labelling has got out of hand. By putting the grape prominently on the front we assume that it is this grape in the bottle. Certainly most drinkers assume this. Why, they tell me, would a wine say it is cabernet sauvignon on the label if it is not? Most of the time, it is true, they don't much care – as long as the wine is to their liking. But if anyone wishes to learn how a particular grape may taste, in a teaching environment or off their own bat by themselves, then the label confuses. In the sense of passing on anything which may reflect a single grape's characteristics it is of no value. Whatever its rating as a blend, its worth as a single varietal expression is nil.

Colonial copycats

So how is it that the practice is allowed? Blending is permitted by those who set wine laws because quite sensibly it can be bad business to rely on a single variety. Chateaux in Bordeaux, for example, may depend on half-a-dozen varieties, which ripen at different times, have varying resistances to disease, and together help create a wine. In this region the *chateaux* or *domaines* call their wines by a vineyard or other name. You cannot discover the grape varieties from the label. This principle stems from the French concept of the grape or grapes being the scaffolding of the wine and the vineyard being the architect. Who puts the name of the scaffolder on the finished building?

When vineyards in Australia, south and north America, New Zealand, South Africa and other places began planting vines and making wines their first attempts were often called after European models. There were commercial reasons for this but also egotistical ones. André Simon, in his 1966 book *The Wines Vineyards & Vignerons of Australia*, wrote of a Captain Elder who made a wine south of Adelaide in 1857 which 'he tried to market as Red Osmondeau'. But it was only when he called it 'Burgundy' did it sell. A century and a quarter later, however, and we find that if Aussie and other New World wines wished to go on sale anywhere in Europe they could not sport phony French or any other Eurocentric names. South African Hock and New South Wales Chablis bit the dust.

In typical parvenu fashion these newcomers could do only one thing to make themselves respectable and accepted. They could make reference to the families already established and recognised in Europe: the grape varieties. We may not be bordeaux, they said sheepishly, but we are cabernet sauvignon. We are not burgundy but we are pinot noir. We are not Chablis but we are chardonnay. And so it went.

Ironically, the success of New World wines, their overwhelming sales success against the old guard, has led not only to Europeans copying their success with anglophone names (Devil's Rock from Germany, Firebird from Moldova, Fat Bastard from France) but also to the popularity of varietal labelling.

Today, examples are legion and utterly misrepresentative and confusing. It is a mess that producers cynically use to exploit their consumers' trust. In January 2008, for example, I was tasting some of the latest offerings from the New Zealand producer Cooper's Creek. My taste buds, grappling with a so-called Hawkes Bay Merlot 2006, forced me to remark to its maker, Simon Nunns, that it was unusually savoury and surely it wasn't 100% merlot. He said the merlot actually contained 12% malbec. That accounts for the meatiness I said. But there was no mention of the malbec anywhere on the bottle. Why? Mr Nunns had a ready answer 'Hard sell malbec. So we just don't declare it.' Would it not have been more honest to label that wine Hawkes Bay Almost Merlot 2006?

I remember, some years ago, remarking to a Kiwi sauvignon blanc producer, famous for his wines, how aromatic and minerally cutting his wine was – even in years when these characteristics were not widely discernible in his region. After we had enjoyed several more glasses of his exquisite liquid, he tapped his nose and leaned across and spoke softly into my left ear.

'Keep it under your hat, Malcolm. But the secret of that sauvignon is the 2% riesling I added.'

I was initially, I admit, rather prudishly shocked. Having once used his wine in a tasting class as an example of highly individual and finely textured NZ sauvignon blanc, I and my students had been cheated — even though his adding the 2% riesling and withholding this information was not illegal in New Zealand. Then I was elated.

What a brilliant move on the part of the producer! I do believe that blending is one of the only truly creative areas of wine making (do not tolerate those sentimental clowns who claim winemaking is an art). This crafty New Zealander was inspired — his wine was all the better for the addition.

And yet he was perpetrating a fraud. His wine was not sauvignon blanc. It was sauvignon blanc and riesling. And it was a totally unnecessary fraud.

For decades we had to suffer amateur wine merchants, arrogant and intolerant of complaints, indifferent to genuine provenance, and lies were routine. Much of this old-boy network, staffed by those too dim to get into the army, too louche to tolerate the priesthood, and too scruffy to become estate agents, has now disappeared. We have instead superbly versatile and kindly merchants with exciting ranges and enticing prices. It is a trade more professional than it has ever been and yet reliant on the scam tactics of second-hand car salesmen. As practically all wines are blends, is it really too much to demand that wine producers straighten out their false labels?

3

PURE WINE

You thought your glass of wine contained just fermented grape juice?

In order to turn grapes into wine, not only has the fruit to be taken from a vineyard manipulated with chemicals (unless it is organic) but during the process of transformation from berry into vinous liquid, and from barrel or tank to bottle, all manner of other things, for better or worse, find their way into the wine. Pesticide, herbicide, and fungicide residues are bequeathed by the vineyard manager, although levels have dropped over the past two decades, and the vast majority of wines are, one hopes, well within government health guidelines. But who tests them? No-one. Supermarket own-label wines may be lab tested for such things before being put on sale, as such retailers have their own reputations to safeguard, but for other wines all retailers must depend upon their suppliers good will.

As far as fruits other than grapes turned into wine are concerned, however, we do have some recent figures. In September 2007 the annual report of the government's advisor, the Pesticide Residues Committee, reported that traces of pesticides were found in 70% of free fruit (and vegetables) for schools. According to the *Guardian* '1.7% – 60 samples of the 3,562 surveyed – had residues above the legally permitted limits.' However, the committee 'concluded that none of the residues was likely to harm school-children's health.' That's all right then.

But what about their parents and the complex cocktail of chemicals which is used on the grapes which go into the wines they drink? Wine berries are not raw fruit and since they go through a manufacturing process some chemicals are largely, but not wholly, eliminated. (In any case, many treatments intended for the vine vanish with weathering into the soil where they only bother earthworms and the like.)

Organic producers, who use no chemicals – though they may have recourse to natural treatments – grow purer grapes (which is far from saying making better wine). They believe the best fertiliser is the farmer's shadow on the soil (though they help by throwing on natural winery waste, pips and skins etc, and natural mulches). And they will eschew the enzymes many modern wine makers use to clarify the juice during the pressing of the grapes in order to ensure an easier ferment. This ferment, with the most pure-minded winemakers, is initiated by wholly natural processes, that is to say the yeasts naturally present on the skins of the grapes and in the winery. Other wineries will use a commercial yeast or they may claim to make a wild-yeast wine but this is a dubious distinction as once a winery has employed a commercial rather than a natural strain of yeast there is, to some extent, a mutation of the natural yeast rather than one wholly created in the vineyard. It may be that a wild-ferment wine is more complex, funkier, but unless the winery has never used anything but the yeasts naturally occurring on the skins of its grapes, the wine will reflect such yeast and not one which might be said to be unique to the vineyard or winery. (Any claim that yeast reflects the *terroir* of a vineyard is even more meaningless unless scrupulous organic or biodynamic farming principles are followed and even with these it is the winemaker who is responsible for the style of the wine not the vineyard unaided.)

When it comes to additives, wine is in a hallowed league of its own. It is different from all other foods in the European Community, and elsewhere in the world, in not being legally compelled to list its ingredients. Producers and marketeers have fiercely resisted the content labelling of wines to the extent that such a move is actually against regulations. The heavily French-influenced bureaucrats in Brussels have legislated to prevent content labelling of wines.

Yet many times the things in a bottle would never form part of anyone's idea of a nice tipple let alone one you would include as the liquid centre-piece of a candle-lit dinner. One major wine producing country and one of its largest markets, Australia and the European Community, established an agreement in 1994 on permitted additives and processing aids for winemaking and wine importing countries. The Australian Wine Research Institute's Analytical Service, as a guide to exporters, publishes a list with 40 or so chemicals that are okay, including bentonite, also used for cat litter. Far more extensive than this list, however, is the one revealed in a letter sent from the office of the Assistant Secretary (Enforcement and Operations) on July 26th 1983 to the Director-General for External Relations, at the Commission of the European Communities in Brussels. It contains over 60 chemicals that are allowable in wine production, including three different types of bentonite. This is somewhat startling information for someone to swallow who fondly imagined you made wine merely by pressing grapes and letting nature do the rest. But if the US likes to add things what about the South Africans? Their official list has 76 chemicals (for the Australian guide to permissible chemicals, and the official American and South African ones, see pages 274 and further below).

The dividend for shopping at the UK Co-op chain

The Australian, American and South African lists are largely the same all over the world, it has to be said, so these three countries are not exceptions. I know of only one retailer prepared to admit to using additives in its own-label wines. This is the UK Co-op.

The Co-op is the only retailer in the UK to defy EC diktat and put ingredients on the back label of all its own-label wines. As long as other wines in a retailer's range conform to all other regulations, it may not bother to enquire into the nature of any wine's manufacture or what its precise additives might be, sulphur apart. Sulphur has always to be indicated and it is always present as an essential preservative in very low amounts and it must say so on wine labels. Wines can be made (preserved) without sulphur but no high street chain or supermarket, as far as I know, has ever, or would ever, stock one. I have seen an unsulphured white wine, from a fanatical organic producer, start to turn horribly brown with thirty seconds of being poured out in much the same way a slice of apple, fresh cut, will pucker and darken within seconds of being exposed to the air.

It is normal now for any retailer to indicate whether a wine is suitable for vegetarians or vegans (i.e. no animal products, like egg whites or fish bladders or milk have been used in the wine's fining or clarification prior to bottling). The list of clearing agents as used by the Co-op suppliers is seventeen strong, used by wineries all over the world, and some are suitable for vegetarians and some are not. The Co-op appreciates, as I do, that there may be no residue of any clearing agent left in a wine (apart from gelatin, unsuitable for vegetarians, which can leave traces) but that it is clearly unethical not to list its use (see for their full list pages 274 and further).

Clearing agents also need to be filtered out of the wine before bottling and so a further degradation of the juice occurs here. As the clearing agents goes so will a degree, perhaps small but certainly significant, of the character of the wine. It is not relevant here to go into a discussion of how clarification may make wines more bland, but it is pertinent to any debate about organics and natural process wine production whose practitioners eschew fining and filtering. Many of the finest wines I have ever drunk have had particles and crystals in them, in some cases to the detriment of any notion of sharp clarity (especially with a white wine). Does this matter? Surely not if the wine is enhanced on the palate as a result.

Leaving such niceties aside, it is good manners for me to stress how forthcoming the Co-op has been in the matter of disclosing the nature of clearing agents used in its wines. The retailer has been extremely open in responding to my interest in this matter. It is an area in which, as an ethically minded retailer, they are deeply concerned.

In 2007, excluding its small so-called Fine Wine range the UK Co-op had 423 wines of which 125 were own-labels. This is 30% of the standard range and this, laudably, makes the Co-op one of the leading own-label wine retailers in the UK. The Co-op's statement on its additive stance and labelling reads as follows:

> It was in 1999 that the Co-op became the only retailer to label the ingredients in wine in support of its commitment to open and honest labelling. This move is technically illegal, but in the consumer's interest. The Co-op called on the Government to change the law and called upon the food industry to follow suit, but we continue to be the only retailer to provide such comprehensive information about ingredients. We always list all ingredients and items used in our beers and wines on the label, so if isinglass is used, it will always be included in the list of ingredients under the heading 'cleared using'. Even though it is not contained in the end product, we believe, that vegetarians have a right to know that Isinglass has been used in the production of the wine.

The EU seems only to be motivated to act on wine labelling when consumers' health is directly threatened. In 2005, the Co-op points out, the EU introduced new legislation on allergen labelling, under which allergens have to be indicated on both food and wine. However, this only covers allergens such as sulphur dioxide, but does not cover some of the other ingredients which the Co-op displays on its back labels. I offer the wording from two of these back labels below, as they appear on the bottle. In the case of the first wine it would be preferable that the filtration agent was named, but I assume if it were unacceptable to vegans or vegetarians it would say so. In a statement, the Co-op said to me: 'A list of wines produced with non-animal fining agents is available. Where we can guarantee that wines have been produced without animal finings we will indicate this on the label, using the vegetarian/vegan leaf symbol accompanied by the words – SUITABLE FOR VEGETARIANS or SUITABLE FOR VEGETARIANS & VEGANS.

Co-op Australian Red Wine

Ingredients: Grapes, Tartaric acid, Tannin, Preservatives (Sulphur dioxide, Sodium metabisulphite)
Made Using: Yeast, Yeast Nutrient (Diammonium phosphate), Potassium tartrates, Nitrogen, Copper sulphate.
Cleared using: Filtration

Co-op Fairtrade Argentine Reserva Malbec

Ingredients: Fairtrade Grapes (Malbec), tartaric acid, Preservatives (Sulphur dioxide, Potassium metabisulphite), Stabiliser (Tannin).
Made Using: Yeast, Antioxidants (Nitrogen, Carbon dioxide), Yeast nutrient (Diammonium phosphate), Stabiliser (Potassium hydrogen tartrate), Lactic bacteria.
Cleared using: Pectinolytic enzymes, Filtration.

I do not propose to add to this list the hundred and twenty more Co-op back labels we could examine. May I suggest you do this if you have the opportunity to visit this retailer? Whatever treatments Co-op own-label wines may have undergone, I can assert that many have sent shivers of delight down my palate. I refer to my tasting notes and I can find no reference to Polyvinylpolypyrrolidone or fish bladders discerned in any Co-op wine. It is important here, therefore, to make quite clear that none of the horrifyingly sourced, manufactured, and, in other guises, dangerous elements used in the making of many wines are toxic. In most cases they leave absolutely no trace of themselves.

What, then, is my gripe here? It is our ignorance, as drinkers, of the use of these agents and the attitude of the wine industry which does nothing about it since it does not side with the Co-op's refreshing and laudable stance. All agents used in the making of a wine should be declared by law on the back label and additives, even it is merely sugar to enhance the alcohol, should be printed double size. Wine is touted as a romantic, natural liquid. It is neither, seen in the light of the list of permissable additives (see pages 274 and further). Many wines are no more natural than any soft drink, and wineries should not be allowed to pretend they are.

One other reason to press for reform here is that I believe precise wine labelling would encourage the spread of honesty to the wine craft in the trade as well as give a boost to biodynamic vineyards and wineries, thus broadening choice to consumers. Consumers, reading the truth about the chemicals used to make wine would be able to differentiate between the various ways of producing wine. Depending on whether they mind finding crystals or other sedimentation at the bottom of their glass, for example, they would be able to choose accordingly – in the same as they choose orange juice with or without pulp.

4

VINES DO NOT MAKE
GREAT WINES

Official: Report of the Royal Economic Society

Terroir is the belief that the vineyards make wines great, not humankind. It is the biggest thing wine experts will tell you about. Yet vineyards grow only grapes. Let me explain the matter with a brief disquisition on the peach.

We can all, I think, accept that a peach grown in Provence will taste different, even if it was the same variety, as one grown in Tuscany. Indeed, we can prove it simply by eating one of each. Similarly, we know that the same variety of apple grown in Kent and Gloucester taste different, one from another. We can narrow it further, fruit connoisseurs maintain: a fruit grown in one orchard can taste different from the same fruit grown in an orchard a few miles away. I can go along with this, because if growing conditions differ then so will the fruit. And the growing conditions in orchards only a few miles apart can vary because the climate and day and night-time temperatures will be peculiar to each; these factors influence fruit development sufficiently to affect flavour (and perfume).

This is an encapsulation of what *terroir* means. But what is the crucial difference between a peach (or an apple) and a wine grape? It is that one is eaten from the tree, and the other is poured from a bottle.

In other words, a huge level of human manipulation is involved with the latter product which is entirely absent from the former. We eat peaches and apples raw, oblivious of what growing practices the producers might follow. But with wine, where the notion of *terroir* is so fancifully and widely applied, not only are the growing practices, viticulture as it is called, widely different but, above all, the creation of the finished wine from the raw fruit is different, often unique to each individual producer. But the *terroirists*, the wine merchants and producers, the toffee-nosed wine writers and so-called experts, want you to believe that in spite of all this individuality and all this science (called oenology) the wine is merely the slave of the vineyard itself; that each individual vineyard expresses itself in the wine so that its *terroir* is distinct. You hear the word bandied about, misused, abused, misunderstood, and so accepted as received wisdom that the wise sages who believe Elvis Presley is alive and living on the moon are rationalists in comparison.

Would you believe me if I told you that no matter what chef is in the kitchen the dishes from a particular restaurant always taste exactly the same because the ambience of the place conferred so potent a presence that it overrode individual style and technique? Of course you wouldn't. You would rightly call me a mountebank and turf me out on my ear.

But the *terroirists* want you to believe exactly this. We wine writers employ dozens of metaphors for the textural qualities of a wine, from velvet to wet-wool, but the *terroirists* specialise in two: they employ flannel to pull the wool over your eyes. Why? To answer this question it is instructive to examine the motives of the various interested parties who maintain the *terroir* fiction.

1. Wine writers, and the high-end wine merchants they buttress, love *terroir* because it is yet more jargon they can use to distance themselves from the drinkers they wish to hoodwink. All professions employ a special language to enforce their speciality and expertise. Wine scribbling is no different.

2. The wine merchants referred to above love it because it enables them to wax lyrical even about even bad vintages.

3. The wine producer loves it because he can do as the merchants do, point 2 above, but above all, above everything else, producers maintain the fiction of *terroir* because it protects real estate values by elevating a discrete, demarcated area to supreme status. This leads

inevitably to high prices, rarity value, and many wines being traded as commodities not as vinous liquids to be drunk for pleasure but amassed for profit.

The war on *terroir* is, then, an unequal struggle. There are a few critics, mostly in the New World, who feel as I do but I must confess I seem to be the most virulent anti-*terroirist* around. Massed against myself and the stragglers behind me are, firstly, decades of acceptance of *terroir* by unthinking drinkers and self-serving experts and marketeers along with a cultural predisposition by many people always to believe the 'answer lies in the soil' argument. Just as humankind manufactured its myriad beliefs in deities from being overawed by the sun and the night sky, so we all tend to believe that things grown are somehow special. It has been the world of wine's most conspicuous victory (of fantasy over logic) that so many people relate to *terroir* without having a clue what it is they are putting their faith in.

Human intervention

In essence, *terroir* is bullshit. As such it is easily the most effective manure for vines, the most easily absorbed, the cheapest to create. This begs the question, what does make the difference to a wine if it is not the soil the vines plants stand up in?

The answer is the winemaker. All truly smart drinkers know this. That is why they follow particular burgundy (or claret or Barolo or Aussie shiraz) producers and it is why, all over the world, the canny tippler wants to know who made the wine, above all other considerations before s(he) looks at grape variety and vintage. The other significant factors that influence wine, apart from the human, are grape varieties and climate. Of course, you need a vineyard which faces the right way and is free draining and may be on a slope. All the rest of the palaver, the stones, the rocks, the minerally bits, the chemicals in the soil, is hokum. Compared with the soul of the winemaker, the soil is of as little consequence to the wine as the type of tree which supplied the wood for the vineposts.

In March 2005, a most illuminating paper was presented at the Royal Economic Society's annual conference. It was prepared by Olivier Gergaud of the University of Reims and Victor Ginsburgh of the Université Libre de Bruxelles. Their findings were dynamite, utterly exploding the idea of *terroir*. It was, these two academics said, not *terroir* which determined the quality of a wine but the 'winemaking technologies.' The two men collected data on environmental conditions and winemaking techniques in 100 Bordeaux vineyards of the Haut-Médoc in 1990, including the top-growths such as Mouton-Rothschild, Latour, Lafite-Rothschild and Margaux.

'In the Médoc region the French *terroir* legend does not hold,' they reported. I would confidently assert that if they carried out the same research in the vineyards of Burgundy, Rhône, Loire and anywhere else in the France, let alone the world, the results would be the same. It is not *terroir* which makes a wine, it is human intervention. Of course, the old-school wine merchants in cahoots with (and dependent upon) French wine producers will have it differently. *Terroir* is everything, they'll tell you. Of course they will. But would you ask a car salesman for his opinion on bicycles? And would you place any faith in his reply?

Terroir, as it is enshrined in the Appellation d'origine contrôlée (AOC) laws in France, and similar regulations in all other European countries (DOC in Italy), have been a consumer con for the simple reason that it is a ruse to protect real estate values not a scale of worth. Many UK consumers say to me 'I open a bottle of French AOC or Italian DOC wine and I know I stand a bigger chance of being disappointed than if I open a bottle which says Australia or South Africa.'

That is the heart of the problem. Yes there is regionality and yes different climates affect grapes profoundly. But designating certain vineyards or vineyard areas as superior destroys credible marketability for it is merely a cunning plan to perpetuate the status of vineyards over the personalities of the various winemakers who will create wine from them over the generations. To paraphrase Edmund

Burke *terroir* is the superstition of feeble minds.

Is the New World trying on the discredited clothes of the Old?
Horrifically, the South Africans are now being tempted to knock on
the *terroir* door. Recently I received the shocking revelation,
courtesy of cyber space. It describes the set-up envisaged for a South
African wine tasting, to be held in London.

> Apart from the individual importers' stands, each region will
> display its best wines, so delegates will still be able to
> experience the taste of place particular to each wine-growing
> area. With biodiversity an essential component of our
> positioning, we do not want to lose this focus. The country
> has the oldest geological formations and the most weathered
> soils anywhere in the world. The Cape Floral Kingdom
> might be the smallest, but it is also the richest on the planet
> and is where over 90% of South African wines are grown.
> These features make it possible to produce an enormous
> range of wine styles across the price spectrum.

What the Cape publicists are saying as they drown in their own
nonsensicality is that it is not dynamic Cape winemakers like
Bruwer Raats and Charles Back who make the difference. It is not
Martin Meinert and Danie de Wet who create the wonderful
diversity of Cape wine styles. It is not Abrie Bruwer of Springfield
Estate and André van Rensburg at Vergelegen who are responsible
for those superbly individual Cabernet Sauvignons. Great
winemakers like Peter Finlayson and Hannes Storm are to blame for
creating outstanding Pinot Noirs? No sir! It is the dirt that holds the
vines up which is responsible for all of this. The dirt.

It is the pigs taking over the farm and standing up on two legs
and swigging whisky with the farmer. Have you ever read anything
so half-baked in your life? Soil and apes and leopards and pretty
flowers make it possible to produce an enormous range of wine

styles across the price spectrum? We have moved beyond George Orwell's world now. We are in Daniel Defoe's. To utter such inanities as the above is to suffer calenture, the delirium which affected thirsty eighteenth century sailors in the tropics. It is a belief that the sea is a green field and the sufferer has only to lie down in it to find relief. I am surprised no-one is citing particular earthworms as making the wine and individuating biodiversity in each vineyard.

In Orwell's *Animal Farm* the pigs ended up becoming the spitting image of the oppressive humans the rest of the animals sacrificed everything to resist. A similar irony is at work in the New World of wine. Having worked so hard to crush old Europe, to take its markets and colonise its customers' taste preferences, they want to be like old Europe after all. Or, rather, some of them do.

In Australia, there are the pronouncements of Brian Croser. He would like to see certain Aussie vineyard areas designated as superior to others, following the appellation contrôlée pattern. Is it conceivable that we could one day see the equivalent of grand cru and grand premier cru sites in Australia? When Australia has done so much to prove that it is the winemaker who makes the wine, not the vineyard site, this is an absurdly backward step.

Mr Croser's is a lone, if eminent, voice, and as far as I know very few of his younger contemporaries entirely agree with him. But they are tempted, of course. Would Jeffrey Grosset, dear old bald-as-a-coot, sharp-as-a-sushi-knife Jeffrey, who concurs with me on this matter in conversation, be persuaded to go along with AOC style regulations if his Polish Hill riesling vines in south Australia's Clare Valley were rated as grand premier cru and was one of only a few dozen in Australia to be so singled out?

Vineyards only grow the raw materials; wine is made in a winery
It is human beings who make wine. Vineyards merely grow the grapes. Grapes are not wine: no more than latex from the Hevea brasiliensis tree is a rubber tyre. Even the Philippe de Rothschild company, famous for *grand cru* Château Mouton Rothschild in

Bordeaux, acknowledges this. On a neck label for one of its subsidiary ventures, wines from Maipo in Chile, I came across this:

> Baron Philippe de Rothschild, masters in the art of assemblage, are now associated with some of the best wines in Chile. As in France, so it is in the New World, it is the winemaker who provides the inimitable finesse that distinguishes a Baron Philippe de Rothschild wine. This man, with a tongue like a tuning fork, tastes the cuvées (or parcels of wine), selects and with infinite care assembles them to produce beautifully balanced wines.

Laugh? I cried. Apart from making the whole of the 1855 Bordeaux chateau classification league, based on vineyard site, irrelevant piffle (which is what it largely is), it is hugely entertaining to think of a winemaker with a forked tongue and his employer openly admitting it.

In their 1999 *German Guide*, the authors Armin Diel and Joel Payne, were deliciously honest when they said of the wines of one of Germany's most celebrated producers, Weingut Dr. H. Tanisch-Erben Müller-Burggraef, that 'the loss of cellarmaster Norbert Breit caused a surprising drop in quality in 1993…' If the vineyards of this producer, some legendary, are so powerful an influence on a wine how was this drop possible?

At times even the most ardent *terroirist* finds it impossible to maintain the fiction. The key-note speaker at a pinot noir conference in Central Otago in New Zealand in 2002 was Anthony Hanson, a senior consultant to the Christie's wine auction company in London. Mr Hanson gave the delegates (I was one) a disquisition on the soils and geography of the Côte d'Or, where burgundies come from, complete with slides of temperature charts and vineyard maps. After an hour of this he pulled the rug completely from under his own *terroir* argument when, as we tasted several burgundies, he remarked that if only Monsieur Gros's Clos de Vougeot had been made by Monsieur Bachelet of Gevrey-Chambertin we would have got a different wine altogether.

Ah, so it's not *terroir* then. It's wine makers which create the differences. I was very grateful to Anthony for the exquisite explanation.

But if he put the skids under his own argument, then the next speaker demolished it altogether. Professor Warren Moran is professor of geography and environmental science at the University of Auckland. He talks about *terroir* as if I had written his address for him. Which shows how eloquent and direct he is as I don't have a millionth of his science and he is far more reasoned and reasonable than I can ever be. Professor Moran is passionate and committed, a thorough academic no-bull-shitter.

'*Terroir* is a marketing tool.'

'We are part of nature and nature is part of us.'

'People are involved with *terroir*' and *terroir* 'is a sum of many things' and, my favourite, 'it is naïve to associate *terroir* simply with soil as textbooks tend to do.'

Do bear these words in mind, and as much of this chapter as you can recall, next time you hear a wine salesman waxing about the beautiful vineyard his wine emanates from. Raise an especially sceptical eyebrow, not to say a deeply disbelieving pair of eyes, as the word *terroir* comes into the conversation or, more likely, you read it in a wine catalogue or find it peppering the text of a wine book supposedly a critical appraisal but nothing, in truth, but an extravagant superficial brochure for the region or country in question. It was said by a famous old 18th century dictionary compiler that 'Patriotism is the last refuge of a scoundrel'. In the 21st century we might usefully rephrase it: *terroir* is the first refuge of any scoundrel trying to sell you a wine.

I once attended a tasting of burgundies of a particular vintage from a well known importer and when I had finished I was asked what I thought. I said that apart from two inexpensive miracles from the Côtes Chalonaise I thought all the famous vineyards, the big names with big price tags, were hugely disappointing and rotten value and not likely to improve in bottle. The merchant took me by the arm and drew me aside.

'I agree,' he whispered, 'but there are enough UK customers who use their eyes to drink and the far-east market will buy anything if it's got a name.'

5

Appellation d'origine Controlee

The great French real estate scam

'In AOC wines many artificial tastes are allowed, which is truly shocking.'

Nicolas Joly, biodynamic wine producer,
Clos de la Coulée de Serrant, Loire

In the previous chapter we examined the falsehoods surrounding the notion of *terroir*. Here we must look at how those falsehoods are applied in countries which enact regulations to protect vineyard names. In France, it is the AOC, standing for the Appellation d'origine contrôlée system. All major European wine countries have similar set-ups. Only the most knowledge wine consumers know their way through the thickets of such wine laws and the shrewdest of these buyers place no reliance on them whatsoever.

I urge you to do the same. There are only two classes of person who can ignore this advice. First is the wine investor. He does not need to bother with discrimination as he only puts his money on legendary labels which, whatever the excitement level of the liquid in the bottles, will always, if his cache is properly cellared and accredited, be able to make a profit. This is emphatically so in vintages largely agreed to be exceptional. (There is no so such thing as an exceptional vintage in fact, in so far as it reflects on every vineyard in a region so blessed. There are only winemakers able to take advantage of the exceptional vintage who make exceptional wine. Talking up a vintage is another trick of the wine merchant in order to dazzle, bamboozle, and trap the unwary and unsceptical customer.)

The second person is the novice drinker who is only acquainted with large-selling high street brands. S(he) will cultivate a small selection of prejudices and stand by them until the wine(s) substantially changes (as happened when the UK's biggest single wine brand, Kumula, from the Cape underwent a quality fall in 2006 and sales declined). Such happy drinkers do not feel the need to read wine books (which may contribute to their happy state). Yet they are far more discriminating human beings than the soulless collector or venal investor.

Having ventured this far into this book you will already have discovered that though AOC pretends to ensure that a wine labelled with the words Appellation d'origine contrôlée is made wholly from grapes of that region or area this is not always the case.

When I first discovered wine and went to France and Italy, Spain and Germany I was thrilled, soppy innocent booby that I was, to hear of the stories attached to many vineyards and what made such discrete areas so wonderful. I tasted the wines and felt, as I did in some (too many!) cases, that my failure to reach orgasm, or even to feel mildly titillated, must be as a result of my own ignorance. 'It must be good', I remember a wine merchant saying to me in 1967, 'because it's Appellation Clos de Vougeot Grand Cru'. When later, visiting the place, I discovered that something like eighty different people each had a piece of the Clos de Vougeot action and could label their burgundies accordingly, irrespective of whether a high norm of excellence was achieved, I began to twig the obvious. French wine laws protect the wine grower. They do not protect the wine consumer.

It gets even more complicated when one considers the graduations of AOC nomenclature in burgundy: apart from Clos de Vougeot Grand Cru there is Appellation Vougeot Premier Cru as well as Appellation Vougeot Contrôlée. As I ventured further into this legal jungle of obfuscation and double-meaning I found that some people who made the less appellated wine in fact turned out feistier wines than the *grand cru* winemakers. It was all very confusing and when multiplied ten thousandfold by all the other regions in France downright impossible to take in and comprehend. And that was just France. Visiting the famous Doktor vineyard in Bernkastel I was told in no uncertain terms that these eight acres formed the greatest vineyard in Germany, not just the Mosel region. Its wines, I was assured, were sublime. Yet not only did I discover that the site's multiple ownership produce different levels of excitement (in one case high, in the other low to middling) but that much sexier wines came from elsewhere in the region not to mention Germany.

What was all the fuss about? Doktor was, and is, just a brand name, without any brand values. It was, and is, just a myth. True, great wine could be made here but so could it in a hundred other places along the same stretch of river.

What made the difference, as touched on in the previous chapter, was not any wine law, be it French or German or anywhere else in the world, but the winemaker. But how do you trap a winemaker? How do you enshrine him or her so that they can be a permanent fixture of a wine? You cannot. Winemakers change jobs. They lose heart. They die. How much more convenient, how much more in tune with humankind's love of legend and the romance of the soil, to make the stamp of authority of a wine to be what it legally can claim is its provenance. Yet it can be stated as an undeniable fact that of all agriculture products wine is the one least able to claim that where it comes from ensures excellence or confers consistency. AOC wine laws, however, purport to legislate for the exact opposite. It is a swindle. The laws cannot be corrected. That makes it a scam and a scandal.

Belatedly, the French themselves now agree with this. In September 2007, two English newspapers broke the news. The *Independent* wrote: 'One in three bottles of appellation contrôlée wines produced in France is sub-standard, according to the French consumer watch-dog. A survey of wine professionals by the organisation, UFC-Que Choisir, concluded that the supposed local authenticity offered by the label 'AOC' – Appellation d'origine contrôlée – has become meaningless.'

The *Daily Telegraph* went a little further. It said: 'Up to a third of wines sold under France's regional appellation system might be from an entirely different region, according to a French consumers' group. The Appellation d'origine contrôlée, or AOC, once a gold stamp of origin and quality, is fast turning into a national joke, UFC-Que Choisir said.'

It has been a joke for so many years it is a bigger joke for someone in France now to pass the remark. How can AOC be anything more than a scam? It is operated and managed by the very people who produce the wines they purport to 'examine'. No wonder around 99% of AOC wines submitted get the nod. One wonders, indeed one shudders, at what the 1% who get turned down must be like. It is significant that UFC-Que Choisir has finally spoken out. Its words carry weight. It is similar to the UK's Consumers Association, with the same independence and aims, but it is older being set up in 1951 (the UK Consumers Association followed in 1957).

However, whatever the level, accuracy, and force of the criticisms made of the AOC system those within it will fight tooth and claw to hang on to its privileges and traditions. Any attempt to sweep the whole thing away wholesale will be resisted, not least because some very gifted, culturally vital and dynamic wine producers work within the confines of the system and, apart from some reservations, support it. In many ways it seems surprising that the iconoclastic, individualistic, anti-authoritarian French go along with the sham. It's rather like religion or the monarchy (in the UK). We recognise it's a tissue of lies, we know it has had its day, we appreciate its huge disadvantages, but, hey, wouldn't it be terrible if it didn't exist? Tradition is just another way of repeating the mistakes of the past.

The AOC is just like an all-embracing nanny-state within a state, tolerated by those who manage to excel, exploited by the far greater number who are second and third rate. If it were to be done away with, however, the excellent producers would surely thrive even more. It would only be the charlatans who would go to the wall.

In the end, like me, the way to cheat the AOC system and all the other European national appellation of origin scams, is to always buy wine using the name of the maker as the key buying decision reference point. Of course, it is useful to know that a red burgundy is going to be a type of wine which narrows down your choice and makes purchase easier. You want a wine which tastes like burgundian pinot noir and there it is. But there it isn't in so many instances (either by virtue of its false provenance or because it is poorly made).

No-one imagines, any more (surely!), that by virtue of being in London on Savile Row an immaculate gentleman's suit can be purchased anywhere along this thoroughfare's short length. Yet if this street in London declared something similar to AOC there would be a public outcry; the haberdashers there situated would be declared frauds. Yet AOC (France) and DOC (Italy) and the rest do exactly the same thing, with, in truth, less rationality.

6

THE RITUALISED LABEL

Château Lafite as the first great wine brand (long before Blue Nun in 1921), and why it can be promoted so brilliantly

> *'Reverence is often no more than the conventional homage we pay to things in which we are not willing to take an active interest.'*
>
> W. Somerset Maugham

Whilst the casual snob or lefty critic believes that all advertising is based wholly on lies this is not the whole truth. Only the advertising for alcohol – brewed, fermented or distilled – is based on lies. Were it otherwise, alcohol would become like religion – unsaleable except to the brainwashed, the superstitious, and the emotionally needy.

Car advertising, for example, may well trade on illusion and status and imagery but nevertheless the product will take you from A to B. Apparel and shoe advertising may play on the label or the perceived glamour of its wearers; but no-one can deny that clothes provide somewhere essential to hide your money and conceal your private parts and who goes shoeless these days? Food ads may strike absurd and declamatory poses but we need the stuff to get through a working day. Even the dire, vomitory superficiality of perfume advertising offers a product which will make you smell. And so it goes. Advertising may be the patina here but these products have an effect which cannot be gainsaid. Further, many of the individual brands within these categories will have a singularity of design or performance which genuinely makes them different from each of their competitors.

None of this applies to any alcohol. Try as hard as you like you cannot find any substance in any drink advertisement. Of course a drink may major on its provenance, be it an Australian wine, Belgian beer, a Kentucky bourbon, or a Scottish whisky, but this merely gives the marketeer and the advertising creator more scope on which to build a more credible basis for all those wonderful lies and preposterous fantasies. An advertiser may offer you an ingredient, such as a rare hop or water from a very particular stream, or, in the case of a hybrid or a cocktail, the very nature of its primary parts (rum, coffee, oranges, cream), but this is just the excuse for associated imagery which is always, not to put too fine a point on it, complete deception. For what are all these drinks at bottom?

A drink is alcohol, and whether it is a grand-cru from Château Lafite or beer brewed by Stella Artois or cognac distilled by Rémy Martin there are dozens of similar drinks which do precisely the same thing in precisely the same way. Only their provenance is individual. What gives each of those products its cachet has been shrewd marketing, clever advertising, brilliant image manipulation.

If you remove these latter activities from the equation, the sums do not add up. Or rather they add up to much the same bottom line as many other drinks of similar base ingredients, provenance and performance. With alcoholic drinks the image is everything. And why? Why have drinks, especially wine, managed to corner an exclusive corner all to themselves where imagery is the absolute ruler?

Because nothing marks out a man or a woman so much, nothing nails them so compelling as a cool kid, a connoisseur, an aristocrat of taste, an aficionado of the hop or the grape, as that bottle on the table (with its label so prominent) or in the wine bar, restaurant or pub. Long before clothes designers stuck their labels on the outside of their products, the manufacturers of alcohol were doing it and doing it brilliantly. Wines and spirits are two of the very few products we can serve at home which immediately reinforce to our guests and neighbours the kind of person we wish to be perceived to be. The label on the bottle is as good as – indeed, better than – a label worn round the neck of its purchaser.

Wine labels, wine names, are, then, almost as important as the actual liquid in the bottle. To an untrained palate, to someone who has miniscule knowledge of wine but has heard of Bordeaux, any liquid short of being toxic which emanates from a bottle marked Château Lafite or Château Pétrus will be regarded as significant. The name alone works the magic.

Yet paradoxically the wine trade has only superficial knowledge of advertising and meagre understanding of what a brand is. In an editorial about brands in *The Drinks Business* magazine in July 2007 Charlotte Hey editorial director wrote: 'Even though the wine trade has been late to jump on the branding bandwagon…' But this is not so. Wine offers up some of the oldest brand ideas in the world. Champagne has been a corporate brand for centuries. Château Lafite for 150 years. The German export behemoth Blue Nun started in 1921. Forty years ago when Grants of St James's launched its Don Cortez wine brand the deputy chairman of the company, Derrick Holden-Brown, was sufficiently savvy enough to remark that the aim was to create 'a cheap no-frills table wine' which would be no more difficult to acquire than 'a bottle of ketchup.' (*Wine Snobbery* by Andrew Barr, 1988.)

Indeed, the same magazine reported in September 2007 that a wine like Lafite is not so much a major brand as a major investment trading stock. There are now wine funds as there are funds in commodities or property and the managing director of one such, the Vintage Wine Fund based in the Cayman Islands, was reported, perhaps in a blatant attempt to talk the stock up, by *The Drinks Business* as remarking that 'The best wines are shockingly undervalued. Lafite, in any vintage, should be more like £1000 a bottle, rather than the current price. Some vintages sell for less than a couple of parking tickets.'

Such a whinge is an amusingly self-serving endorsement of the current ludicrous fashion for buying a label rather than a liquid and it is ironic that even some of the diehard wine snobs of the world of wine criticism are, somewhat late in the day, beginning to realise that their perpetual banging on about the so-called 'great names' of wine has only fuelled this craze for treating wine as it were a stock market item or a property investment.

Good idea down the drain

When I was shooting a TV series[2] for the BBC five years after my first wine guide was published, I wanted to take two bottles of red – a major Bordeaux and a Bulgarian cabernet sauvignon – and swap the contents. I then planned to offer the wines to a group of people who regarded themselves as knowledgeable and film the results with a secret camera. I was fairly confident that with an indifferent vintage of, say, Lafite (£150 a bottle), and a serious Bulgar cabernet (£5), each in the other's livery, a lively discussion would ensue which would prove the power of a name to alter an experience which should only be judgemental as regards the palate. My TV producer (a timid soul) was not keen on this idea, however, saying it was improper. Maybe she was right. But I have no doubt some people would rave about the claret, until it was revealed to be a fiver's worth of Bulgar's blood.

What we see prejudices what we taste. Ridiculous? Not at all. And experts are just as fallible as anyone else. In my opinion, often more so, because many experts (in taste or style areas) are slaves to their imagined expertise.

In 2001, Frédéric Brochet, who was working towards a doctorate at the University of Bordeaux's Faculty of Oenology (wine science), conducted two hilarious and hugely illuminating experiments to prove how what we see influences what we taste. In the first embarrassing test, 54 wine tasters were given two glasses each of red and white wine. However, both wines were the same white wine except the one coloured red had been changed with an odourless and tasteless food colourant. The *soi-disant* red inspired the usual litany of clichés from the tasters (who, being wine students, were about the level of wine enthusiasts, French – for what that's worth – but not experts perhaps in the English sense of the word) including 'jamminess' and 'red fruit'.

Brochet's second inspired idea was even more embarrassing for the tasters (57 of them this time). He poured a very ordinary Bordeaux into two different bottles, one labelled with the classification *grand-cru*, the other as *vin de table*. Dazzled by the grand-cru designation on its label the *vin ordinaire* was variously described 'agreeable, woody, complex, balanced and rounded'. The poor *vin de table*, however, in spite of being precisely the same liquid, was considered to be 'weak, short, light, flat and faulty'. Forty of the tasters reckoned the *grand-cru* wine was up the mark, whereas only 12 said the *vin de table* good enough to merit praise (and 5, as far as I can work out, said nothing).

Okay, so the tasters involved weren't national newspaper correspondents or international celebrity critics but they were connected with wine, as far as I can make out, and so not complete chumps. But they were largely made to appear so.

The blind leading the blind

I have, in blind tastings (where the bottle's design and label are covered up), seen Pelorus, the New Zealand sparkling wine (£15) preferred to Krug and Dom Pérignon (£75/80) and, in one memorable tasting I did for ITV and the Trevor MacDonald show, a bottle of carrier-bag wrapped Casa Lapostolle Cuvée Alexandre Merlot (£16) was favoured over Château Pétrus (£350) wrapped up in a paper bag. Only when the labels were revealed was there a debate over judgement. If I had switched the contents of these bottles, and the labels were not hidden, I am confident that people would rave about the more expensive offering every time.

Such is the power of the name, the label, the talismanic magic of an object perceived to be legendary. If I hold out a lump of sugar in my palm and offer it to you, you will sense sweetness in your mouth. Sadly, this is many drinkers reaction when forced to contemplate a bottle of German wine no matter how complex, dry, and exquisite the liquid inside. It is not just novices or beginners who react like this.

In a London tasting I heard the *Times* wine critic, Jane MacQuitty, say to Stephen Spurrier, a wine consultant, as, standing next to me, they regarded a bottle of California wine, 'Oh, it's got the name Gallo on it. I could never taste a bottle with the name Gallo.' Stephen gallantly concurred. But when I tasted the wine I enjoyed a vivid experience, which no amount of labelling as Ernest & Julio Gallo Sonoma Frei Ranch Cabernet Sauvignon, could blunt. It was a stunning wine.

Richard Neill, who wrote on wine for the *Daily Telegraph*, in my company, declared that it was clear which of the two masked zinfandels we were drinking came from the revered Ridge estate and which was from Ernest & Julio Gallo's Barrelli Creek vineyard. He knew the identity of the wines. What he did not know was which wine was in which covered bottle. He got it wrong, on this occasion, nominating the Gallo product as superior, that it must be the Ridge wine, because it was clearly the more pungently sensual of the two. Ridge, needless to say, enjoys hallowed status amongst wine nerds. Gallo, never mind the excellence of certain vintages of its Sonoma vineyard wines (like Frei and Barrelli), does not. (Gallo's many other offerings are bland and largely mediocre, which only reinforces the company's image of third-rateness amongst experts.)

Repute is everything with wine. In attempting to persuade an Australian man that he should serve Aussie sparkling wine at his wedding (in the UK), I served him several examples of this along with an assortment of champagnes. One wine stood out. It was Aussie. But his wife-to-be put her foot down. She was having champagne. (Luckily for his finances I managed to persuade them to keep the Veuve Clicquot for the toast and then go on to a much cheaper – and in my view more attractive – supermarket own-label champagne. Since the wines were being served wrapped in napkins no-one was any the wiser. I forbore to point out that a wine called

'Widow' Clicquot was, in the circumstances, inappropriate.)

A rich American who entertained me in his home in London offered a galaxy of expensive burgundies but none was outstanding. When I returned the favour at my house I served a pinot noir, from a jug, which he declared was among the best he had ever tasted, confident that he had in his glass a legend. Indeed he did, but when he was handed the bottle he was truly shocked to discover it was a reserve Romanian pinot noir, of mature antiquity, at £4.99 the bottle from a wine merchant of whom he had never heard: budget supermarket Morrisons.

If all this sounds too anecdotal to be presented as hard evidence that people drink labels, in January 2008 it was reported that research at the California Institute of Technology showed that the more a wine costs the better, to some drinkers, it tastes.

The sample was small, just 21 volunteers, but the results were predictably the same as the French research on labels. The 21 drinkers tasted several cabernet sauvignons and were asked to rate the ones they reckoned superior. The wines were tasted blind, no bottles were visible, but the tasters were told the prices. The prices bore no relation to the wine in the glass, however. A £45 bottle of cabernet was said to have cost a fiver and a fiver bottle of cabernet was said to have cost £22. Interestingly, scans were taken of that area of the brain associated with pleasure and decision making and in every case the expectation of the more expensive wine being better, and seeming to taste so, was borne out and the less expensive wine was rated as being less good. Antonio Rangel, who led the research team, told the BBC News website that the experiment showed how 'expectation can affect the actual encoding of the pleasantness of the experience.'

It is easy to be critical of the findings of this research. The number of tasters is very small and the research was carried out in the USA where price and apparent prestige perhaps matter more to consumers than in other places. This may be true, but the findings back up my experience in the UK, and elsewhere, where even so-called experts are swayed by price. The point is never to drool over the label but savour the liquid and assess it on its merits in the glass. It is for this reason that many wine tastings are conducted with labels covered as blind tastings, and there is no doubt that in many circumstances this approach has a great deal to recommend it.

In a glass clearly

I should add that I do not exempt myself from the weaknesses with which I charge other experts. Faced with that Lafite and that Bulgar, unmasked, I have no doubt I would be trying hard to discover nuances in the former which I would not expect to find in the latter. Renown, fame if you will, acts an excitement to the senses which obscurity does not. Confronted, many decades ago now, with the most facially beautiful woman in the world, Claudia Cardinale, I dismissed her as crude and over-cosmetised. I did not know it was she until twenty minutes later when she was no longer in my sight. Had I known who she was when I regarded her I would have been smitten. It is no different with any expert and any label of a celebrated wine staring him in the face.

It is this which the advertiser and marketeer can count on. Most people will simply follow others lead, accept received wisdom, pay lip service to the perceived 'correct' way of doing things. And this is as true of party-givers like Jeffrey Archer, who always served Krug because so many of his guests were impressed by its sheer cost, as it is of the man at lunch who exclaims 'I'll think we'll have a premier cru today, Charles, as we're celebrating'.

You are what you drink as much as you are what you eat. Perhaps more so. Drink is never served without ritual and hokum attached and it is this which makes it such a profitable area for con-artists and those trading wholly on perceived excellence not actual.

All brews, ferments and distillates carry magic. It is microbial magic to begin with but this transference of power by which a grape, or a cider apple, or a mere vodka potato becomes an elixir, directly parallels the metamorphosis which the drinkers of such potions experience. We bring a belief to every alcohol we use or consume and the most talismanic are perfumes and fragrances even though each is supposedly unique made from a formula special to itself (unlike alcohols taken in to the digestive system). Perfumes are outside the scope of this book and, on the basis of their individuality, beyond the reach of my thesis – except to point out that I cannot name a single perfume which rather than offering the aphrodisiacal route to purchaser satisfaction trades on its ingredients.

Wines are no different from certain perfumes and clothes labels. This is why the French luxury-brand company, Moet Hennessy Louis Vuitton, the LVMH group, considers certain wines as mere snob appendages. Employing 60,000 people world-wide and with an annual income of $16-billion, this beautifully manicured and managed business puts wines in their place on the list of the must-have accessories of the unthinking rich. What do fragrances from Christian Dior, Guérlain, Givenchy or Kenzo have in common with fashion and leather goods from Fendi, Loewe, Marc Jacobs or Thomas Pink? As much as watches (or jewellery) made by Chaumet and TAG Heuer have in common with Château d'Yquem, Cloudy Bay, Krug, Dom Pérignon or Veuve Clicquot. They are all businesses (and the list here is only a selection) owned and managed by LVMH. That list will certainly grow. There are plenty more luxury wine brands LVMH can acquire.

In ethos, the luxury brand is just like a mass-market label, though one made to a different manufacturing specification and sold at a higher price. In some cases, of course, the differences may not be merely superficial and, certainly with wine, we would expect Château d'Yquem at £200 a bottle to perform more spectacularly than a modestly priced Spanish sweet wine such as Moscatel de Valencia. However, with a crushingly unctuous pudding it might be that the latter wine is more soothingly compatible. It is certainly true that between those two prices there are scores of sweet white wines able to perform brilliantly.

And herein lies the reason why the well-heeled snob goes for the d'Yquem nonetheless. He has heard of it. It is very expensive. Yquem suggests you know a lot about wine even if all you know is how to pull out an ample wallet to pay for your bottle and have no idea what it tastes like and whether it might suit the food you are serving. More crucially, even if he hasn't heard of it, those to whom he will serve it most certainly have and they will be aware of its cost. That knowledge, that residue of fantasy in the brain, is what the luxury brand seeks to manipulate and maintain. It is, in truth, consumer totalitarianism. Choice, the free exercise of discrimination, plays no part. This is what makes the brand business so insidious and the intelligent wine drinker takes no part in it. Rather than trust the seductive design and chic style of the label, he or she will rely only on their taste buds and ignore the chicanery of packaging.

7

THE CURSE OF THE CORK

*Infecting wine for centuries,
yet why do wine snobs love it?*

There is a serial wine killer on the loose. This killer cunningly and subtly ruins a proportion of wines, possibly as many as 10%, and affects 100% of wines. This killer goes under the name of Cork.

Cork taint, for which the cork industry is desperately trying to find a cure, is caused by a rogue chemical called 2-4-6 Trichloranisole. It is created as a result of the chlorine cleansing the tree bark undergoes before it becomes a wine seal.

However, tainted wine is only one of the problems which cork confers on a wine. Since no single cork, however untainted it may be, is the same as the one lying next to it on the bottling line, each cork makes each bottle different. Some times the variations are wide, sometimes very small. But all corks, especially those inserted in wines designed to be cellared for a few years, cause variation between bottles as cork is an inherently unstable seal. You truly do not know what you will get with a wine sealed with a cork until that cork is pulled. Thus if we continue to use natural cork, even if cork taint was eradicated, bottle variation would still curse wine. Bottle variation makes one person's judgement on a wine irrelevant and misleading. Cork makes a mockery of critical appraisal of certain wines because, by allowing random oxidation, the bottle the critic tastes will be different from the one you buy.

Plastic corks – infernal things! – do not cause taint but they are difficult to extract, impossible to put back, and they are not designed for any wine which can be, or should be, cellared for future enjoyment.

It is a scandal that in the third millennium we have a product sold world-wide which is so uneven in performance thanks to its seal. Sticking a cork made from tree bark in a wine is like producing a modern motor car with a starting handle. Would you accept the viewpoint that in spite of electronics and an onboard computer, a starting handle, inconvenient nuisance that it is, keeps the romance of motoring alive? This is the argument many sentimentalists would like wine drinkers to embrace. No other edible or drinkable item is made with such a hit-or-miss attitude. Would beer drinkers tolerate a failure rate of one can in ten? And their favourite tipples being different from one pub to the next? Would soft drink fans cheerfully tolerate similar failure rates and variations in taste?

The answer is no. And a very resounding no. But because wine has the aura of a special liquid, a liquid representing ritual and tradition, too many drinkers accept these problems as part of the price they have to pay to participate, afraid they will be dismissed as dilettantes.

Screwcaps

The answer, both to cork taint and inconsistency, is screwcaps. Does such a seal kill the romance of the wine? Not if the fruit in the bottle is sexy. The romance of wine surely lies in the liquid in the glass not in the maintenance of old-fashioned rituals. A screwcap is the firmest guarantee that the wine in the bottle will be in the condition its maker intended. The vast majority of red and white wines benefit from aging without the need of air getting in via their seals.

The cork industry has made a belated attempt to clean up its act, to get rid of the rogue chemical Trichloranisole, but it has not acted speedily enough to satisfy the larger British wine retailers and supermarkets which have increasingly turned to plastic alternatives. In late summer 2007 it was reported that less than 10% of Sainsbury's own-label wines were bottled with natural cork. The retailer said to the wine trade magazine *Harpers* that its priority was 'to deliver the wine in the best possible condition' and that since using synthetic stoppers it had experienced 'a 75%/95% drop in complaints.' At supermarket Tesco, which led the revolution in UK retailers turning to screwcaps (thanks to its then female-dominated wine-buying department, which was not prepared to tolerate so much cork-spoiled wine), the percentage is even higher. Indeed, producers tell me that if they can screwcap an excellent wine and the wholesale price is right, Tesco will always seriously consider putting the product on shelf. Other major retailers are following suit, all recognising that consumer acceptance of screwcaps is growing.

Of course, the screwcap is not perfect. Indeed, with some wines it suffers from a maddening overperfection. Take the Chilean wine Errazuriz Merlot 2006, for example, which I tasted in summer 2007. This wine, now screwcapped, performs, moments after the top is screwed off, like a mumbling choirboy unsure of his lines or his position. It seems gauche and clumsy. But leave the wine, firmly re-screwcapped (after a large tasting sample has been poured out), for twenty four hours and a lovely svelte luxurious firmly confident merlot emerges. How is this? The screwcap has held back the wine (it being so young), and it needs air to be fully lithe, characterful and true to its grape. This is not good news to someone who opens the wine at the dinner table and expects instant gratification, but at least the wine is in perfect condition if you let air get to it. Decanting for six to eight hours should do it. (Just removing the seal and letting the wine stand and so-called 'breathe' will not do the trick.)

Terrific PR stunt

What has been one of the cork industry's naughtiest responses to screwcaps and plastic closures? To concoct, via its PR agency, a harrowing fairy tale of the disaster which will visit the fauna of the cork forests if plastic corks and screwcaps dominate the market.

It is a specious argument which ignores the fact that cork has many uses beyond wine. The cork spin-doctors claim that the eagles and feral pigs who depend on the cork oaks, magnificent trees no-one can deny, will die if the forests are no longer commercially maintained to produce the crop from which cork is taken to manufacture wine seals. Does anyone suppose for one second that those pigs, eagles, owls, okapis or whatever which feed amongst those tree trunks, will give a hoot whether the cork is peeled off the trees every decade?

Screwcaps not only guarantee a taint-free product but also, unlike natural cork, ensure that each bottle of a wine will age, will develop in complexity, in the same way. Each bottle of wine is a live performance, but why should the performance differ from bottle to bottle and in some cases be awful? Bottle variation is the problem cork can never solve.

If you think I exaggerate consider the words of Michel Laroche, veteran Chablis producer, who addressing a seminar organised by dynamic London wine importer Bibendum in September 2007 said 'screwcaps are the perfect closures…' True, he said this applied more to 'aromatic whites' than reds, which is where he is wrong in my view, but he did point out that that a cork permitted 30 times more oxygen ingress into a wine compared with a screwcap – which is why he is bottling his Chablis mostly under screwcap.

The delicious idiocies of wine snobs

Certain wine commentators and wine merchants adore cork. They love it because it gives them an area of technical expertise denied the average drinker. It offers a further hurdle for the ordinary drinker to pass. It ensues the so-called 'expert' has another language to unravel, an added mystery to pontificate about, a further area of obfuscation and uncertainty to which he can lend his expertise. Screwcaps rob the snob of an important metonym: for the cork and its instrument of removal stand for tradition, mystique, difficulty and trial.

The White Queen, you will recall, told Alice she had the habit of believing six impossible things before breakfast. The wine snob believes twice this number before he has even got out of bed.

One such, the philosopher Roger Scruton, wrote that 'No

screwtop can match the use, beauty and moral significance of a cork' (New Statesman, 2005) and doubtless the more rational reader of that magazine who encountered the article went his way without giving such pompous proclamations, however entertaining, any more heed.

The cork has nothing moral in it. Cork is, in truth, an amoral seal as it permits not only faulty products to go on sale but inconsistent products to be paid for and opened. It is because of snobs (the wine trade still boasts the breed), who sanctify the cork by peddling poppycock about the pseudo-religious element it confers by being inherently unstable, by publicising the canard that a screwtop reduces a wine to the level of an alcopop, that there are drinkers, keen for clarification on the subject, who are suspicious of the screwcap.

It is interesting that many proponents of cork seals never search for reasons why the idea of shoving a chunk of tree bark into a wine bottle is not only often unhygienic and wildly erratic, but instead go in for character assassination on its most serious rival. I have, over the past 15 years, sampled screwcapped wines up to 32 years old. Some, it is true, suffered from seemingly excessive sulphur retention, perhaps because their winemakers were still using levels they employed with cork-sealed wines, but these are teething problems. There are other associated problems with the anaerobic environment bequeathed by the screwcap. However, I have sampled only one hopelessly undrinkable screwcapped wine in this time (Knappstein Clare Valley Riesling 2002, opened in July 2008). The cork cannot compete. The corkscrew is fast becoming as obsolete as the cigarette holder.

Doubtless, the old fogies of wine wish also to retain the 750ml bottle. But this too is outdated. Most wine need not be packaged in glass and certainly not in three-quarter-litre bottles. Why 750ml? Because a glass blower, centuries ago, could only blow a bottle between 730ml and 750ml in a single puff and modern mass manufacturing methods adopted it as the norm. Yet wine is slicker packaged without the risks associated with cork in a pint size (and in a tetrapak, say) or in a plastic pouch of two litres (for parties and picnics), or an aluminum can. There are also 3-litre wine boxes, which are a splendid idea (making a purposeful addition to any mantelpiece). It is only tradition and ritual, and the tedious stuffiness of the wine trade, which maintains the idiocy of wine in glass bottles. Our grandchildren will stare at bottles and corks under museum glass and chuckle.

8

ORGANIC WINES

A con to extract more cash from the consumer?

The word organic has become a shibboleth. Does it gain you admittance to a world of tastier, healthier wine? Not exactly. Certainly there should be no trace of pesticide, fungicide or herbicide residue in a certified organic wine and the grapes will not have received artificial fertiliser. However, such residues can be very low in non-organic wines. A conventional vineyard red blend, costing £3.99, which is vivacious and full of fruit is surely to be preferred to a dull organic cabernet sauvignon costing £5.99. (There are vineyards all over the world which use natural products instead of chemicals but refuse to become certified organic. They want to have recourse to the chemical option in an emergency. This is something of a cop-out. They should come clean and eschew chemicals altogether.)

The biggest abuse of chemicals (the use of chemicals at all, to be pure about it) takes place in vineyards which have the most to lose. It is obviously in the commercial interests of, for example, Bordeaux, Burgundy, Champagne, certain tracts of Australia, parts of California, south America and Africa, for a consistency of vintage to be achieved at whatever cost. Thus chemicals are routinely applied. This is one reason why wines from these places can be so uniform in style and flavour. The vineyards can be large, the personality of the vines subsumed under a chemical blanket, and individuality is rare, quirkiness unheard of.

Organics helps individuality, for in natural yeast, the product of the home vineyard, rather than a commercial yeast which others also use, lies the secret of an individual wine. The mono-culture of such vineyards also encourages the very pests which the chemicals they use are designed to eliminate. They do not. The chemicals merely temporarily suppress; they teach the vines to be not naturally sturdy but to be feeble addicts begging for the next fix, and the chemicals leach into the water table (and affect all other growth in the vineyard). If chemicals were banned tomorrow, the world would be a healthier place.

Never forget that the use of chemicals in vineyards leads to one of the biggest cons in wine: that each and every product of an individual vineyard is an individual statement. Chemicals mar any pretence to individuality. Read any blurb from any wine producer or lackey wine merchant aiming to sell the producer's product. It will trumpet the specialness of its vineyard(s). It will not mention the use of chemicals (thus making any claim to express a vineyard's *terroir* even more mendacious than it is already). They ban drugs in sport. Why not ban them in wine? In sport, you have no choice (unless you cheat). In wine, you can cheat legitimately. That is the disgusting legacy given us by the agro-chemical industry.

Organic equals tastier grapes, but not always tastier wine
Why don't organic methods (and the tastiest wine grapes I've ever chewed have been organic) always produce better wine? Because it's one thing to grow organic grapes; another thing to have the skill to turn the juice into something thrilling. Only a proportion of organic wines are better, or even as good as, non-organic. Too many are dead boring. It is surely right to reduce grape growers' dependence on chemicals which aren't in tune with nature. However, until more organic growers can turn their beautiful fruit into exciting wine there is not much point.

It is also important here to make a distinction between a 100% organic wine and one which labels itself made from organic grapes. The latter wine is not organic, it is crucial to note; only the raw material has been certified. If the winery is not, or the methods used infringe organic principles (like using enzymes to clarify the must), then the wine cannot be called organic. I believe that many consumers are misled in these circumstances, assuming the organic grape wording to imply an organic wine.

In my view, no wine should use the word organic on its label unless it is 100% organic, both in grapes and winery practice. It is wholly legitimate that organic grapes growers expect more for their grapes and it is perhaps true that organic methods in the winery may require greater vigilance, more care, certainly less dependence on additions and adjustments to modify the wine, and thus any wholly organic wine is expected to be more expensive.

The organic option is a price worth paying for nature and for the health of the planet and its inhabitants. Of that I am in no doubt. But organic is only a price worth paying for the consumer if the wine is superior in performance. If only all organic wines were as complex and as sturdily individual without being whacky as, for example, those of the Catalan producer Albet y Noya then I would be a happier wine critic. This is what this producer has to say and it is one of the least hysterical and most measured of depictions of the organic process of grape growing I have come across.

The quality of an organic wine (even more than for a non-organic wine) starts in the vineyards. The principal character-istics of organically grown grapes are the lack of chemical residues and ideal sanitary conditions. If you add to that low yields in the vineyards, you not only improve the quality of the grapes, but also improve the sustainability of the vineyards as the vines are naturally more resistant to plagues. Organic regulations therefore prohibit any kind of treatments with synthetic chemical products (herbicides, pesticides or fertilisers). The following treatments are applied at Can Vendrell: Instead of chemical fertilisers, the vineyards are treated with green composts. The organic material recycled from the organic water treatment plant, composted cellar residues and shredded vine shoots maintain the soil's balance. Every autumn we sow a mixture of three grasses between the vines that contribute a balance of nitrogen, carbon and cellulose. These grasses are cut in the spring, and after being left for a fortnight to decompose, they are ploughed back into the soil.

Although organic regulations still permit the use of copper sulphate – the traditional 'bordeaux mixture' (limited to 4kg of active components per hectare) at Can Vendrell we use Copper hydroxide, which has a lower copper content and is more active at low doses. Nonetheless, Albet i Noya are increasingly substituting these treatments for a biodynamic mixture of sulphurous clays, equisetum (horsetail) extract, nettles and marine algaes. This mixture has proved effective against mildew but also indirectly helps prevent botrytis. The use of sulphur is permitted for treatments against oidium [fungus]. Depending on the time of year and the temperature we use liquid sulphur (in suspension), soluble sulphur or sulphur dust. Organic farming combats cochylis, the larval state of the totrix moth with *bacillus thuringiensis* – a microbe that when eaten by the larvae secretes an enzyme which stops them from feeding. As in all organic treatments, timing is of the essence. To ensure these treatments reach the grapes, the vines are green pruned, removing excess leaves to give the grapes sufficient ventilation and exposure to the sun. This process also improves the quality of the grapes as with increased exposure to the sun, the skins produce more pigments, giving the resulting wine more colour and more mature tannins. Finally the grapes are selected during picking ensuring only the healthiest grapes enter the cellar.

These treatments can represent an increment in costs of around 10% over and above the cost of conventional viticulture, although depending on the characteristics of the vineyards the differential can be somewhat higher.

Less than 1000 producers farm this way. They own a fractional percentage of the world-wide total of vineyards. This places the would-be Utopian, myself, in a dilemma. I want the world to be organic (bio-dynamic is better yet). But I also want my wine, and any wine I feel comfortable in recommending, to be excellent. It is not always the case that the two go hand-in-hand.

What is bio-dynamism? Let me state first of all that my opinions are not formed by romantic idealism but experience. That experience has taught me, in France, California, Australia, and New Zealand that the most beautiful to look at, the most stunning to chew, the most gorgeous to taste, have all been grapes grown by extreme organic methods, so-called bio-dynamism. Only in a few cases, however, have the resulting wines been as exquisite. Bio-dynamics follows the precepts of the Austrian thinker Rudolf Steiner (he of scholastic fame). It is based on polyculture, so the vineyard must grow a great many other things than grapes. It also involves phases of the moon and the movements of the planets and it relies on natural remedies and vineyard treatments which, for many people, are mere mumbo-jumbo or agricultural witchdoctory. For such people, the idea of burying a cow's horn full of dung in a vineyard and expecting it to make a difference is nonsense. I can only say taste the grapes which result. Taste them side by side with the same variety from an organic or conventional vineyard a few miles away. Is not the impact on the palate not superior? Is not the structure of the berry more interesting?

I can answer yes to both questions.

The Utopian's dilemma, then, deepens; its horns get sharper. What advice can I offer to resolve it? I suggest organic and bio-dynamic winemakers become more ambitious winemakers, to relate what they do to the market place not just to a sentimental notion of what is ethical for the vineyard, and to taste the best wines to see how good, perhaps, their own could be.[3]

9

HIGH ALCOHOL

The curse of wine making and wine drinking.
Low alcohol, the curse of wine retailing.

I do not like alcohol. Yet I write about it for my living. The secret of wine, with its huge world-wide appeal, is that it is the first and only alcohol which we do not taste when we drink it. What we taste in proper wine is fruit. Proper wine masks alcohol and when it is not proper, not proper wine, when we get whites over 14% with no balancing natural sugar and acidity and reds up to 16.5% with no balancing natural tannins, we have imbalance. The alcohol is revealed. This is a wine fault that is intolerable; bad for people's livers; bad for moderate drinking and the thoughtful consumption of wine. It is a disregard for civilised values.

There is in wine circles a permanent debate about Power versus Finesse and to my mind and palate, and to the hundreds of wine drinkers with whom I have discussed the topic, it is finesse which is preferred. Power may be measured by a wine's ability to go with food, and often delicate wines of great finesse are fussy liquids in this regard, but only those attached to alcohol, and its edgy sweetness, can admire brutally alcoholic wines as most are too jammy to go with anything but the most crazily robust dishes which they cannot overwhelm.

Over the years, in written and verbal debate with *Guardian* newspaper readers and buyers of my annual wine guide to supermarket wines (*Superplonk*), I would estimate that only some 3% to 5% of those drinkers were vociferous in their delight in high alcohol wines and eloquent in their rebuke of me for my denigration of wines of 15+% abv (alcohol by volume). They looked, conspicuously on the shelves, for high alcohol in wines. I suggested they simply pour 4-star Shell into bottles of Ribena. I hope they did not take this advice seriously, indeed I know they must not have done so for they continued to survive and glug and to plague me with their enthusiasm by letter and when we met face to face on the street as they were leaving their raffia sandal making classes or whatever it was their other appetites led them to indulge in. They were, perhaps needless to add, all men.

Some of these men share much in common with certain male wine writers, who are also not fazed by high alcohol in wines. Indeed, such promulgators actually encourage high alcohols in wine. The otherwise sane and delightful UK scribe, the *Daily Mail*'s Matthew Jukes, so admired Battle of Bosworth White Boar Shiraz 2004 from McLaren Vale that he listed it as one of his top 100 Aussie wines of the year in 2006. When it was sent to me to taste I found it, at around 15+% alcohol, undrinkable. It was repugnant; to consider it a real wine was as absurd, to my palate and mind, as placing a pile of wet cement in the same class as Michaelangelo's statue of David. Matthew, it is true, did warn his readers that it was '… Herculean. You will need a helmet and gloves to attempt this wine, and a chaise longue nearby after a glass' but this hilarious imagery, its metaphors not so much mixed as kaleidoscopic, only dares people to try it when the responsible critic would surely warn his readers not to go anywhere near it.

When I challenged Matthew about this wine, in October 2007, he said 'I hold my hand up. I feel a bit guilty now about writing it up, but when I tasted it I was unaware it was so high in alcohol.' Perhaps when he tasted it, it being so much younger than when I did, it was feistier and the alcohol was masked. I have great admiration for Matthew's palate so this is a one-off lapse, comparable, maybe, to the Portuguese wine I recommended in the *Guardian* in 1990 which inspired readers to liken the abrasive malodorous liquid to wool socks freshly peeled from a footballer's feet after a strenuous game.

The problem of high alcohol in wines is very much a modern

one. It has been said, by authoritative commentators, that global warming has so increased the sunlight which berries soak up that sugar levels are higher than they have ever been. The sugar is turned into alcohol by yeast and with more sugar in the ferment creates wine with higher alcohol. Whereas I was brought up, as an autodidactic student of wine in the 1960s and 70s, to regard 13% as high, 13.5% as impressive, and 14% as huge, such levels over 13% are common across almost all wines nowadays and some drinkers regard it as evidence of a thin wine in the bottle and 12% or 12.5% as hardly being wine at all. Yet when I first encountered beaujolais and beaujolais nouveau in Paris in 1968, some years before these wines became ruined by commercial yeasts and the reckless additions of sugar to increase alcohol levels, I found utterly captivating reds of between 9.5% and 11.5% which not only went with a considerable repertoire of foods but did not get you unbearably sozzled.

Below I refer to the American critic Robert Parker's nigh addiction to high alcohol wines. He is as at home with such liquids as a hippo in mud. Mr Parker, in one edition of his wine guide, rated highly the Turley Moore Vineyard Zinfandel 1997 and it was 17.1% alcohol. What is a Turley wine of 17+% going to be consumed with? Certainly not any food I can think of. One compatible use, almost certainly, is to accompany a suicide as he lies in a warm bath listening to the gloomiest passages of Mahler with a razor to hand and if I were forced to live in a world where such wines were the norm I would certainly consider following his example.

Drink more wine but consume less alcohol
How can we combat globally warmed or otherwise unnaturally high-in-alcohol wines? Winemakers can adopt practices which reduce alcohol, not by weird spinning cones and mechanical means but, as one thoughtful South African producer suggested to me, by the harvesting of some vineyards, or part of a vineyard, when the grapes are under-ripe, with less sugar to turn into alcohol, and blending them with grapes picked later which have more sugar to

turn into alcohol.

Another way of reducing alcohol in wines is to reward lower alcohol wines by reducing their excise duty, by banning all chaptalisation (adding sugar for fermentation), and encouraging the use of natural yeasts instead of the latest lab-created monsters designed to allow yeast cells to survive above 17% alcohol. In the UK we have cripplingly high taxes on alcohol and tobacco. Only one is a poison, tobacco. The other, consumed sensibly, is a health drink. Only excessive alcohol makes wine a poison, or there is a bodily intemperance which creates dependence, alcoholism, because the intake cannot be moderated.

I would suggest that wine merchants cease constantly quoting wine writers who praise high alcohols and that we publicly disavow the judgements of such critics. No subsidies would be allowed to any wines over 14% alcohol, and for every half-percentage point above 12.5% I would increase the duty payable and, if possible, increase any sales tax. (In the UK, Vat is 17.5% on wine. In France, and other wine growing countries in Europe, the equivalent sales tax is miniscule. I recommend upping sales tax on all wines above 12.5% and above 14% to make the tax swingeing.)

All this must not, however, be taken to mean that I am in favour of some of the so-called lower-alcohol wines now creeping, like a plague, on to UK wine shelves. In July 2007, Sainsbury's launched a new range of own brand lower alcohol wines labelled Ten%. I confess I liked this labelling approach, certainly to get the range off the ground. Eventually, with the Utopian ideals I have sketched out above, all wines will be lower in alcohol and labelling of such starkness regarded as unnecessary (or even unhelpful). Sainsbury's range comprised Australian Chardonnay, Australian Sangiovese/Shiraz Rosé, Italian Pinot Grigio, and South African Chenin Blanc. Tesco, never to be outdone, came out with Van Loveren Light White 2007 (9%) from the Cape, Plume Chardonnay 2006 (9.46%) from the Midi, Van Loveren Blanc de Noir 2007 (12%) and Plume Syrah/Grenache 2006 (9.34%).

At the very sound of the pentasyllable, Low Alcohol Wine, a shiver of revulsion courses up the spine and creeps across the palate of the Bacchic enthusiast. Not because we relish intoxication, but because by designating a wine thus it is a besmirchment of the sensual experience of drinking. Wine is already the only alcohol one consumes without being aware of alcohol. It is wine's unique characteristic (it has others, not germane here). We embrace wine's fruit! Faultless wine has richness and texture, complexity and stimulation. But subtly. All these things can be found in the world's sleekest white wines, German Rieslings, where there are examples from 7.5% to 10% alcohol. Who needs a Low Alcohol Wine category?

However, today's drinkers ignore German Rieslings but not, British supermarkets Sainsbury and Tesco hope, the wines mentioned above. Will drinkers like these wines? If my palate is anything to go by definitely not. The Sainsbury Rosé 2007 is inoffensive and simple to the point of oblivion on the finish. Useful for putting out fires but not quenching a thirst. The Sainsbury Chardonnay 2007, pusillanimous from nose to throat, is a hollow mockery of this gallant grape. The Sainsbury Chenin Blanc 2007 is perkier, however, reflects its grape variety aromatically, but its dryness tends to austerity rather than elegance. The Sainsbury Pinot Grigio 2006 is also a prim wine, has a suggestion of varietal fidelity, but, as with the other three, is docile, lacks mid-palate aplomb and is distinctly bony on the finish. Each is bad value for money at £4.99. Curiously, however, perhaps they represent an argument for sealing wines with corks rather than screwcaps. The latter splendid advance is wasted on Sainsbury's Ten% range. Corks might at least taint these wines and give them some character.

Julian Dyer, a Sainsbury's wine buyer, defended his new babies thus: 'We've seen a real increase in sales around lower alcohol wines as consumers move towards lower calories and a healthier lifestyle. It seems that our customers are looking for slightly less alcohol but do not wish to compromise on quality or taste – these wines deliver perfectly. Our research shows that customers are put off low alcohol

10

WINE IS GOOD FOR YOU

But only if you relish the fruit, not the alcohol

'… bureaucracy, the rule of no-one, has become the modern form of despotism.'

Mary McCarthy

Did the committee from the Royal College of Physicians, commissioned by the British government in 1987, which arrived at the so-called 'safe drinking guide lines', having made their unscientific recommendations, go round the corner to a wine bar and celebrate with a terrific jeroboam of old claret? One suspects the answers to this question is no. Certainly the latter individuals had nothing to celebrate because according to physician Richard Smith (as reported in *The Times* of October 20th 2007) who was involved in the 1987 farrago at The Royal College of Surgeons, the guide-lines – how many units of alcohol it was safe weekly to consume – were based on figures which had been 'plucked out of the air. They were not based on any firm evidence at all. It was a sort of intelligent guess by a committee.'

Plucked out of the air! It seems beyond belief that any government would accept guide-lines from a committee without asking to look at the evidence behind its findings. The evidence, of course, did not exist. Thus the idea that a man drinking more than 21 units a week and a woman more than 14 units a week were endangering their health by so doing, was, and is, not based on hard evidence. This was later recognised when the figures were revised upwards to 28 units a week for men and 21 units for women. Yet who knows if such figures are accurate? They fail, for one thing, to take into account individuality and pretend that drinking limits are like speed limits: proven dangerous when exceeded by anyone. Each drinker is different, with an individual metabolism. Some people should not drink at all. Some people can manage twice the guide-line limits and lead a healthy life.

If the people who rule over us with their barmy pronounce-ments and crazy statistics had ever enjoyed wine properly how could they have acted, and continue to act, the way they do? Not only is the UK alcohol duty on table wine obscene, preventing many people who would benefit from a daily wine regime from enjoying a regular glass by compelling them to see wine only as an occasional luxury, but the lies about safe drinking demonise what is, enjoyed properly, the world's most wonderful health drink.

As pointed out in the previous chapter, wine is the one alcohol we don't taste when we drink it. What we taste in properly balanced wine is fruit. It is this fruit which makes wine so good for us. The evidence for the beneficial effects of moderate wine drinking is vast and if it did not exist I hardly believe the doctors of the Swindon General Hospital's cardiac unit, for example, would give its angina patients two glasses of Chilean cabernet sauvignon a day. If this sounds a strangely joyous use of NHS money let me further add that funding for these mild west country orgies comes from the hospital's charitable trust. The health benefits of wine, particularly red, were appreciated even by the Americans during Prohibition as, in that insane era, angina patients could acquire red wine on pre-scription from pharmacies. I do not propose to bore you with reams of documentary evidence but I will just quote from a single conference, a wine and health congress which took place in Bordeaux in September 2007. Attended by the 'pioneers of alcohol related research', according to the digest Alcohol in Moderation (AIM) which reported on the congress, this reiterated the evidence showing 'the protective effect of wine on the cardiovascular system and total mortality'. AIM reported that 'Scientists from many countries met to discuss and analyse the latest findings regarding wine, and particularly its polyphenols, and the wider issues regarding moderate alcohol consumption, diet and health. There is no question that wine and especially red wine is a potent source of antioxidants, or that alcohol assists the solubility of these antioxidants... What was clear from data reported at the conference was that people who begin to consume a Mediterranean diet, especially when including the regular consumption of wine, showed a marked improvement in health.'

'But somewhat surprising,' AIM added, 'was a report of a recent study at Harvard University showing that even among the 'healthiest' men (non-smokers, lean, ate a Mediterranean diet, and exercised regularly) those who also drank moderately had their risk of a heart attack lowered, indicating an independent protective effect from alcohol.'

Wine is now by far the most popular alcohol in the UK and is increasingly seen as a necessary adjunct to a civilised lifestyle. Even the retailers are jumping on the health bandwagon with the introduction in 2006 and 2007 of the Red Heart Australia and Red Heart Australia brace of reds. Claiming to have an antioxidant level higher than leading branded wines, these two wines cost £4.99 the bottle.

Without doubt, the perceived healthiness of wine over other alcohol has contributed to its increasing popularity. In spite of the overall consumption of alcohol in the UK falling 5.3% over the past two years, wine has grown steadily in popularity. Data from Customs & Excise reveal that UK wine consumption has gone from 14% of the population in 1980 to 18% in 1990 to 29% in 2006. Quite how this last statistic squares with figures which, given in the summer of 2008, say that 84% of the adult population enjoyed at least one glass of wine in the previous month, I do not know. I always claim 75% of Britons are wine drinkers.

In spite of wine's popularity, the government prefers to tax it unreasonably and scare people with phoney safe-limit figures. It is time for a change of policy or, failing that, a change of government. No-one has put it with more clarity than New South Wales GP and

11

WHY WINE MERCHANTS DAREN'T TELL YOU THE TRUTH: EVER

'One of the most salient features of our culture is that there is so much bullshit.'

Harry G. Frankfurt, On Bullshit, 2005

An ex-employee of a leading wine merchant once told me that with scant knowledge of the subject after leaving university she was hired by a leading London dealer to phone customers up and sweet talk them into buying expensive cases. She was encouraged to meet these men and, being an attractive blonde, she was showered with offers of dates by her customers and was soon flogging lots of cases of extravagant wines. If she did not know the answer to a question she was told 'to make it up'.

'What do such customers know about wine or care to know?' as a wine merchant put it to me. 'They have heard of a few select names and if a glamour puss catches them at the right moment, after receiving some fat City bonus, then they are easily able to blue £40,000 on a few cases of wine.'

I am not suggesting that all wine merchants are as devious and manipulative as the one just referred to, but there is no doubt that no wine merchant is above economy with the truth and beyond romancing in order to keep the reputation of a wine label high. The truth is that wine is not timeless. It is the product of different conditions each year, it is unstable in quality, yet if any merchant is to retain the loyalty of any producer he has to sell the wine. Given the choice between speaking the honest truth, which would see a wine remain unsold, and spinning a yarn which keeps sales buoyant, what merchant is going to play the saint and chew dry bread?

Unimaginable wines

It was Benjamin Disraeli who said there are lies, damned lies, and statistics. May I offer an adjustment? There are liars, damned liars, and wine merchants (in their own way the wiliest of statisticians).

Daily, as the wine catalogues thump on to my door mat and I peruse their fevered paragraphs as they heap praise on the wine producers they represent, one marvels that there can be any bad wines made in the world. The language used is regularly misty, sentimental and overblown, and often employed to depict wines the fruit of which it is impossible to imagine actually existing.

Take this typical specimen from a list of burgundies offered by Notting Hill merchant John Armit: 'Great Corton Charlemagne with all the masculine intensity you expect from this Appellation.' 'Masculine intensity'? Does this mean the wine screams abuse at football referees? Could it refer to the wine's habit of never lowering the lavatory seat after use? Perhaps Mr Armit meant to imply what exactly? I do not know, though I do get the impression that the wine's grapes were difficult to squeeze.

I do not believe the writer knew exactly what he meant when he wrote what he did. I have every confidence that his poor customers (or rather rich ones since they are being invited to stump up £690, excluding duty and Vat, for a case of this intense masculine experience) have no idea what the phrase could mean either, and, if they are sensible, they will pass over the listing. The fact that Monsieur Patrick Bize, who made the Corton in question, genuinely manages to fashion, now and then, some of the more sensual interpretations of Burgundy you'd never know from the description.

There is also, readers may recall, the phrase 'waterish Burgundy' in King Lear though in fairness to the wine this is a Will-owy pun referring as it does to the Duke of this region finding his passion for Cordelia diluted when he realises she has been disinherited by her barking mad dad. Burgundy in those days, when the play was written in 1605 (let alone a thousand years earlier when the play is set), was notorious for its myriad streams, rills and brooks.

Supermarkets (and major high-street chains) are not the worst offenders here as none of them, even when it prints a consumer wine list, goes into extravagant detail about each producer, preferring the lazier option of throwing clichéd wine notes together.[5] The sort of wine merchant mostly referred to in this chapter, though, is the one or two shop merchant, some with a local following but many able to deliver nationwide. Some are members of a select little band. Others sell to restaurants or small merchants at wholesale prices (and even here, where it might be said professional is talking to professional, the fantasies abound).

Such merchants represent producers with whom they have had, in some cases, relationships stretching back decades. They have no option but to fluff their producers' labels because if they did not they would lose the business. This is why the producers are always 'prestigious', or the winemaker the 'most talented, award-winning, a master' or 'amongst the most exciting' or, when the writer is really stuck for something rational he says that so-and-so is 'completely dedicated to expressing the personality of the *terroir* and relentlessly pursues excellence' or 'owned by so-and-so who also has the fabulous chateau X' or 'makes wine in the vineyard' or (very popular this) 'his vineyards are on the same latitude as Bordeaux (or Burgundy or Hermitage etc)'.

Almost every adjective as applied to any wine in any wine merchant's catalogue, therefore, must be approached with extreme scepticism. These descriptions are either made up or simply impossible to verify by research or are meaningless as indicators as to what the wine tastes like, or whether it is really any good. However gilded, the words are no better than the kind of falsehoods real estate agents used to employ (before it became illegal in Britain), and that the producers love to hear written about themselves. These producers read their merchants' write-ups, too (or have them translated for them), and so it is crucial for the wine merchant that only honeyed words are written.

It is for this reason, plus the paucity of writing talent and style amongst merchants (though in Britain there are exceptions like Yapp Brothers on its Rhône wines, Adnams, with only the occasional lapse, on anything, and Lay & Wheeler when its buyer Simon Larkin is describing different vintages of Billecart-Salmon champagnes), that all merchants love to employ quotes from wine writers.

Robert Parker, in particular, is popular, or failing him the *Wine Spectator* or failing that there is dear old Jancis Robinson. Parker's point scoring system is loved by wine merchants as they know that any wine to which they can legitimately append a 90+ rating will fly out of the door, no further verbal sales adornment, in some cases, being necessary. What everyone fails to note is that the Parker rating can apply to a single bottle, tasted some time ago, and that not only will the wine have changed in bottle but if it is sealed with a cork, and the vast majority of wines experienced by this taster (Parker) are so sealed, then without doubt each bottle of any wine of any age will be different from the wine to which Parker awarded a high or indeed a low score.

'Every wine in this star-studded list is a peach.' Do they mean, sweet and ripe? Druitt/Porta Italica/Hallgarten (April 2007) on their Italian wines.

'They set out to put the essence of the best vineyards in the area into a bottle.' Yes, but do they grow any of the grapes? Genesis trade catalogue (September 2007) of Brewer-Clifton a Santa Barbara California producer.

'… may be the finest Duhart-Milon made ever! best consumed between 2010-2030 92 points.' Wait another 24 years? With a cork in the bottle? Richard Kihl catalogue (December 2006) quoting Robert Parker.

'… in the same ownership as Lafite.' Please. Spare us. *The Wine Society* (July/October 2007 catalogue) on Château Rieussec 2002.

'It's graceful and poised, in a more feminine style with a long, fine and pure finish.' Is this a wine or a writing implement for sexists? Uncorked wine catalogue (winter 2006/7) quoting sarahmarsh.com.

'Winemaker Dave Guffy… believes in "making wine in the vineyard".' Nonsense. He makes wine in a winery. Enotria catalogue on The Hess Collection wines, California.

'Lying Abroad.' What does it mean?' A rare touch of modesty. I'm sure a wine merchant can lie at home too. Tanners vintage report on Bordeaux 2006.

'Austria has a latitude similar to that of Burgundy.' And Thierry Henri used to live parallel to my street. Does that mean I can kick a football? Adnams (June 2007).

'Jean-Charles exhibits an adroit sense of purpose and unwavering tenacity − his pursuit of excellence results in tremendous precision and a fundamental quality which is recognised all over the world.' Aside from this being semi-literate babble (what else can tenacity be but unwavering? In what way can precision be tremendous?), it is utterly meaningless. Corney & Barrow (2007/8) on the burgundy producer Domaine Bonneau du Martray.
What really takes the chocolate-coated biscuit from this wine merchant with regard to its burgundies is Corney & Barrow's next entry in the same list.
'… at your request, we have introduced a clear and simple marking system. 10–12 Above average to good wine 12–14 A

good to very good wine 14-16 A very good to excellent wine 16-18 An excellent to outstanding wine 18-20 An outstanding to legendary wine.'

The crafty writers state that 'wines are judged within the context of a vintage and value for money'. For a wine merchant to make such claims is utterly absurd, wholly misleading and to be wholly disbelieved by its customers. How can wine rating 10 be above average? Incredibly, the burgundies from the 2006 vintage, from the estates the merchant represents in the UK, all, except one (which scored 15-plus) scored a minimum of 16 points, many got 17 and 18, and several 18-plus and 19. The 15 producers listed, offering some 90 different wines, all so seductively rated and described, may well be committed, skilled winemakers. But to exploit a rating system like this is to demean it. Be as sceptical about so blatantly biased an approach as you would be towards a set of exam papers marked by the parent of the child sitting the exam.

'The grapes from this *vieilles-vignes* wine come from vines which are up to 85 years old, meaning lots of flavour and depth.' The age of a vine is irrelevant to flavour and depth, only the yield of grapes is significant along with the winemaker's skill at handling the fruit. I have tasted wine from vines 8 years old alongside the wine from vines 90 years old, from the same winemaker, and the younger wine was deeper and more flavourful. Vintage Roots catalogue (2006/7) on the wines of Château Pech-Latt.

'Your glass will brim with subtle hints of spring blossom from the ever popular Gallo family vineyards.' You mean, they pick the blossom all that time before the grapes are ripe? Amazing! Thresher (summer 2007) on its Pick of the Season, but perhaps chosen because its producer is so powerful?

'All three bottles have a bit of bottle age and are drinking beautifully. A real treat at a terrific price.' So for God's sake take them off our hands, please, before they get any older. Tesco wine club magazine (September 2007) written for gullible supermarket customers.

I have scores of catalogues and almost any page of any one offers examples of prose like that above. Whilst it is easier to dismiss it all as mere careless, unconsidered blather, the empty boasting and flannel of the wine merchant, it disguises a profound problem: wine merchants believe what they write and some readers believe what they read. It is almost as if it is expected of the wine merchant that he talks so high-falutingly, so mysteriously, so richly in clichés.

12

VINTAGE

*A subject about which more rubbish is talked than
sex, politics, football and religion*

The French have always been geniuses at manuring their vines with bullshit and there is never a shortage of wine writers to rally round and lick their boots. If it isn't claims of the superiority of French vineyards – all that sacred soil and so on – it is the purity of French wine laws. The bullshit reaches its apogee of aromatic intensity, however, when vintage declarations are made which claim that a specific vineyard area has come up with its vintage of the decade or, in the case of the Bordeaux 2000 vintage, the greatest ever.

When such claims are enhanced by critics like Robert Parker, who has a status amongst US wine buffs similar to that of Elvis Presley amongst dead–popstar–worshippers, then Bordeaux châteaux can ask any money they like for their 2000 wines (which in many cases the buyers will not even have tasted and evaluated personally). Never mind that each vineyard makes its own wine in its own way and thus human factors predominate over all others. Never mind that each bottle is sealed with a cork which will ensure a percentage of faulty wines as well as huge individual bottle variation between the same wines as they age. Never mind reality. It is all about perception. No US wine collector will be able to sleep at night knowing he does not have representatives of 2000 vintage Bordeaux in his cellar.

But, and it is a deliciously massive 'but', how can any such a person, patriotic to his Gucci soft-soled slip-ons, contemplate purchasing wine from the fickle and fiendish French? From the nation which, quite sensibly, would have nothing to do with the Iraqi invasion? Relations between the two nations are not at an all-time high and it is, in some quarters of the States, seen as an anti-American act not only to acquire French products, let alone ask for them in restaurants, but even to use French words in conversation (French Fries have, I believe, been replaced by Brit Chips).

I have been studying wine merchants lists, magazines and brochures, and auction catalogues, since 1966 and only once, in all that time, have I read any horribly critical words said about any vintage. The Henekeys & Backs of Norwich catalogue of winter 1966/7 remarked of Bordeaux that 1963 is 'A wash-out in every sense.'

Do those words stand as a beacon of rectitude and honesty in a sea of deception and gloss? Or do they amount to yet again a stupid blanket verdict of little value? As it happens 1963 was indeed a disaster throughout Bordeaux as widespread rain throughout September caused rotten grapes and this could not be masked even by chaptalisation. However, what I learned at that time, as I was beginning to travel to France and other European countries, that some producers managed to make more than passable wines. I can recall only Leoville-Lascases of that year as being attractive, and there may have one or two more, and therefore I came to the view that generalisations were baseless. All that mattered, and matters, is the individual producer.

Yet even Waitrose, a British supermarket wine retailer of greater integrity and less cynical ruthlessness than most, saw fit to trumpet the 2005 Bordeaux vintage as 'once in a lifetime' and, laughably, 'The vintage of the century' in its 2005 '*En Primeur* Bordeaux' offer brochure. Whilst I could readily appreciate that the weather conditions of the summer and early autumn, the crucial period prior to grape harvest, were exceptionally dry and clement in 2005, it is totally fatuous for embroiderers like Anthony Rose of the *Independent* newspaper, whose words were used as an advertisement in the brochure, to write '2005 came flying out of the blocks with the grace and vigour of a Kelly Holmes and looks set to turn into a vintage with the staying power of Paula Radcliffe. I cannot recall a time when young red Bordeaux tasted from the cask was marked by such wonderfully pristine, balanced and richly-textured fruit.'

No-one can judge any wine's staying power until it is tasted in the bottle never mind cask. Wine writers in Britain are peculiarly susceptible to penning high flown prose about vintages in barrel. It is a national disease. Attempting to be definitive about a wine before it is in the bottle is imprudent; each producer will treat each wine differently (with regard to fining and filtration and perhaps blending manoeuvres). There is also the effects of the barrel aging on the wine. This is best judged after the wine has been released for sale and has been in bottle for a little time. The golden rule is always to wait for a wine to go on sale before opening your mouth and being oracular.

Climate change and hot air

In between the 2000 and 2005 vintage hyperbole there was the year 2003, especially in Burgundy. This is only the third new Millennium vintage I have tasted in depth and it confirmed how impossible it was to offer intelligent coherent sweeping views. Indeed, there was more rubbish talked about this vintage than any for years.

Why?

The answer is tannin. 2003 was a monstrously hot year and Burgundy is not supposed to be the Costa Brava but in 2003 it was and the grapes, to protect themselves, grew thick jackets of antioxidants in their skins. As the colour leaches into the wine from maceration so do the antioxidants in the form of tannins. 2003 was a year which threw up monumental tannins in the wines and growers, *negociants*, wine writers, and, crucially, wine merchants were, and many still are, all in a tither – mostly because they have never tasted tannins, and low acidities, like this in burgundies before.

Acid production in grapes, and photosynthesis, are affected by high temperatures and lack of water (irrigation being forbidden in Burgundy) and this is why the tannins were so high – small berries, thick skins, reduced acids – especially on south-facing vineyards. (In some cases, berries were not ripened properly. It is important to realise that sun does not create ripeness regardless; if you cannot water a vine and the heat is extreme the plant will close down internal systems to survive. With photosynthesis thus curtailed, how can berries get properly ripe?)

Another important, massively important, factor: once you fine and filter a wine you remove character. Once you stick a cork in the bottle, tannins can be absorbed or aspirate out, and fruit, with less acid, fade. So how full of character will the 2003 burgundies, out of their misleading casks and contained within glass, be within a few years? Will the tannins last? Will the fruit fade before the tannins are softened and ameliorated?

Of course, acids had to be added to the must (as it was in 1997, another warm vintage). This is now routine in France. Yet it is a practice the French once vehemently derided the Australians for always following. However, with global warming the French have no choice, in some cases, and increasingly so, but to use tartaric acids to balance the grape musts before fermentation. Perhaps the best clue to who made the best wines in this vintage – now that drinking them is under consideration – is to ask when the producer picked the grapes. Paradoxically, those who waited for true physiological ripeness in their grapes, with properly ripe pips throwing out less harsh tannins, may make the most graceful wines. I do not know the answers to the questions this throws up.

These are some of the fundamental concerns for this vintage in Burgundy. They cloud every judgement anyone can make about it.

However, despite the furore, I do reckon the 2003s will, for the most part, be better drunk now rather than being kept longer. But I say this because, although I am a lover of pinot, I also adore tannins and I do not associate the two – pinot and tannins. I do not associate them so strongly as one would, say, with cabernet or syrah. It's rather like seeing the phenomenal Manchester United (at time of writing) footballer Ronaldo (to indulge in sporting metaphors) middle-weight boxing and doing it rather well but only in parts. Do you advise him to give up football and box or stick to what he knows best? If hot vintages become routine in Burgundy, then the sinuous footballer will become an aggressive pugilist, but we must wait and see whether the learning curve this will dramatically initiate will be perilous or smooth. I fear the former.

Burgundy is a conservative, very traditional area. Change is not lightly welcomed. Yet change was forced on the producers in 2003 right from the start. The so-called *Ban des Vendanges*, the first official day of picking, was proclaimed on the 18th of August (in 1996, for example, it was more than a month later). Yet some pickers had been out for 2 or 3 days before, forced to believe it was crucial to pick the grapes early because of the sun (up to 40 degrees centigrade). Many pickers were on their annual August holiday as picking is normally much later, so I assume, but do not know, that there were not as many people available as normal to do the work.

Later pickings benefited from irrigation from God; rain did fall towards the end of August, and cooler weather arrived by early September. And so those who picked in early September may make more robust wines in the long run. As for the white burgundies, with the exception of the odd one, I am sceptical of the 2003's ability to have produced widespread beauties of classic proportions.*

Hyping the millennial hype

If the hype about the 2000 French vintage was marvellous to behold – and 2003 bewildering – the 2005 was overwhelming. Though I might poke a little fun at certain commentators it was notable that there was consensus.

But underpinning this kind of febrile unanimity are the powerful market forces which compel commentators to take part in the circus. French vintage declarations are a spin-doctor's dream, for, particularly when the weather has been spectacularly clement, only little elbow grease needs to be expended to create dizzying rates of spin. Certain wine writers feel a compulsion to take part, rub shoulders with the barrels, and to issue their orotund verdicts. If it does nothing else, it ensures that a wine region gets good column inches in the press.

If one were to charge these commentators and critics as merely being the stooges of French PR executives, they would look at you in hurt despair and surprise. We are independent, they would cry. We form our own opinions, they would insist. This is true, yet merely by going beyond the role of spectator at the circus and becoming a performer, they add weight to the hype. Indeed, they are the hype – outside of that generated by the producers themselves and the exporters in whose interests it is to enthuse over the vintage because the wines have to be sold. And if they can sell each year at a higher price than the year before, so much the better.

This is why it would, in my view, be much better for wine critics to be less flamboyant with their praise, more circumspect with their views, and not allow themselves to be merely part of the PR machinery which is wholly designed to inflame drinker's imaginations and set them all dreaming of becoming wine investors or collectors or merely able to have an opinion, albeit someone else's, on a particular vintage.

In both 2004 and 2006, I was regularly asked by people who were otherwise restrained intelligent human beings what I thought of 2003 burgundies (and should they buy) and 2005 bordeaux (and should they invest). It was as if not to ask me was a dereliction of rationality. How could these modest fellows (it is always men who do the asking) not want to know what I thought?

Take the 20th April 2003 edition of the *Observer* newspaper on the 2000 Bordeaux vintage. All the top and middle end UK newspapers waxed lyrical about the same subject, and the gush was not untypical. Under the headline 'Bordeaux beats boycott with 'best vintage of all time', the *Observer* said:

Just when it seemed safe to boycott all things French, they turn up with perhaps the greatest wine ever the 2000 Bordeaux. Even when early samples were being tasted from barrels in 2001, the vintage was hailed as potentially the finest from the most famous of regions. At the top end of the market, bottles are going for more than £200, but a trickle-down effect is fuelling demand in the £5 to £15 bracket

Chris Hardie of the Majestic chain of wine merchants told the *Observer* 'It really is a delightfully ripe and fruity vintage, which reaches out to new wine drinkers while still reflecting the classic Bordeaux style.' At rival Oddbins warehouse in Glasgow's West End, wine manager Ross Buchanan reported brisk trade and said more exclusive labels, such as Château Margaux, would sell for £200 a bottle. 'Loads of people are coming in and asking about the 2000 Bordeaux', he said, 'among the general public, as well as connoisseurs, it's the most talked-about wine in years'

The excitement surrounding the 2000 vintage became a frenzy in the United States. The nod of approval from one or two key American specialist publications can send prices and reputations soaring. King among the critics is Robert Parker. He first tasted the 2000 Bordeaux in barrels years ago, and called it 'a phenomenal year that might turn out to be one of the greatest vintages Bordeaux has ever produced'. In 2002, Parker tasted the wines again: they fulfilled his prediction. 'This is the greatest vintage Bordeaux has ever produced,' he raved.'

To its credit and his, the *Observer* wine critic, Tim Atkin, was quoted in the article and he sounded the only note of intelligent caution by saying: 'Much has been said about the 2000 Bordeaux and it is a great year, but I think it is too early to herald it as the greatest ever or even the greatest since 1961.' Wise words. The fuss over Bordeaux 2000 generated a vast lather of confusing froth which did not wholly represent substance beneath. (That the most expensive specimens may, as Mr Parker opined, be tremendous I cannot really say as I have not tasted enough of them to offer an opinion in depth.)

The surest measure of the vintage hype are the merchants. Here is Lay & Wheeler, in July 2006, on a famous 2005 bordeaux red:

> 2005 Château Cheval-Blanc, 1er Grand Cru Classé (A), St Émilion at £2625 per 6 bottles in bond. Both rich and full, and the tannins seem fine and well-masked. Such a fine nature here, near perfect poise. Sophisticated and elegant, a fine Cheval-Blanc. order now – it may well prove to be your last chance to secure certain wines in this outstanding vintage.

A curiously muted and confused write-up (a longer one was available on the firm's website) and difficult to decipher. Is it not impossible to be rich without being full? Does one want one's tannins to be well-masked? What is a fine nature in this context? Sophisticated and elegant is an interesting conjunction; it suggests that if you don't like the wine, having splashed out over £437 on a bottle (excluding duty, vat and delivery), you lack the sophistication and elegance required to appreciate it. Of course, keeping the wine for a few more years, in the six-pack, will result in six different wines as each cork in each bottle will ensure variation in aroma, flavour, complexity and body. What an absurd lottery!

A collector's item: a wine merchant's puff
At the London wine merchant Corney & Barrow, its description of the Bordeaux 2005, which customers were encouraged to consider buying *en primeur* (that is to say still in cask, before it goes into bottle and becomes a different liquid), was fulsome not to say feverish. It was a lengthy, deliciously indulgent, erudite write-up, of which I can only provide a portion here, but the writer, the urbane Adam Brett-Smith, did provide subtle pointers where danger lurked

(which I have italicised where worthy) and to any perceptive Corney & Barrow customer this should have been enough to inspire exceedingly wariness at getting carried away. However, I suspect most well-heeled customers eagerly jumped in with both feet, cheque book open, mouth agog. Let me give you a tour of Corney & Barrow's prose:

> The best wines in 2005 – and there are quite a number of them – exhibit power, richness and concentration, a significant structure which will guarantee and require extended cellaring, and a hallmark of sometimes dazzling freshness and purity of form.

'*Require extended cellaring*' means that only customers of serious wealth need concern themselves with the wines as they need a proper temperature-controlled cellar. 'Dazzling freshness' means the tannins are stark and any tender palate will be outraged. This emphasises the need for the luxury of the cellar in order for the wines properly to mature and lose their 'dazzling freshness.'

> The unique qualities of the vintage are the combination of such spectacular ingredients and a bar of consistency set very high indeed. Assuming that these embryonic offerings are handled sensitively pre-bottling, customers will find themselves in possession of something very great indeed.

Assuming that these '*embryonic*' offerings are handled sensitively pre-bottling is a key proviso and as written cannot be bettered for style and efficacy. It reveals that the wines are embryos, thus not fully formed and will develop in ways no-one can truly predict. Crucially, it also points out that the wines will be going through another stage of manufacture: being taken from a cellar, perhaps fined, possibly filtered, handled in various ways, and then bottled on a mechanical bottling line. The word assumption conveys, then, guesswork and the presence of imponderables. In other words, beware!

> If there is a certainty about the quality of the best wines...
> This is not an 'early drinking' vintage, nor does it have the
> seductive, addictive charm perhaps of 1982, 1990 or even
> 1989 vintage legends.

'*If there is*' clearly offers the reader the chance to pooh-pooh the hype though in following this with 'a certainty about the quality of the best wines' a wicked ambiguity is set up – the writers clearly would love to claim perfection for all the 2005 bordeaux he has to sell but cannot. '*Not an "early drinking*"' indicates that if you don't like any of the wines when you open them, unable to contain yourself, expect not to enjoy what you taste. '*Seductive, addictive charm of previous vintage legends*' allows the reader to both reflect on their deliciousness and their spectacular rise in value since release.

> The wines possess very high levels of concentration, richness
> and extract with significantly high tannins and hallmarks of
> focus, intensity, purity and freshness owing in part to
> excellent acidity levels. These are the qualities that the
> growing season offered quite naturally, and they required
> sensitive and above all neutral translation.

'*High levels of concentration, richness and extract with significantly high tannins*' repeating an early point that these wines will not be easy to like in their youth. 'Quite naturally' so no sugar additions were necessary. 'Sensitive and above all neutral translation' again warns the reader and potential buyer that these are moody untamed monsters.

Those who sought, through winemaking, even greater

extraction, more profound colours and higher tannic levels have produced disturbing, often grotesque parodies of ingredients that needed no such initiatives.

'*Grotesque parodies of ingredients*' is a subtle nudge at *terroir*, I am delighted to note, as it makes clear that some winemakers did well, others badly, and that any wines owes more to its winemaker than climate.

There were a number of wines we tasted in both the northern Médoc and more sadly St Émilion that we did not understand and whose future development we simply could not visualise – these were the wines to avoid. Nevertheless the consistency of quality in 2005 remains very high.

'*These were the wines to avoid*' means that all the wines Corney & Barrow have to offer are the opposite and exquisitely chosen exemplars.

Demand for 2005 will be driven by both traditional European markets as well as the USA and Asia, with our first sightings of prospective Indian customers amidst the circus of the 'big band' trade tastings in Bordeaux during April. The drug of *En Primeur* is more powerful than ever... the more traditional markets will look back on 2005 and indeed preceding good and great vintages as possibly the last 'Golden Era' opportunity of wine buying, in particular of the great classed growths of Bordeaux customers should not ignore the more gentle but still classical charm of 2004, or the dangerous, irregular but supremely exciting 2003s. I believe the latter may – in some cases and communes – exceed the quality of 2005. In summary, when 99% of the world tells you to do this or to do that, there is often wisdom in listening to the small voice who suggests, perhaps mildly, to do a bit of the other.

'*First sightings of prospective Indian customers*' points to the fact that inexperienced hugely wealthy greenhorns are interested in the 2005s and so customers who hesitate to purchase quickly, before even tasting but relying wholly on the merchant's opinions, will be disappointed. '*Possibly the last "Golden Era" opportunity*' wonderfully flags that time is of the essence. 'Buy now whilst stocks last!' is a cruder way of putting it. '*Listening to the small voice*' means believing in Corney & Barrow.

In that much undervalued category fall the vintages of 2004, 2003, 2001 and even 1999. 2005 will be expensive. Once again the curtain rises slowly, the scene is set, the plot unfolds and the outcome remains, as so often a matter of conjecture, doubt, fear and optimism. Theatre indeed, with a full and expectant house.

'*2005 will be expensive*' means you going to pay a lot and that not to do so would be foolish. Only the most expensive wines, perforce, will show high rates of investment return. '*Theatre*' indeed, with a full and expectant house is wonderful writing clearly revealing the writer's own inner turmoil that he is once again merely an actor dancing to the script of the major château proprietors as they rake in the dosh.

In spite of everything that such prose strives to be – balanced, not soppy or stupidly enthusiastic (note the lack of facile metaphors which often convey nothing but a writer's poverty of style and imagination) – the reader is left in no doubt: Bordeaux 2005 is irresistible. It cannot be ignored. It must be acquired.

The Alsace points the way
But if any blanket vintage statement confirmed that one must taste the wines before considering purchase, and rely on individual wine

makers not wine merchants, then it was in Alsace in 2006. The official French report began honestly and simply: '2006 will go down in history as a vintage which produced good quality wines thanks to masterly wine making skills and in spite of a difficult year.'

There you have it. In a nutshell.

Forget *terroir*. Ignore vintage. Taste the wines from producers you trust and whose wines you have enjoyed in the past. It is all about wine making skills and these can be poor, mediocre, good and brilliant. It is always about wine making skills. They matter more than whether a vintage was phenomenal or wretched, whether the wine merchant was lyrical or grouchy, and they transcend anything any wine critic can think or express in words.

13

BoGoFS

How the wine consumer is bamboozled

Actually, not all consumers are so stupid. (Or are Novacastrians sharper than the rest of us?) Anyway, on September 14th 2007 there I am in Newcastle, having driven up two of my children to go to university in the city, and I find myself in a newsagent's shop, early morning. There's a small woman by the stash of papers and she's looking through the tabloid pages of the *Daily Mail* and she snorts in derision and barks at me 'They must think we're daft to believe this twaddle.' I get my usual paper, the *Guardian*. She snorts again and brandishes the paper at me. What I see is not a news item or an article but a full page advertisement and naturally I am interested because it shows seven bottles of wine with the headline 'Less than half price at Morrisons – corking!'

When I buy the paper and examine the ad in detail I do not mind admitting I am rather shocked. It is patently obvious that supermarket chain Morrisons is perpetrating a fraud. How can a bottle of Charles de Villers Brut Champagne cost £23.99? It is hugely overpriced. Perhaps even at the price the ad trumpets it has been reduced to, £11.79, it is overpriced. It is a con. The wine has been artificially inflated when first put on sale to establish a phoney basis for then flogging it later at its real price. This is also true of the other bottles from the Codornieu Reserva Cava (an absurd £9.99 to £4.79) and the five other wines, including brands such as Rosemount and Incyon, each artificially overpriced at £7.99 and reduced to £3.79/99.

This utterly destroys any true brand values which could be established by any wine thus exploited as it is only the retailer who benefits in this regard. The supplier may, of course, sell a lot of wine in a short period but he will not be able to create true brand personality. It is surprising that Rosemount and Incyon, from Australia and Sicily respectively, allow themselves to be used in this way in Morrisons advertising as both have tried to establish themselves as decent brands in their own right. Rosemount, it is true, has hugely lost its way, but Incyon, in spite of its stupid name (or perhaps because of it), continues to turn out some deservedly popular wines. Pricing like Morrisons, not to mention the advertising, will eventually destroy both brandcredibility. Or should, at any rate.

Pricing cons are now routine with supermarkets and high street chains (particular the British chain Thresher's). If all consumers were as on the ball as that woman in Newcastle then perhaps the practice of overpricing in order to fake a discount price would be discounted. However, why are such scams permitted? In Britain, the wine trade's regulatory bodies have been incredibly feeble in taking any action to put a stop to it. It is now a feature of almost every major retailer's wine shelves.

Even an innovative product like Arniston Bay's 1.5-litre pouches (which I applaud) were launched (as they should have been), not at a proper price at Tesco but an outlandish £8.99. Some time later this price was reduced, to a per-bottle equivalent of £3.24, making it a bargain only by virtue of an honest price for a reasonable wine. The original £8.99, however, was ludicrous. When I invited the marketing director of the importers of this wine, Keith Lay of Erhmanns, to comment on this he stayed silent. Doubtless he was wary of upsetting Tesco which dictated the pricing terms to him on the probable basis of take it or leave it, mate.

All major supermarkets work on a percentage margin. The practice of fake pricing allows them to maintain these margins yet at the same time provide a point of difference, either on shelf with a prominent discounted price displayed or, as with the Morrisons ad, to use in paid publicity.

These margins are generous and, from the data I have assembled, work out as below. (Note: acquiring sales info like this is almost as difficult as acquiring Chinese military intelligence. All retailers refuse to reveal such things. I had to resort to sleuth tactics.): Tesco 33%. Sainsbury 35%. Asda 32%. Somerfield 33%. Waitrose 35%. Majestic 30%. Oddbins 40%. Co-op 30%. Morrisons 35%. Thresher 45%. These margins are as they were up to the summer of 2007 and so may have been adjusted since. Essentially, they give a very good indication. These margins are by far the largest in the supply chain. The producer of a wine selling at £2.99 at Tesco, for example, has to let it go at 0.46 Euro a bottle. (Freight, UK duty and Vat have to be added on to that 0.46 Euro, which is around 32p, so the biggest profiteer in the deal is the British exchequer. It is an insane merry-go-round – especially when you bear in mind the grotesque subsidies which allow a producer to flog a wine at 32p a bottle.)

It is also, in the view of one of the UK wine trade's most established legends, Allan Cheesman (now chairman of Berkmann Wine Cellars but for almost 20 years previously the head of Sainsbury's wine department), 'almost criminal' for supermarkets to pressurise suppliers by insisting on such generous margins for themselves leaving so little for the makers of the wines. In a revealing interview, in September 2007, with the wine trade magazine *Harpers*, Mr Cheesman, said '1.25% isn't a big enough margin for any supplier. It's almost criminal that suppliers are expected to run a business under that sort of pressure.' He then went on to characterise supermarket wine buyers as 'prima donnas' and that 'I really question the honesty and integrity of some of them.'

In late December 2007, the managing director of Waitrose was quoted as using the word 'duping' in connection with certain of its rivals' discounting schemes. He was alleged to have said that Tesco and Asda underwrote the cheaper prices on the discounted products by hiking the prices of others.

One dedicated supplier of wines to supermarkets is the London merchant Bibendum. I happened in the summer of 2007 to find myself drinking with a wine salesman who told me that when he was headhunted for a job there he thought he'd pull their accounts from Companies House so he could see the financial health of a company which might employ him.

'I was enlightened by discovering,' he said to me, 'that in 2006 the company's turnover was £170-million and its declared profit was just £385,000. I didn't take the job.'

I pointed out that maybe Bibendum's directors were merely paying themselves fortunes, driving luxury cars and flying private jets, but the salesman shook his head and said he though it was related the profit margin they were making.

Who knows the truth here? All I can say, in the face of what is merely an anecdote and a few figures, is that there is no getting away from the fact that the small margins available to wine suppliers to supermarkets is hurting the wine industry.

Early in 2008, the British wine importer Orbital, considered one of the brightest and most innovative around, run by some superbly experienced wine industry guys, owning some well-respected wine brands (Stormhoek from South Africa and Camden Park from Australia), went into administration, its three major directors and 10 staff all losing their jobs.

How could this happen? Somewhat stupidly (it has to be admitted), Orbital sold a load of Stormhoek sauvignon blanc and pinotage to Tesco where it went on sale at £4.99 at what must have been a punishing profit margin for the supplier. The same wine was more sensibly priced at £5.99 at Sainsbury's and Waitrose who immediately threw the wine off the shelf when they discovered their arch-rival Tesco had undercut them in a way with which they could not compete.

Magnified evil

Small supplier margins also restrict choice, force more and suppliers to merge or to seek takeover opportunities, and in the end it will lead not just to fewer and fewer suppliers but to an homogenisation of product which will inspire fraud and encourage mediocrity.

As mentioned previously in this book, for certain wine suppliers in Australia, in the face of the worst drought in living memory, to have access to enough grapes for their supermarket products they could be forced – and I have heard allegations that some already are – to ship grape juice in from South America and elsewhere and fraudulently pretend it was their own Aussie born and raised product. Thus we see here the evil connection between possible deception and how supermarket trading practices encourage it.

The difference, the real bloody minded difference, between wine and all other food and drink products on sale in the supermarkets is that wine is historically the product of a particular vintage (year). A non-vintage wine (like many a champagne) can buffer this irritation by blending several years to counteract variation in flavour, but most other wine is subject annually to the vagaries of the weather and the winemaker. To achieve the consistency of product, in the face of the meagre profit margins which suppliers have no choice but to accept in order to sell in major quantities, I can see a future where country of origin and vintage will, for many brands, be as irrelevant as it is to Coca Cola. When that day comes I will hopefully be dead.

In the years between 1989, when I began my career as a wine writer, and now, a whole new supermarket monster has emerged, a totally realigned wine industry has evolved, and a new wine drinker has been born. It would be impossible for anyone today to contemplate writing a column solely devoted to supermarket wines, as I launched in March 1989 with 'Superplonk'. No conscientious wine writer would contemplate the venture and no respectable journal would publish it. One of the most compelling reasons for me to relinquish my annual wine guide, 'Superplonk', and all related activities, including a website with 25,000 subscribers, was the encroaching sense of boredom and despair I was experiencing at having to taste so many wines, along with so many brands, of nil personality. There are still some good wines on sale at supermarkets, and I will not ignore their virtues, but the fact is it is difficult to muster enthusiasm for them in light of the extortionate tactics of certain of their sellers.

He who pays the piper…

The president of Wines of Argentina, the generic body representing the producers, actually went on the record in September 2007 when she remarked (in the pages of *Harpers* trade magazine) that 'Supermarkets want to pay less than ever with a strong pound. We can't sustain such low wine prices when we have such high inflation.'

Susana Balbo, the president in question, will, if things get worse, find out the horrible truth as did the Bulgarians before the Argentineans: UK supermarkets will simply drop you as a first choice supplier if you don't dance to their tune and meet their price points. It is a ruthless, unsentimental, and severe attitude and done in the name of the retail mantra 'putting our customers first'. The French were shocked (and still are, with many producers still frothing at the mouth at what they see as 'perfidious Albion') when Australia overtook them as number one wine in the UK market a few years back.

The Aussies, in their turn, will find out the true nature of their relationship with UK supermarkets, and how rapidly they can be given the elbow, if their homeland drought crisis worsens, Aussie grape production plummets, and prices rise. The Aussies will discover that 'shiraz' is now just an international brand and if UK supermarkets insist it must go on sale at £4.99 it will do, but if the country which has made the grape famous cannot supply its wine for less than a retail price of £6.99 then it will have to come from eastern Europe, north and South Africa and southern France, Spain and Italy.

I urge the Aussies to lessen the prospects of this disastrous doomsday scenario occurring by urgently talking to their government, which has so far matched the lack of rain by a drought of political ideas to solve the problem. In ten years time the Aussie wine industry could be so small, unless water is found (desalination plants are the only answer) to irrigate the vineyards, that it will be the most spectacular reversal in vinous fortunes in history.

This is how crucial supermarket pricing is, for with 75% of all wine in Britain being sold in supermarkets at an average price well under £5, no wine producing nation is strong enough to survive as a major force if it cannot widely meet those pricing criteria.

How do you fancy a glass of pinot grigio at 0.8p a bottle?

I was astounded, actually rendered speechless, when in late 2007 I was told the following story by a major UK wine merchant, who wishes for obvious reasons to retain his anonymity.

'We had a 32,000 case drop into Tesco. Pinot grigio. When we worked out our profit on the deal it was £1200. £1200! It was crazy. We slept on it and said no thanks. It wasn't worth doing business with margins like that. The cost of the actual wine, by the way, was 0.8p a bottle. The cork, label, bottle all cost a lot more than the liquid.'

When I delved into this a little more I discovered that it was probable the wine was what is called EU Intervention Stock. In other words it was surplus wine which the producer was subsidised to destroy but didn't. He collected the money (I was told this may have been a Sicilian scam) for throwing away wine but instead sold it on.

How much is that doggie in the window?

All supermarkets also deal in so-called BOGOFS, buy one get one free, and here honesty and integrity really do get thrown out of the window. For British supermarket Somerfield, it underpins their whole wine offering. It is another method of discounting, it shifts more wine, yet the initial sales price, a single bottle, is almost invariably well be above what would be considered fair.

The arch exponents of such fake pricing is the Thresher's chain. This retailer, in order to compete with supermarkets, introduced in 2006 a 3 bottles-for-the-price-of-2 deal right across all its lines with the exception of fortified wines and champagnes. All the single bottle prices were utterly ridiculous.[6]

It is has been estimated, by the UK wine trade, that two thirds of all wine drunk in the UK has been purchased in a discount promotion (not necessarily the same as a genuine discount, as we saw). Indeed, a spokesman for Constellation, the world's largest wine company, said in 2006 that for many brands in the UK the reality was that 80% of sales were made at half-price. We Brits are suckers for a bargain. Is it in our blood?

The same newspaper the advertising sales department of which was happy to take Morrisons' shekels and be party to the supermarket chain conning its readers, in 2006 actually criticised the pricing practices of UK wine retailers. The *Daily Mail* quoted Jean-Manuel Spriet, CEO of Pernod Ricard UK which owns Jacob's Creek, who said: 'it just leads to the impoverishment of the wine trade. The practice of 'marking up, only to mark down' has been rife for years The supermarket pretends to be offering a 'great discount' on a £7.99 bottle of wine, but the real price of the wine is £3.99. ...suppliers make the wines designed for sale at £3.99, introduce them at a higher price, and then bring the price down. They start at £7.99 and are discounted down to half price, which is crazy.'

Many suppliers, perhaps a majority, possibly 100% (if they 'had the balls to speak their minds' as one member of the wine trade put it to me), hate discounting like this. They loathe BOGOFs, but feel they have no option but to supply the wine if they wish to stay in business. In recent years, some have concentrated great effort on other markets than the UK, particularly the USA, where supermarkets and discounting do not rule the roost. It is surely no coincidence that the most successful New World producers, like Charles Back of Fairview in South Africa and Jose Zuccardi of Familia Zuccardi in Argentina, have introduced new products which they refuse to sell to supermarkets but offer only to restaurants and small wine merchants. 'I hate the British discounting system,' said Senor Zuccardi to me in the Autumn of 2007. 'It cheats the consumer and corrupts the values of my brand name.'

All of the bigger, more sophisticated producers like José Zuccardi feel the same way (we can exclude the monster conglomerates like Constellation and Gallo from this as they structure their whole businesses around supermarket discounting). Indeed, José once took one of his most exquisite reds, a £9.99 tempranillo, off Tesco's shelves because the retailer wanted to knock two quid off the price (and expect the supplier to stand the loss in profit).

I once came upon a famous Chilean winemaker walking down Bruton Street in Mayfair, on a lovely sunny day, and his own normal sunny disposition was distinctly cloudy. 'I went to see Mister Soandso at Safeway supermarket this morning,' he told me. 'All he could talk about was price points and built-in discounts. He didn't seem interested in tasting my wine.'

Three days later I saw him at a London wine fair which had been the primary purpose of his trip. He looked his usual radiant self. 'Yesterday my wholesaler took me to see the buyer at The Wine Society. He spent half an hour tasting my wines before he mentioned a word about money. I wish we didn't have to deal with supermarkets.'

It wasn't always like this. In a wonderful exposé in 2007 about supermarket wine pricing *Guardian* wine critic Victoria Moore quoted one of the UK wine industry's stalwarts: 'When it comes to wine offers, we're living in a fool's paradise,' she reported Allan Cheesman as saying to her. 'I think perhaps some of this is my fault,' Mr Cheesman went on to claim. 'During the late 1990s and early 2000s at Sainsbury's we began promoting wine. The difference was that those were genuine promotions. Today many wine offers are created artificially. They aren't what you'd call genuine promotions at all. But unfortunately, there are an awful lot of special-offer junkies out there and it's slowly strangling the wine industry.'[7]

The City pages of the *Guardian*, August 25th 2007, reported that '… competition watch-dogs have found hard evidence that the big supermarkets use their muscle to bully suppliers and extract unreasonable price cuts. The Competition Commission leapt into action after unearthing email evidence that the big two supermarkets had been threatening suppliers and demanding cash payments to finance this summer's round of price wars.' Tesco and Asda, the ones implicated, denied 'all such wrongdoing.' The Competition Commission in a previous enquiry on this subject quoted one supplier as telling it that 'it would be commercial suicide for any supplier to give a true an honest account' of the nature of its commercial relationship with supermarkets. The *Guardian* quoted the Commission as revealing that 'a climate of fear' prevails. I know. I have found it extremely difficult to get any supplier to level with me.

I now consider certain supermarkets as no more members of the wine industry as a result of their having wine shelves than they are part of the British Parking Association because they have customer car parks. Many of the finest, truly committed and knowledgeable professional wine buyers, the real individualists, once employed by the likes of supermarkets Tesco, Sainsburys, Asda, Somerfield, Morrisons, Thresher and Oddbins have left – some to work for the suppliers, some to run their own wine merchanting operations.

As the so-called Apostle of Plonk, I am not against value for money, but I am opposed to cheapness for cheapness's sake. Phoney discounts and fake offers should be banned, producers should get a fair price for their wines, and supermarket wine buyers should not be slaves to cheapness at any cost but devoted to value for money. That was the way it was when I became a wine writer and, sentimental old fool that I am, I'd like to see those times back again.

14

THE PROFESSIONAL SUPERMARKET BUYER

Who needs to know one wine from another?

'We're becoming the toilet of the global wine industry.'
Simon Farr, co-founder and head of
Wine Strategy, Bibendum[8]

Scoffed at by a (small) band of wine critics and PR people (larger in number) who said it was hyperbole, this wine correspondent of the *Guardian* wrote in his column, in the late 1990s, that someone somewhere was penning the obituary on 'The Death of the Supermarket Wine Buyer'.

The day would surely soon dawn, I wrote, when such an individual would be surplus to requirements. For if there is no need for anyone buying wine professionally to know the difference between cabernet sauvignon and sauvignon blanc let alone that zinfandel is a Californian grape and steen, a South African, why employ expensive specialist personnel?

In Spring 2007, in the columns of the wine-trade magazine *Harpers*, the obituary was re-published. Some wine buyers for major retailers, I wrote, had become like tobacco buyers in similar employ. What buyer working for any supermarket today needs to know why Virginia is so called and what makes it distinct from, say, Sobranie tobacco? Today's buyer does not even need to smoke. The buyer needs know nothing beyond the names of the brands her customers die for. At the time of writing, the head of Somerfield wine department, Angela Mount, left in disgust because its senior management no longer felt any need to employ so talented a woman in a highly paid position (when they could, as they have done, simply move the beer buyer over). My prediction had come true. Somerfield, awash with brands, no longer needed a wine buyer to list them.

Mrs Mount was a whizz at creating Somerfield own-labels. Anyone who ever guzzled her Argentine sangiovese, well under four quid, will know that here was a lively mind who made Somerfield a place to find bargains. But the higher management decreed: why fund such a person, who can negotiate in six languages for our customers, when we need speak only one: brands. Do we stock ten different types of baked bean, management asked itself? Do we ply forty-four various loo rolls? No. At a stroke, Somerfield blew its chance of being a genuine contender-with-a-difference and became just another dreary retail business whose wine aisles were wholly predictable.

Somerfield lost not just a wine buyer. It surrendered the chance to be a business worthy to compete with the other supermarkets and give its customers reasons to buy wine there rather than at Waitrose, Tesco and Sainsbury, etc. It didn't, of course, need to compete, for in the end it was sold to the Co-op in 2008 and Somerfield will disappear as a retail brand name.

If a supermarket is to retain difference for its buying public, it can only be via own-label brands. Wine is not really a commodity, as the vibrancy of Waitrose and the relevance of Sainsbury provide proofs. Wine needs talented individuals to blend and to package it and if any retailer no longer believes that this comes from within but is more easily sourced from without, then it is nothing more than a corner shop and we all know what is happening to corner shops.

Simon Farr of Bibendum, quoted above, an individual involved in creating some truly outstanding brands (like Argento from Argentina), was in no doubt, when we conversed in January 2008, that the once gloriously diverse and quality-conscious UK wine retailer, staffed by real specialists who love wine, is almost a thing of the past. Argento, for example, is a huge international success, and may well take the US by storm because Bibendum will choose to concentrate on that market rather let its thinking be dominated by the UK because the profit margins are higher, the pro buyers are easier to deal with, and there is more appetite for this innovative and highly creative wine merchant's style of thinking.

This is why his remark about the UK wine industry, 'We're becoming the toilet of the global wine industry,' is a serious one and deeply meaningful for the British consumer. A dozen years ago, such a comment about the UK wine scene, suggesting that the crappiest wines in the world are increasingly the norm, would have sounded preposterous. The UK was, at that time, the lifeline for the most excitingly made wines on the planet and they were widely on sale.

But with the increasing paucity of professional buyers who know their onions (or, in some cases, do know their onions when they really ought to know their grapes), and the emphasis on cheap branded or supermarket own-branded wines made to a price point and not a quality standard, where is the excitement for such a talented individual and such a dynamic wine merchant? If the UK is not as exciting for Bibendum as once it was, then the outlook for the knowledgeable home buyer of wine at supermarkets and high street wine chains is far less thrilling as a result.

Not all brands are fit to pour down the toilet
Brands are useful for introducing people to a category of taste when there is no other mentor. But, unless it leads elsewhere, with the brand also begins the death of individualism and variety.

I have lectured Master of Wine students on the positive role certain wine brands – like Jacob's Creek in the UK or Concha y Toro in Japan – have played, and are playing, to introduce new drinkers to wine. This service makes them unpopular with those wine writers who need maintain certain fictions in order to survive. Novice brands make the wine scribe's input otiose and her livelihood precarious; they provide no free lunches. I like brands at this level.

It is when they become Brands – the Bully with a capital B – that we must be alert and frustrate their growth. A few years ago, for example, champagne label Veuve Clicquot served legal notice on a small bubbly maker in Tasmania, Stefano Lubiana, because of an alleged similarity of the colour of Lubiana's label with Clicquot's orange livery. It defies belief? Not where Brand defence is concerned by its owners.

Wine is the one alcohol product people place on their dining tables. This is why it is so crucial to drinks-giants' portfolios who possess the money and ambition to build international mass-market Brands. The Branded wine is a huge corporate asset, even though shareholders are in their turn often bullshitted by presentations which seek to represent their investments as nigh-impregnable because their company can satisfy every aspect of the drinkers' whims at all stages of life, all times of the day, all drinking situations.

The Brand cannot be taken for granted and requires, like some Moloch, constant feeding by its managers. If it fails to adapt to societal changes it is doomed. I see hope in these failures – hope that society is not in thrall to Brands – but as one Brand dies, like some dinosaur, another takes its place (Levis is dead long live Gap!). Brand designers will claim this is proof of the democratic credentials of brands but what is democratic about one flock of sheep supplanting another?

The Brand, any Brand, eventually dies if not nurtured through crises. In wine Blue Nun, once a significant Brand, tries to survive by relabelling. It will fail. Gallo, however, is a hipper brand name even though this product, or range of products, is not yet quite the Brand its makers would like it to be (because the advertising has never been able to disguise its hysteria and at the basic level the wines lack excitement). Jacob's Creek, in reality a no-account piddle of dank water, used to have Gallo beaten as a brand without spending a fraction of Gallo's ad budget. Jacob's Creek used to be an exciting brand at a decent price. Once it strayed over six/seven quid, however, its attractiveness, measured on the palate penny for penny, palls.

Daily massage

With wine branding, there is a problem not present in Brands in other fields. This is the inescapable fact that wine is a different product every year, unlike, say, Coke, or Rice Krispies which can be made precisely to the same formula or recipe year in year out or, like Nike or Gap, the products can be made, for peanuts, by ruthless sub-contractors in the so-called Export Processing Zones in third world countries.

Implicit in a Brand is a continuance of its real or, in truth, its perceived values. Perception, as in so much else in life, is more important than reality where the Brand is concerned. Prestige wine Brands require constant marketing massage to keep their message supple. One of the most crucially important aspects of Branding is, as Veuve Clicquot disagreeably demonstrated, the maintenance of tradition, or the appearance of it at least.

Thus, it is only natural that wine companies like Penfolds (happily digesting wine producer Rosemount to become even larger) and Hardy's continually try to develop successful Brands and it is why drinks conglomerates Allied Domecq and Diageo want to buy successful Brands (and sell underperforming or irrelevant ones like Oddbins). Penfolds Grange is a Brand, possesses all the loyalties associated with Brand worship, and the Rawson's Retreat range has this ambition too though it is struggling to make it.

The greatness of a wine Brand is the extent to which loyalists are prepared to forgive, that is to say actually drink bad, indifferent, or even palpably rotten-value vintages and still claim to enjoy them. No other type of product has this problem. (Champagne has solved the problem by non-vintage blends which ensure consistency.)

If a wine must be seen to be perfect all the time, how can it get round a bad vintage? This is where the magic, the insidious magic, of Branding comes into it (leaving aside any necessary manipulative practices of the winemaker).

If Brand Management and Brand Massager have done their jobs then the wine Brand stays 'the same' even for the consumer though the wine may be significantly different from batch to batch. This also alleviates the further problems of individual bottle variation, cork taint, and the varying factors which make a wine one day marvellous and the next banal.

The Brand, the successful Brand, is proof against the varieties of level of performance cork confers. The Brand Massagers, especially certain hoity-toity wine writers, also assist here by disseminating the idea that it is variability which makes certain wines (expensive Brands) great and therefore gambling on each bottle's quality is what proves individuality. This lie is actually peddled as wisdom by certain addle-pated wine gurus.

Château Lafite, possibly the world's most overrated wine yet biggest wine Brand, is proof of this and all the other wine Brands want to be Lafites: proof against anything the competition can launch and against changing tastes and fashions. With a bottle of Lafite on your dining room table, your guests can label you a con-wa-sewer. That is the pinnacle to which all wine brands must aspire. If all wines had to be decanted by law, prestige Brands would suffer. That label on the table is the key to the aspirant consumer's soul. The fatuous Opus One, the Mondavi/Rothschild product now owned by Constellation Brands the world's largest wine conglomerate, is an attempt to extend this nigh-metaphysical franchise.

If only so many of us wine writers weren't such chumps, such trumpeters of the fancy Brand hype, perhaps more consumers might be less susceptible. In Britain, the discussion of Brands is a vulgar subject. Not so in France where intellectuals without muddying their academic credentials advise marketing organisations and advertising agencies on the hidden significance of red when it comes to women choosing a motorised Brand or the shape of the bottle when men decide on a brand of after-shave. We should teach drinkers to cultivate scepticism instead of encouraging them to be fleeced. We should drink wine.

15

CHAMPAGNE

The biggest brand of all with the biggest hype

The greatest Brand in wine is champagne. It is the only generic brand stocked by ALL wine merchants. It is the only generic brand demanded by name. It is the greatest success story in wine. Champagne is a creation of the most deliciously outrageous marketing hype. Merely to say to someone 'A glass of champagne, darling?' is to join an exclusive class.

That is why champagne asks so much of your pocket. To be cheap would defeat its object. Cheap champagne? An absurd an idea as a one-legged centre-forward. The low-end chain Woolworths, when it introduced its own-label fiver-a-bottle champagne, in the summer of 2007, had only a short-lived product on its hands. Even its buyers knew they were not really living a champagne lifestyle by purchasing it. Why? Because it was too easy to buy. At not much than a packet of 20 cigarettes it presented no difficulty of acquisition.

Champagne, though it had been introduced into London in the 1600s, became, during the momentous years of Queen Victoria, the wine of many historic moments. It was the symbol of celebration and success. It was a long and exciting reign and though the Queen died champagne did not; never since to lose its exuberant image. The Champenois have, since then, ferociously insisted on their right to the name. The word 'champagne' is enshrined legally and the champagne houses have aggressive lawyers ready to crush trespassers world-wide.

The famous champagne houses like Moet-Chandon, Bollinger, Ruinart, Billecart-Salmon, Charles Heidsieck, Mumm, Lanson, Krug, Laurent-Perrier, Roederer, Pol Roger, and Veuve Clicquot

Ponsardin, assiduously manage their images.

Champagne Mumm, for instance, paid a fortune to be the official bubbly supplier to Formula One races a season or so past. Lanson, for the Millennium celebrations, offered bottles of its product encased in chain mail designed by Paco Rabanne: a mere £320 in silver and £1450 in gold (excluding Vat).

True, champagne does cost a bit to grow. Most of the vineyards are independently owned and these growers (18,000 of the blighters) have the producers over a barrel – a great many barrels in fact since every year around 250-milion bottles of champagne are turned out. In other parts of France they jovially explain the unique wealth of champagne grape growers thus: *Quelle-est la différence en champagne entre un vigneron pauvre et un vigneron riche? Le premier lave sa Mercedes a la main, le second la fait laver au garage* (What is the difference in Champagne between a poor grape grower and a rich one? The former washes his Mercedes himself, the latter at a garage). If you think this is just a joke, and not a reflection of real wealth in the region, muse on the fact that in 2008 the Champagne authorities, anxious to produce more product, extended the area legally able to call itself Champagne. 40 villages, previously on the edge of the region (and much of it wheatfields) will henceforth be able to grow champagne grapes. Land which was once worth £4000 a hectare has jumped in value to – and please hold your breath – around £800,000 a hectare. All this with the full connivance of the National Institute of Appellations d'Origine. Small wonder I describe the notion of appellation contrôlée and terroir as a real estate scam.

In its finest manifestation, of course, champagne is a remarkable concoction. The greatest sparkling wine I have ever tasted was a champagne: Alain Robert's mesmerisingly subtle yet emphatic Les Mesnil, a blend of old and young vintages priced around £90 a bottle and sold in France in only two outlets.

Some of the big champagne houses are also meticulous. Laurent-Perrier uses old vintages in its non-vintage blends and it adds less sugar (so making a more classic, elegant style). Charles Heidsieck puts a *mis en cave* date on certain of its brands, thus clearly informing you of how long the wine was aged in the cellar. These wines are not cheap.

Yet Tesco's, Waitrose's and Sainsbury's own-label supermarket blends of Blancs de Noirs Brut champagne are not only better than the famous name Brands, they are much cheaper. But what bride would tolerate her lifetime of happiness being toasted in a bottle with Tesco on the label?

Champagne is many things to many people at many prices. But if it is not necessary for you to make a statement, do not be bamboozled by the hype. Sniff, swirl, taste and consider – and make up your own mind. You may, like me, come to believe that many sparkling wines are just as good if not finer than champagne, and that all that stands in the way of accepting this is what is in the glass.

A little white (and sparkling) lie

The attitude of champagne producers to their over-hyped products has led to one of The Great Lies of wine. This is the utterly ludicrous suggestion that such a wine goes with all sorts of food and is even a perfect partner for chocolate. True, some champagnes go with smoked fish, others with certain shellfish dishes. I once used a bottle of cork-tainted Krug as an ingredient in a rather sexy moules marinieres and I can also reveal that champagnes dominated by the pinot noir grape are at home with soft-shell Vietnamese crab.

But the Champenois, the big name producers, insist on making all sorts of extravagant claims about the compatibility of their wares with dishes which no-one in his or her right mind would offer in a lifetime of food/wine matching. Taittinger, in its Christmas 2006 publicity push, suggested its bubbly could amicably cosy up alongside honey roasted quail and *girolles* mushrooms, charcoal grilled john dory and cockles, *and* strawberry crème brulée!

Not to be outdone, the 2007 new year card from Gosset champagnes reckoned I'd be on to a good thing if I matched scallops and caviar with its 1998 Celebris, consumed mocha-perfumed and balsamic-vinegared foie-gras with its Grand Reserve, and tucked into fruits in jelly with its Grand Rosé. How, I wondered had Gosset's PR department come up with that scenario? Champagne with a high chardonnay content can go well with fish and chips, but this is totally nuts.

I also have great reservations about the idea that several glasses of bubbly wine are an aid to digestion in a rich meal. I would suggest it has the opposite effect after two or three glasses. I found this out personally in October 2007 when I drank seven different Beaumont des Crayères champagnes with a meal which consisted of wholly incompatible elements (from guinea fowl with red cabbage to smelly cheeses through to caramelised rice pudding). I was not the only person at this lunch to find himself gagging for a glass of still white or red wine. Yet this champagne house had present a highly qualified British wine consultant and food expert who should have pointed this out: no normal human being can enjoy a meal dominated by gassy, acidic wines which disappear under the richness of the food ingredients.

What's in a name?

Britain has long been daffy when it comes to champagne. This country's affair with the liquid began some centuries ago when the nobles and rich merchant class began to enjoy the tickle of sparkling wines and French monks indulged their cravings. But it was in the year of the Diamond Jubilee, 1897, that Britain imported more champagne than at any time in its history, and we have, two world wars apart, never looked back. In just seven years, between 1992 to 1999, we increased our annual champagne drinking in the UK from 14 million bottles to 32 million and in 2008 it is anyone's guess how much of a vast increase on that latter figure will be revealed when the latest statistics come out.

Figures like that always suggest champagne is the world's most consumed sparkling wine. In fact, it isn't. Cava, the Spanish bubbly made using the champagne method, individually sells more world-wide. Taking the sparkling wine market as a whole only one bottle in a dozen consumed world-wide can call itself champagne.

The only difference between much champagne and other sparkling wines is often very little or nothing. Bubblies from regions of France other than Champagne, and many of the sparkling wines made in New Zealand, Australia and the Americas, can all be witty expressions. The Italians have their often exquisite Prosecco, the Germans (per capita the world's biggest drinkers of sparkling wines) their lean-but-not-sparse sekt, and local bubblies are made in California, Oregon, Chile, Hungary, Australia, South Africa, New Zealand and several other places.

The only difference in quality between such regions and Champagne is that these upstarts cannot legally employ the name champagne on the label, though they may use the same methods and often have finer grapes to choose from.

The truth of this latter assertion can be proven when you taste, alongside the Moet Chandon Champagne product (£21), the same company's bubblies from elsewhere at half the price Chandon Australia Brut and Chandon Argentina Brut. Both manifest, in my view, the superiority of their grapes. The same goes for Mumm Cuvée Napa from California, richer and more persistent in flavour than its French uncle.

Tours, where the sparkling wine is made from that richly exciting but massively undervalued grape the chenin blanc (sneered at, incidentally, by the champenois) is one reason why a Crémant de Loire Brut, is so deliciously crisp and unpretentious. Crémants d'Alsace and Bourgogne can also be fine specimens (and two of the nattiest bargains to pick up at the ferry ports).

I am a great fan of the major supermarkets' Cava Brut (under £5), invariably dry and elegant, and also its rosado sister (also around a fiver) which is even more attractive with its extra tang of subtle fruitiness. The finest Cava of all is often Albert I Noya's Can Vendrell Brut (£7.50 or so).[9]

There are many Australian bubblies but one of the best was Pirie of the 1996 and 1997 vintages from Tasmania. It cost around twenty quid from small wine merchants. I once drank the 1995 vintage, at home, in competition with Taittinger Comtes de Champagne 1990 (£75 the bottle) and it knocked the latter in to a cocked chapeau. But even finer than Pirie is the bubbly from the Cloudy Bay people in New Zealand. Called Pelorus, this finds its way onto several supermarket and high street wine chains shelves for around £15 and is superb.

Three of the most surprising places to find sparkling wine grown are India, Ethiopia and Hawaii. I've yet to taste either of the latter two. I thought I'd got hold of a bottle of the Hawaiian product, made from grapes grown on the slopes of an extinct volcano, but the promised bottle never turned up. The Indian product, called Omay Khayaam, is no more than passable (and so we shall pass over it).

One of the finest sparkling English wines I've tasted was Nyetimber, made in Sussex from chardonnay grapes. It came in a magnum for £50. Alas, the vintage which so impressed me, 1996, is long gone and subsequent bottles have not been a fraction so incisively elegant.

My hope for New Millennium is that these other sparkling wines start to make bigger inroads into champagne's dominance of snootiness. If nothing else, at least the New World producers don't inundate one with silly menus and trumpet how brilliantly their wines cope with food. And yet, with sparkling shiraz, the Aussies possess a most exciting way to relieve the banality of the traditional British Christmas lunch. This bubbly beats cracker jokes, silly hats, and tonsil-tennis under the mistletoe hollow. Okay. Maybe not the mistletoe.

THAT'S FIFTY QUID WE CAN POCKET. THANKS!

How supermarkets make a profit on every wine you loathe

I feel rather foolish writing about this as it reveals my complete naivety. When I began the first supermarket-exclusive wine column in the UK in 1989 (in the Guardian) one of things my research had established was the huge difference between such retailers, multiples as they are called, and traditional wine merchants. My postbag was full of it.

At a traditional wine merchant one approached the taking back of a bottle with apprehension. *Guardian* readers regaled me with their horror stories. Indeed, it was not just at the Purpleconk & Flabbycheek (est. 1899) type of establishment that the returning bottle was regarded with suspicion and its returnee interrogated: high street chains like Victoria Wine and Oddbins were also villains.

'Well, of course the wine is off, madam. It's been opened twenty four hours.'

'It was off when I opened it. Can I have a refund please?'

'I don't know about that. I'll get the manager over. He might, if he's in a good mood, consider replacing it.'

But at the supermarkets you strolled in and even if the label was not stuck on to your liking, or you simply found the liquid not to your taste, you got your money back. (Apart from the now defunct Safeway, where readers reported that they experienced interrogation and initial resistance.) At Tesco, Sainsbury, Asda, Morrisons, Waitrose, the Co-op, Somerfield (then called Gateway), Marks & Spencer, even Budgens, the returning bottle was not the object of hassle, embarrassment and dispute. This was one reason why I liked super-markets as wine merchants. They didn't argue with their customers.

Now, somewhat belatedly, I know why. They don't argue with their customers because they can profit by any returned wine by not only charging the supplier of it for a new one, or most likely simply by adjusting a future invoice, but by levying an admin charge, greatly in excess of the cost of the replaced wine. The poor supplier gets hit with a double whammy. Now this is perfectly legitimate if the supplier has created a faulty product, but often the complaint is simply 'I don't like this wine now I've tasted it', rather than this wine is corked.

Is this a scandal or simply standard shrewd trading practice by the supermarkets and high street chains to ultimately benefit us, their customers. You be the judge. This is what one of the few suppliers prepared to talk to me on the subject said, when I visited their winery (the name and location of which I shall take to my grave as I have no doubt that if I were to reveal either they would be immediately delisted by Tesco):

The other day we were charged £58 by Tesco for a returned bottle of wine. There is a £25 admin charge plus other costs of returning the bottle.

If the customer doesn't like the wine we also have to pay.

One Tesco customer complained 3 times in 3 months. He said the wine each time was corked.

Tesco are not pleasant people to deal with.

Sainsbury's once forgot a wine of ours in the warehouse. The product was made to be drunk young. Now we are getting complaints as people drink the wine.

A woman found a bottle with a fly in it. We had the bottle flown here and we had it tested. The lab said the fly would have disintegrated if had been there when the wine was bottled. The fly must have entered the bottle in the UK. It cost us a lot of money.

Someone once said they found a nail in a bottle of ours.

Armed with this information, I asked people I knew at some of the supermarkets what happened when a customer returned a bottle. Tesco said this: 'The cost and hassle of physically returning the wine to the suppliers would be more than the cost of the winedistribution systems are designed to flow one way only – to store. Even if we did not return the wine the cost/ hassle of just collecting info on returned wines and the admin in allocating these by supplier would not be worthwhile – I do not think we could actually tell you how many bottles were returned as faulty. Even if the number is in the hundreds or indeed thousands this is in the context of circa 400 million bottles sold annually – and an overall turnover approaching £50 billion.'

Someone, then, is lying to me. Is it Tesco? Or is the supplier? In any case, I have never in 20 years as a wine journalist encountered such a reluctant attitude, almost a wall of silence, when I tried to investigate this area further. No-one wants to talk.

This is what Thresher said in response to my questions:

'Thresher Group operates the Wine Buyers Guarantee. This is a no quibble guarantee to replace any bottle that the customer finds faulty or simply does not like. The guarantee has been in operation for some 10 years and aims to make sure that the customer is always satisfied with their selection. Costs are not reclaimed from suppliers unless the customer describes a particular fault with the wine [corked, oxidised etc]. If it was purely just not to their taste then Thresher swallow the cost of the replacement bottle. All complaints of faults are charged back to supplier where we receive a response form from the customer stating what the fault was, this is logged at store level and monitored at Head Office so that we can check for a pattern of faults or returns on any given wine and investigate accordingly. Bottles are destroyed at store level.'

Waitrose replied in a similar vein:

'We accept wine back with no questions asked, and issue a full refund. Wines are sent from branch to Head Office for analysis and comment… We do not routinely charge suppliers, and only pass on a charge if we are confident that there is some fault of the supplier (wines with the wrong back label – wines obviously re-fermenting etc.)'

The wine buying head of Waitrose, Justin Howard-Sneyd said to me: 'We only charge the supplier if we are confident if we are comfortable it is their error. We get around 4 to 5 bottles returned a week.'

Somerfield said: 'It is our policy to always give a refund if a customer returns a bottle of wine to store The store retains the bottle of wine, and the supplier is contacted regarding the problem. They then arrange with the store to collect the bottle in question, this is at the supplier's expense. The supplier is also asked to contact the customer direct regarding the outcome of the complaint, and provide a full report to Somerfield regarding the issue.'

At the Co-op, chief wine buyer Paul Bastard, said 'For every duff bottle we get back we charge the supplier for the cost of the wine. Sometimes we add an admin charge, sometimes we don't. I do not believe in penalising smaller suppliers unfairly.' As Paul saw it, he was in partnership with certain suppliers, most definitely his own-label ones, and felt they should be treated accordingly. One supplier representative, however, remarked to me that of all the supermarkets she had dealt with the Co-op were a close second to Tesco for the tight efficiency with which they ran their returns operations.

Supermarket Morrisons' reply to my enquiry was a little ambiguous: 'Should a spoiled wine be returned to Morrisons, we would simply exchange the bottle for the customer. The final decision as to who is financially responsible for the spoiled wine is made between ourselves and the appropriate supplier. Should an isolated incident such as this occur, the decision is based on the quantity of returned wines.'

I responded with: 'What is the financial burden on the supplier for the exchanged wine? What is he charged?'

The reply was as opaque as I had expected: 'Unfortunately we can't go into any more detail than what I've already given you as that goes into contracts we have with our suppliers which is commercially sensitive information.'

Someone I approached at a supermarket wine supplier initially said: 'It is with regret that I cannot find anyone willing to talk. It appears that there is far too much loyalty to customers.' Customers in this context means supermarkets. However, this person did go on to tell me that at certain mail-order wine merchants the cost of any returned is covered by the large margin they trade on.

At such 'certain' mail order companies, customers fund their own 'no quibble' returns policy via the high prices they pay. There is also a different psychology at work. The customer whose wines appear on his doorstep takes a different attitude from someone who acquires them by pushing a trolley around wine aisles. In the latter instance, as someone employed at Sainsbury told me, this retailer has even reimbursed a customer's bus fare as the man made such a fuss about the bottle of wine he was returning. I was unable to discover if the bus fare was passed on to the supplier, plus admin charge, plus Vat.

But are the suppliers fighting back? The summer of 2007 saw increasing media coverage of the bullying tactics of supermarkets when it came to those suppliers it can with impunity intimidate. Not for nothing has there been gradual consolidation in the wine world as the industry seeks to emulate what has been forced on other industries: the need to dictate terms to the retailer and not the other way around.

When, in 1989, I first tasted the Gallo wines newly arriving in the UK I asked Allan Cheesman, then head of Sainsbury's wine department, why he was stocking such manifest mediocrities. He replied that the amount Gallo was spending on TV advertising, some £5-milllion if memory serves, along with this company's marketing presentation had convinced him that he had to stock the wines because customers would go elsewhere if he didn't.

Since then, Gallo has been overtaken as the world's largest wine conglomerate by Constellation. There are other large winery companies also and the logic of their size, the economies of scale, the budgets available for marketing and advertising, the ability to compel retailers to stock the wines has changed the face of wine retailing in the UK.

Not all big companies, however, play this game wisely. It was widely rumoured that the reason Penfolds got into financial difficulties a few years back, and were taken over by the Fosters beer group, was a direct result of spending so much money forking out for so-called 'gondola ends' in the wine aisles. This prime position for a wine, or a selection of brands, almost guarantees consumer take off (especially if it comes with some kind of inducement or 'discount') and since these can cost thousands of pounds per store a huge sum was given to leading supermarkets by this company in order to boost sales. Sales which, when it came to the bottom line, it was making insufficient profit on to make the deals viable.

The so-called Supermarket Code of Conduct. Another con?

The active interest the UK media is now taking in the relationships between retailer, buyer, and manufacturer is beginning to unsettle some supermarkets. They are getting touchy on the subject. They know perfectly well they are arrogant bullies but this hardly sits well with the cosy grocer image they wish to project to their customers. In August 2007, Grant Thornton, an international business advisory and accountancy group, published its findings into supermarket/supplier relationships. Its press release had the title 'SUPERMARKET CODE OF CONDUCT OFFERS NO PROTECTION ACCORDING TO THREE QUARTERS OF FOOD SUPPLIERS.'

Wine is a food and one assumes that wine suppliers are treated the same as a supplier who sells a supermarket ready-made meals or fresh lettuces. If so, Grant Thornton's research makes uncomfortable reading for the retailers and disquieting reading for suppliers and any British government regulators concerned to see fair play, if not the consumer. 'More than half (52%) of the UK's food suppliers to supermarkets are unfamiliar with the provisions of the Office of Fair

Trading's (OFT) "Supermarket Code of Practice", reported Grant Thornton, 'and among those that are, over three quarters (76%) don't believe it offers any protection from the increasing power of supermarkets and the financial effects this is having on suppliers.' Grant Thornton surveyed company directors in the food supply chain and found that 'more than half (52%) of the respondents believe the code is not enforceable because it does not encourage suppliers to raise a formal complaint against supermarkets for fear of losing their supply contract.'

The press release went on to quote a Grant Thornton executive who said that 'the results of the survey and, indeed our direct experience of advising food suppliers, clearly show that examples of unreasonable behaviour do go on and are putting a huge financial strain on food suppliers … (and) the code of conduct designed to protect them is hardly worth the paper it's written on because of its ambiguous terms and the lack of effective enforcement. UK suppliers penny-pinching clients who, through their market power constantly chip away at price, demand contributions and credits for unsold goods. Yet, there is little they can do about it. If they complain the likelihood is that they will lose the business through de-listing.'

Grant Thornton then went to reveal how monstrously Asda had treated one of its major suppliers, Ferndale Foods. In 1995 Ferndale had a huge ready meal contract with Asda worth some £40-million a year and it effectively underwrote Ferndale as a business. After ten years with Asda, Ferndale was given the boot with a mere 12 weeks notice (following an 8-month tendering process which Ferndale assumed it had successfully negotiated). The contract was awarded to Northern Foods. The management at Ferndale, with admirable toughness and commercial élan survived and the company now supplies healthy meals to Sainsbury's and Waitrose. It has not gone under. But no thanks to the so-called Supermarket Code of Practice. Asda (and Northern Foods) will no doubt say 'that's business'. But it stinks. Ferndale had invested hugely in plant and people and both were under threat. I offer this case history as an example of the sheer nastiness of supermarkets in their dealings with suppliers.

How deeply wine producers loathe British supermarkets

The UK's largest grocers and wine merchants have their suppliers on their knees before them. That this is hugely resented by the wine producers but which they are powerless to resist was superbly illustrated in late Autumn 2007 when Dan Jago, Tesco's chief wine salesman, gave a speech to an audience composed of members of the Australian wine industry in Melbourne. In this speech he ticked the Aussies off for alcohol levels and over-reliance on heavy fruit and advised them to make their wines 'more refreshing'. He also said how concerned he was that the 'energy' had gone out of the Australian wine offering. 'Make no mistake,' the ebullient Jago threw out, 'There are queues of people outside my office with wines from countries that have no drought, no water problems and no supply problems.' In other words, stop whinging, do it the way I'm telling you, or I'll go elsewhere.

The delegates to the conference sat there, swallowed hard, and those that supplied Tesco kept their mouths firmly shut. Except for two brave souls who spoke out.

Rick Burge, Barossa Valley winemaker, spoke, according to *The Age*, 'for many' when he barked: 'The British have a grocer's mentality towards wine. They want Australian quality at Chilean prices. I don't want to be dictated to about flavour by a British supermarket.' Fair enough. However, it was alleged by the paper that Hunter Valley winemaker Bruce Tyrrell went a great deal further than this. Mr Tyrrell, it was reported, responded to Dan's speech thus: 'He's a wanker – he should go back to selling dog food. For years, the Australian wine industry has been supplying the British with technically correct wines that have good colour and are full of flavour, compared with the Europeans, who have been supplying them with technically poor wines with no colour and taste like cat's piss.'

Mr Tyrrell has since denied very unambiguously he said this, stated that he was misreported, that *The Age* got it wrong and he was going to sue them. Indeed, in *Harpers* wine trade magazine five days after being so wickedly misquoted, Bruce Tyrrell wrote how relevant he found the Tesco wine man's speech, saying 'I found myself very much agreeing. Jago ably described the wines of our area. I must applaud Tesco for beginning to make a broader range of Australian styles available.'

Whether that range will continue to include any Tyrrell wines is in the lap of the little tin gods (that is, the trolleys of Tesco wine drinkers). It is also, of course, in the lap of a major god: Mr Jago himself (who has never bought dog food in his life, unless it was for the family pet). But knowing Tesco, as long as Tyrrell wines fly off Tesco shelves he will not lose out in the immediate term by being so egregiously misquoted.

Unlike McDonalds, who agitate expensively to get the expression Mcjob (menial low paid work of nil prospects) removed from the airwaves and dictionaries, Tesco, in the UK at least, is not an American-style mega-corporation addled by fundamentalist zealotry, prickly and publicly reacting to every critical comment. (Its overseas subsidiaries, as in Thailand for example, are a different matter. There, aggressive and litigious sensitivity appears to rule.) However, if I were Mr Tyrrell I'd certainly start to schmooze some of the other UK wine importers. Some day, mate, you'll need them more than you do now.

17

A FORTUNE FOR A PIG IN A POKE

Wine Auctions

Until all wine which is auctioned is sealed with screwcaps, the practice of acquiring wine in this way, however impeccable the provenance and honourable the auction house, will always be a lottery. The odds are not stacked in the buyer's favour. Since you cannot return any faulty wine bought at auction, let alone any which does not come up the high standard expected, you can find yourself cheated. Or certainly cheated if you judge the wine by its performance in the glass and not by the impact of its venerable label on a dinner table.

Auction houses are very sensitive to criticism because they have no idea what is in the bottles they sell. Of course they may taste a sample of a particular wine, they will go to prudent lengths to verify where the seller bought it and that the wine has been cellared properly, but for the bottle, or case, or indeed cases, of wine which are actually purchased only the final buyer will know how good, or bad, it is when s(he) gets it home and opens it. No other item sold at auction carries such risk of disappointment. This is why much of what changes hands at auction is never drunk but traded as commodities. Some collectors are teetotallers. Most are mere speculators. Wine lovers buy only the wines they feel they can afford and wish to drink.

I was, a decade ago now, given the chance by a BBC television producer to comment on a wine auction at Sotheby's. It would form part of news programme about auctions and the TV producer was keen to know if the wine on offer was any good in relation to the anticipated high prices. As it happened, I had already been invited to attend the pre-sales day tasting in Sotheby's Bond Street premises and so I went along and sampled several veteran burgundies and bordeaux, one handsomely mature white Rhône, and made my notes. I no longer, alas, have these notes but I recall some of the wines, from noted burgundy houses (wines eight to fifteen years old) and renowned Bordeaux châteaux (up to twenty five years old). The only wine I could honestly report I would personally buy and feel comfortable recommending was a white Châteauneuf-du-Pape which was estimated to be sold around a mere £15 a bottle. In fact, I thought I would gamble the BBC appearance fee on a case as the latter was almost enough to cover the cost (excluding the 15% buyer's fee added to the final price which I had forgotten to include in my calculations). By bidding for the wine, I would actually be part of the live auction. However, rather stupidly when the producer telephoned and eagerly asked my views on the wines I told him the truth. 'Hugely over-rated, massively overpriced,' I said, 'and only one of the old clarets had any vague life in it and one of the old burgundies. The only living wine at a humane price is the C-d-P blanc.'

He was delighted that he might get a lively programme but like me he spoke, alas, plainly. He phoned me back a few hours after we had spoken and said the programme was dead. Sotheby's had demanded to know what Malcolm Gluck was going to say about the wines and so he told them. They said that that being the case they would not allow the BBC to film. End of TV programme. End of story.

Prudent management by an auction house anxious to preserve the mystique and perceived excellence of its reputation? Without doubt. In any event, had the programme gone ahead it would have done nothing to dint Sotheby's or any other wine auctioneer's repute. Buyers would have bought those wines whatever I may have said. And they continue to throw money at auction wine in ever increasing amounts.

Here is what Christie's, the other well-known London auction house, said of one of its sales in 2007:

In this thrilling sale a single case of the famed 1961 Hermitage La Chapelle broke the record for the most expensive case of wine ever sold at auction in Europe – and in the process set a world auction record for a case of wine from the Rhône, achieving a eye-popping £123,750 for 12 bottles. Thirst continues unabated as international demand for the very finest wines continues to make auction the most attractive route to market for both buyers and sellers. This Autumn, we may very well see the record for any case of wine ever sold at auction, six magnums of Mouton 1945 sold at Christie's Los Angeles in September last year for £183,511, broken as the wine market continues its expansion…

As it happens I tasted Hermitage La Chapelle 1961, about 12 years ago. Was it worth £10,370 a bottle in 2007? I wouldn't have given you a fiver for it in 1995, though I could quite see that had I drunk it perhaps in 1971 or 1975, and not when I did (in circumstances which now completely escape my mind), it might have been a truly vigorous and vivacious, complex and thrilling liquid.

To consider that it is worth, as a wine to be drunk, ten grand a bottle in 2007 is totally insane. It is obscene. It has nothing to do with wine; everything to do with rarity, collectability, prestige, and with people in the world who have so much disposal income they can fritter away a fortune in the snap of two fingers (or the click of a mouse). I suspect – and it is an uninformed guess – that the wine was bought by someone running a very upmarket London restaurant, where it would go on sale at £25,000 the bottle and be bought by a bonus-soaked City slicker or a Hollywood thespian on $10-million a movie. On the other hand, it might be sold on, to someone in Asia who, though he has to spike his red wine with Cola to make it palatable, would be able to throw a dinner party where the wine would be served and be talked about for decades.

Has any of this got anything really to do with wine? No. It has only got to do with status and conspicuous displays of wealth.

In any case, any case bought at auction will contain only a proportion of old wines which will be outstanding or even satisfying or even decent enough to drink. Being sealed with a cork, and with wines many years old, ensures huge variation bottle to bottle. My personal experience of this is extensive but let two anecdotes suffice to signal the dangers.

In 2006, four bottles of Château Haut-Brion 1989 were opened, auction price around £4000/5000 a case. In 2002, six bottles of Château Margaux 1976 were opened. In both cases, the owners of the wines being rich men with an interest in wine, eyes were opened and minds were changed. The Haut-Brion contained one bottle which was thrillingly sublime; one of the greatest clarets I have ever experienced, only to be compared with Château Cheval Blanc 1947 tasted in 1966 and Château Margaux 1947 tasted in 1967. Of the other three bottles, two were deliciously drinkable but no more so than a £15 Chilean cabernet and one was loose and unkempt. In the instance of the Margaux again only one bottle was really interesting, though it was not great, and of the others one was badly cork tainted and undrinkable, two were dull and disappointing and a further two were okay but over the hill.

Still want to buy old wine at auction? You must be mad. And many people of course are. Those City slickers with their fabled bonuses are now actively targeted by the auction houses. This is how Sotheby's cosies up the City boys:

> Where do you start if you are considering entering the wine market and investing a percentage of your bonus in liquid joy? Should you buy now, or wait in the hope of picking up some bargains when the time comes? Should you be buying 2005s or have you already missed your chance? Our view is that the current strength of the market is likely to continue and if you want to get involved then you will have to go long

on the very best wines. There is still value out there: 1998 and 1999 prices are looking good and 2001 is a much under-rated and under-valued vintage they may offer a certain return in the short to medium term and, if chosen well, delightful drinking. Do not rely solely on your merchant/broker to invest on your behalf. Many brokers and merchants source their stock from auction themselves, so why not cut out the middle man? Buying from Sotheby's gives you far more control over your investment. Our experts are here to offer advice on all aspects of buying and selling at Sotheby's and to advise you on your investment. We take pride in sourcing our consignments and only sell wine where the provenance is perfect. We check all wine older than 15 years for levels and label condition and younger wines if particularly high value…

When I read this I contacted the auction house and asked: 'May I enquire Sotheby's policy on faulty wines purchased at auction? Is there any chance of recompense if wine is corked, oxidised, otherwise marred, of indeed if any bottle's contents is not in perfect condition?'

Sotheby's replied:

Where any wine is out of condition we tend to look at each case individually. It may be a reflection of the storage conditions, although we do not sell wine where we are not confident the wine has been stored properly. We will usually ask for a second bottle from the same case to be brought in and tasted so we can make a judgement on its condition. If we agree that the wine is not showing as it should we may taste another bottle to see if the problem occurs throughout the case. If we believe that this may be due to poor storage, we will invariably go back to the vendor for a full refund. This happens very rarely. We would not knowingly sell any wine which may be out of condition and we physically check all cases pre 1990 as well as visiting private collections in situ to verify the storage conditions. Most buyers of old, fine wine adhere to the maxim of *caveat emptor*. We will entertain serious complaints regarding any faulty wine but will look at each case on an individual basis.'

In other words, once a wine has gone on sale you take pot luck if you want to open it and drink it. If you want to cellar it and flog it on to someone else in a few years and trouser a profit then it is a different matter. As long as your cellar is certified impeccable, you cannot lose on legendary wines of acknowledged stupendous years.

The only wines I would myself consider acquiring via an auction would be old whites. In particular, German rieslings. There are various technical reasons for this but two are dazzlingly paramount:

1. Red wines sealed with a cork lose tannin structure and fruit. Since each cork is a separate, wildly unpredictable artefact each bottle in a case, or cases, of the same wine from the same vintage will vary.

2. Rieslings being white have no tannin to lose. They have high acidity and sugar. Apart from the overtly tainted cork which ruins the wine, some 5 to 8% of examples, rieslings can withstand oxidation via a cork and although bottle variation is inevitable it is not miserably destructive as it is with any red or whites made from other grapes like chardonnay and viognier. In sum, if a Hollywood beauty wants to keep her looks and charm well into late middle age, into old fogeydom indeed, then she should crave to be a riesling not a cabernet sauvignon or a nebbiolo.

For these reasons I have bought old Germans up to 30 years old. I have also enjoyed beautifully wrinkled Aussie rieslings (screwcapped) of similar antiquity, middle-aged Aussie semillons, grüner-veltliners from Austria, viogniers/marsanne/roussanne blends from the Rhône and Languedoc of up to 10 years of age, and chardonnays from France. However, none of the latter can hold a candle to the German riesling as the most profitable wine in the world to cellar.

I speak of profit in the glass. Anyone who has properly cellared, since vintage release, ten or fifteen year-old cases of Pétrus or Latour will always make a monetary profit as such wines are the subject of collecting frenzy and consistent price index rises. If you can acquire such wines you cannot lose money, even if the wine in the glass is corked or otherwise uncongenial. But these wines are commodities. They are not liquid delights so much as speculators' darlings. They are largely the preserve, once in the glass, of the super-rich and the super-stupid. Wealthy Russians, Singaporeans, and far eastern commercial potentates often add Coca-Cola to them as they find them too harsh as liquids for their immature and honey-dentured palates. What a thrill it must be to pour cola into a glass of wine from a £5000 bottle of Château Pétrus 1982! It makes a man feel so powerful it must be an aphrodisiac more potent than any distillation of tiger's penis. And, unlike those potions, one can advertise one's consumption, and wealth, by showing the world the label.

18

RESTAURANT WINE RIP OFFS

Why your wine waiter is not your friend.

It seems that the customer is always right in all trading transactions except when s(he) enters a restaurant. Restaurant mark-ups on wine are generally so awesomely high one would think that customer satisfaction would be easy to aim at but no; the more rapacious the restaurant when it comes to wine the trickier it is to negotiate the wine waiter.

You might also think that someone such as myself, often known to a restaurant management, would have an easy time sending a wine back for being corked. Again, but no. My judgement on faulty wines have often been questioned, in some cases strenuously, by restaurant staff. The most unpleasant confrontations have been where the establishment has its own wine cellar, has paid for its own wines and does not have a wine merchant to whom they can return any faulty wine and claim a refund.

At Pied-a-Terre, the Michelin-starred eatery in north Soho in London, lawyers got involved as a result of my refusal to accept faulty wines. At the Sugar Club in Notting Hill (before it moved to Soho), three Kiwi wines on three separate visits were all corked and each time I had to order second bottles and have a side-by-side tasting in order to convince the management the first bottle was dodgy. In the chapter which follows this one, I write in detail of the hugely embarrassing scenes which developed when I sent clearly faulty wines back at two famous restaurants.

A London wine merchant of my acquaintance recounts the story when with a UK burgundy importer they went for lunch in Beaune but not at the importer's usual restaurant. The importer knew the local wines intimately, so when the first bottle was corked confidently he sent it back only for a tricky situation to arise when it came to getting a replacement. This finally arrived, was proclaimed fine, and the meal finished. When the bill arrived the waiter had added two bottles of wine to the bill. The importer protested and said he would only pay for one. A lengthy argument ensued which ended when the waiter's boss called the gendarmes. They arrived and to their surprise were offered glasses of both wines in order they could tell the stupid Englishman they were no different. But the wines were different. One was corked, one was fine. The police said this was a civil matter and they could not intervene. The importer finally settled the bill, deducting the price of the faulty wine.

Now let us visit Le Rascasse in Leeds, where I am dining with Jerry Lockspieser when he was managing director of wholesale wine merchant Bottle Green. By the time we had sent back the third half-bottle of Château D'Yquem the sommelière was a worried lass. She called a halt and said she was going to send the whole batch back to the wine merchant.

What is so different about my last example? Yes, that's right. The wine waiter was a woman.

Men are the problem. Most men treat wines as if they were their own children. Women, in my experience, treat wine on the evidence of their own senses. They do not equivocate. They do not sentimentalise. Women are also simply better equipped tasters than men. We poor men really have to work at it, but most women are born with the gift of smell and taste.

Wine waiters, let us stress the gender, can give us headaches greater than any wine they might serve. (Small wonder I campaign to have all wines screwcapped. Death to the corkscrew! Long live the screwcap!)

My advice to anyone who is the slightest bit dissatisfied with the condition of any wine in a restaurant is to send it back promptly. Why else are you invited to smell and taste a wine when it is opened in front of you? In the slickest restaurants wine is opened by the sommelier out of sight and, if faulty, not even served to you but another bottle opened. In most cases, however, the bottle is uncorked at table. Note if the person serving you smells the cork. In some quarters, notably hotel schools in the USA, they counsel that smelling the end of a cork is irrelevant. Certainly smelling a screwcap is, but I smell the end of every cork I extract from every bottle and I almost invariably insist on doing this when I am eating out. Why? A cork is supposed to be a neutral seal; smelling the end which has been in contact with the wine will tell you if this neutrality has been besmirched. It is the most immediate clue to the state of a wine. A good cork should smell only of wine. If it smells of anything else – cardboard, mushrooms, wallpaper paste, a dirty leafiness – then this a clue as to whether or not taint has got through into the wine. Often a cork just smells of cork (which is bad enough) but has not affected the wine in any way which would be hugely noticeable aromatically. Sometimes a wine is oxidised (even slightly and it is a fault) and the cork has little aroma; but the wine will be loose and overly oxygenated.

Things would still be as bad if restaurant wine prices were not so astronomical. This is an area in which I have some experience as I personally supervise and design the wine lists of three London restaurants and in each the wine prices are reasonable. I refuse to supervise any restaurant wine list where the management wants to add 200% or 300% or, in some cases, 450% marks-up on the wines it sells. The waiter who brings you a bottle does no more work when the wine costs you £20 or £200, but in the second not only is the Vat on the final bill higher but so is the service charge. It is scandalous, venal, unfair, and crooked.

Yet restaurateurs at the swankiest joints defend their profiteering simply by pointing to the rent and rates they are forced to endure and the high overheads of running an expensive establishment. One hugely up-market London restaurateur said to me: 'Listen, Malcolm, your crusade about restaurant wine prices may make sense in places not in prime locations but for each chair you see here,' and he made a sweep of his arm to indicate the 120 covers he has capacity for, 'I must take £10,000 a year in order to break even.' So. This guy's rent and rates were £1.2 million a year. Add on running costs, staff overheads, raw materials, and it is easy to see why wine is the easiest way to make inroads into these expenses.

If you wish to eat at celebrity joints, posh restaurants with huge mark-ups on its wines, then feel free so to do, but be aware that you are subsidising outrageous profiteering. When I see a bottle of Pelorus, the sparkling wine from Cloudy Bay in New Zealand, at £52 the bottle on the wine list at, for example, Tamarai the Indian restaurant in London's Covent Garden, I feel I am being ripped off and so I decline to eat and drink at such an establishment at my own expense. Pelorus used to be available in supermarkets for around £12/14 and its wholesale price, available to the restaurant, will be a great deal less. Amongst many other pricing horrors, Tamarai also lists Delamotte Blanc de Blancs champagne at £66 and Schloss Vollrads Riesling at £38.

Not everyone is as appalled by these mark-ups as I am. The *Independent* newspaper gave this restaurant its Best Wine List in London award. If one gasps at the Tamarui profit margins on wine one gags with astonishment at this newspaper reviewer's sense of judgement. Further proof, as if any were really needed, that wine awards are almost always not only irrelevant but absolutely no guide to true worth. The ex-vat trade price of the champagne is £17.50 and the Vollrads is £6.23. At the Frontline restaurant in Paddington, on the other hand, the Delamotte is listed at £35 and at the Cây Tre restaurant in Shoreditch the Vollrads is listed at £19.50. Not all restaurateurs, even in trendy parts of London, are out to rip you off. It has been pointed out to me on numerous occasions that I should consider writing a restaurant guide entitled RESTAURANTS WHERE THE WINE LIST PRICES AREN'T A RIP-OFF. But though the idea hugely appeals, I have to point out that it would be a conflict of interest. At both the latter two restaurants mentioned above I select the wines (which is how I know their trade prices). I am not, as a result of my stance on list pricing, going to carve out a lucrative career as a wine consultant.

19

THE SHOCKING TRUTH

Some people in the wine business can't even taste wine

Many people lack the olfactory selectivity and the aesthetic finesse to judge between good and no-so-good wines. The label is all they have to go on. They simply can't tell the difference between something genuine and complex and something shoddy and have no interest in cultivating the passion so to do.

This does not mean that they do not enjoy wine, or clothes, or hamburgers; they do, but the process of choosing which ones is not based on taste as it affects the sensory system. These people are in no way divided by class or income; what divides them is choice based on development of the palate and the nose and that part of the brain which is involved in signalling pleasure when something is imbibed. A man may spend £800 on a duty-free bottle of Château Pétrus and, against airport and customs regulations (and most human preferences), open it and drink it with smoked salmon and shellfish at a bar (this happened with a Japanese wine lover at Heathrow in 1999). Will the pleasure he got be based on a unique compatibility of flavours? It's not impossible. However, more likely his pleasure came from the flaunting of his ability to spend money how he liked. This is a mightily egregious example, red bordeaux and shellfish, but there is a parallel, in the disregard for how things actually taste, in the person who drinks lager with his tandoori chicken or orange juice with her cheese omelette. I recall the habit New Yorkers had, when I lived amongst them, of consuming iced water at meals and which destroyed any chance of them tasting any food let alone wine.

Mine host, the wine bore
During an official tasting/lunch of dessert wines, hosted by a well

known wine lover, at London's famous Michelin-starred Le Gavroche restaurant, I asked a waiter to replace a half bottle of Château Climens because it had manifestly been tainted by its cork. The well-known wine lover appropriates the bottle and smells it and proclaims that the earthy undertonality I describe as taint is a feature of the estate's wines. Upon discretely confronting Thierry, the then sommelier of the restaurant, he agrees the Climens is sick and he replaces it immediately. Why was this well-known wine lover so ill-equipped to analyse wine? All will be revealed soon.

At a tasting of Alsatian wine I came upon a wine which was vividly corked but upon asking the man who had poured it, brother of the wine maker, if I could taste the same wine from another bottle my glass was seized and the cork taint I accused it of ascribed to minerals. I regained possession of the glass and asked a passer-by how she liked the alleged minerals. She grimaced the moment the glass was under her nose.

At an international wine trade fair in London I was invited to taste a rioja by its UK marketing manager. I said give me an hour and I'll be back. When I returned the bottle was two thirds empty and upon insertion of nose in a glass it was obvious it was badly corked. The marketing manager said none of the dozen or so other visitors who had tasted it had uttered anything but nice words. The wine maker was called over. He seemed to think it might be the wood when I proclaimed it faulty. I left the stand before my sides split.

The crux of the problem is simple yet dramatic. Not everyone has the same genetic capacity to smell and taste. The research published in 1997 by Dr Linda Bartoshuk at Yale University gives a fundamental insight into the issue. Human beings are divided into three groups, according to how many taste buds they have per square centimetre on the tongue and in the mouth. Super-tasters have an average of 425, medium-tasters 184, and non-tasters have 96.

How many of the people in the latter two categories are,

perhaps, working in wine? Writing about it? Flogging the stuff? Making it? I estimate that at least one third of my readers, when I was the *Guardian*'s wine correspondent, had fewer than 200 taste buds per square centimetre. This does not mean they could not enjoy wine. But it does mean they were unsusceptible to its subtler nuances and many of its faults caused by corks. This does not illegitimise them as wine drinkers but it surely made them unfit for employment in the wine industry or restaurant trade.

If the Yale research has any validity it forces upon the most superficial thinker, and observer of the human race, the obvious truth that most people lack the sensory faculties to care deeply about what they drink and therefore they do not care to develop their palates to differentiate beyond the most crudely disparate and uncongenial partners (e.g. coffee with coq au vin is a pretty unpalatable liaison but some people enjoy coffee with cornflakes or muesli at breakfast and some, as I have seen, drink it with a tuna sandwich over a hurried lunch).

Let me hasten to add that I am very far from trying to assert here that anyone who is less than a 'super taster' is committing some social crime by this. Still less am I wishing to set up a charter which would seek to legislate on taste (the red-wine-with-meat, white-wine-with-fish school of outdated idiocy). I am also not trying to push the idea that people shouldn't enjoy what they drink and eat because it offends a code of higher 'Wine Connoisseurship'. Just because someone is tone deaf, can't read music or play an instrument, and couldn't whistle Dixie to save his life, does not mean he will not get pleasure from a passing jazz band and enjoy moving his limbs in time to the music.

Another crucial factor to bear in mind here is that each of us has a different disposition to taste and smell. And there is scientific evidence to back this up. In August 2007, the authoritative science magazine *Nature* published the results of research by scientists at New York's Rockefeller University. It was a study of 400 people and how they reacted to 60 various aromas. The key, apparently, lies in a single gene – something called, somewhat unromantically, OR7D4 – and the individuality of this within each human metabolism means we each smell things in our own way. One example given was that one person can detect the smell of male body odour as urine which another person will define as vanilla. Our olfactory abilities are, then, wholly genetic, individual to each of us, and genuine.

In any field of activity there is only a small minority who care to spend the time, money and effort to become accomplished or even vaguely discriminatory in developing this individuality. The flamboyant crowd which insists on Krug at their Christmas parties and Lafite at their dinners is lazy in this regard, but let no-one gainsay the enjoyment they fiercely accrue. But if they had sufficient taste buds and, what's more, cared to use them, then they might be more discriminating. No crime. Just indifference.

Even a winemaker may lack the judgement to know what he is serving up. I swear every particular of the following anecdote is truth, as recorded in my South African notebook at the time.

Sunday 18 February 2006

The good folk at Hunter's Retreat, owners David and Esther Jordan, also have not only a farm but a small winery Manley Private Cellar. I walk up the drive, past the cows, past the cars parked for Sunday service at the little chapel on the farm's land, and find a door into the winery. No-one seems at home. I shout. The answering voice is no echo and soon ex-sea captain David Jordan appears with his monster of a ridgeback hound and we find ourselves in the tasting room. David and Esther met in 1978, both recent divorcées, on a yacht sailing to the Caribbean and never looked back for 15 years until they came back to South Africa and bought the farm. Bruce Jack, who used to be one of the most dazzling boutique wine conjurors on the Cape wine scene until he sold out to the world's largest wine company Constellation, has bought grapes from here, cabernet sauvignon for his Dark Horse Shiraz, so there's no doubting the quality of the fruit.

'May I taste some wine?' I ask.

'Let's see what's open,' says Mr Jordan.

A 2004 bottle of shiraz, 14.5% abv, is produced and some poured in my glass. I regard the colour, sniff, taste a bit, spit.

'Goodness! You don't get a lot of visitors here to your tasting room do you?'

'Um. No. No. Lot a lot.'

'How long as this bottle been opened?'

'That? Let's think. Um. I opened that on January 29th.'

My jaw drops.

'Is it not good? I'll get a new bottle it if you think it's not at its best.'

The wine is porty, oxidised, hanging on for dear and life and contemplating a future role, in the years to come, as vinegar.

'No. No. Don't go to any trouble and expense on my account. Can I taste the cabernet?'

It is poured. I regard the colour, sniff, taste a bit, spit.

'How long has this bottle been opened?'

'Well. That's a bit fresher. We've had that open since February 2nd.'

My jaw, having done its exercises for the morning, has now lost its capacity to drop. The wine is like tannic blackberry soup with a touch of curry leaf. A 2005 Merlot I taste is also not fresh but by then I'm past caring what these wines taste like. If the man who made them can't be bothered, why in God's name should I?

Bearing in mind the two scientific research results touched on in this chapter, and my own collection of anecdotal evidence, it seems to me that each person's reaction to a wine is so individual as to make all tasting notes of a wine by a taster useless as a definitive guide. Such notes are merely impressions. They cannot be held as sacred truths.

However, just as we do not expect those with vertigo to train as an airline pilots or claustrophobes to study for careers in submarining, why should those with the genetic disposition not to detect wine faults or to appreciate a healthy wine's complexities become wine waiters, wine tasters, or wine writers? It seems, though, that the world of wine does contain pilots with a fear of heights and submariners scared of enclosed spaces. The only difference is that they do not know they suffer from the disability. Worse, they inflict that disability on us every time we eat out or read their views. It is an invisible plague.

The answer is simple: every relevant person in the wine trade, in the restaurant business, and wine journalism should be tested, scientifically, to determine their fitness for their role. Nothing fancy or prolonged. A basic DNA analysis might be enough to eliminate the incompetents. I do not know of a single wine merchant or restaurant or newsprint publisher who expects those entering the wine world to prove any fitness for their endeavours whatsoever except to show enthusiasm. It may be entertaining that there are those claiming to be wine writers who can barely put a coherent and original sentence together; it is surely intolerable that within their ranks also lie those whose ability to taste and smell wine is the equivalent of near-illiteracy.

20

RESTAURANT CRITICS

Why send a eunuch to review a brothel?

The following matter is so trivial when compared to the pressing problems the globe faces that it will hardly send shock waves through the nation but it might – and such is my vague hope – cause some of the editors who commission the work to either find more versatile people to do it or instruct their writers to broaden their remit. The it I refer to is the reviewing of restaurants.

How many food critics appear to know anything, or care, about wine? If they do, they don't much show it. One glittering, much-lauded reviewer, A.A. Gill of *The Sunday Times*, is even a teetotaller. A teetotaller!? You might just as rationally send a eunuch to review a brothel.

Any reviewer worth his/her salt would surely study the wine list of any restaurant before the menu not afterwards (if they give it any attention at all). I am often sent, by energetic PR people, details of a wonderful restaurant and it is sometimes later reviewed well by a critic, but a perusal of the wine list, via an email attachment, instantly indentifies the place as not being, to my mind, fit to patronise.

With all this in mind, let us look at the treatment the Vineyard at Stockcross has received, vinously, at newspaper reviewers' hands. Easy to lampoon with its arty opulence and dependent upon much corporate guesting to survive, this country house hotel near Newbury is nevertheless a richly rewarding place to visit. Chef John Campbell knocked up for me, in a single meal, lamb sweetbread risotto, salmon with lentils and foie gras, suckling-pig terrine (sublime!, and years of research went into it), an Anjou squab with celeriac, Galloway beef with an onion tart, and a brulée of strawberries with olives. The six wines which accompanied this remarkable dinner were no less complex but the most toothsome was from the proprietor's vineyard in California. The Vineyard at Stockcross is owned by Peter Michael who among other hobbies has Classic-FM and his La Carrière Chardonnay 2002 from the Knights Valley is a nigh perfect example of the wood-wrought style and I rated it 19 points out of 20 with that salmon. At £125 a bit rich for a superplonker like me. But then someone else was paying.

Yet can you find me one newspaper reviewer of this establishment who has done its wine list justice? Terry Durack of the *Sunday Independent* did at least mention the Oregon Pinot Noir he drank, but he didn't reveal much more. Of course the Vineyard's nosh is ambitious. Chef Campbell's kitchen is enormous (even running to a chocolate room and massive slow cookers for the meat stocks), but the cellar, over 2000 specimens strong, contains equally compelling reasons to eat there. The prices are high but the wine list (at time of writing) contains bargains though I can find no reviewer who pointed them out.[10] All that newspaper reviewers have managed, winewise, is this:

> Even if the wine list was not among the best in the country and was merely a standard compendium, the Vineyard would be worth patronizing for its cooking.
>
> Jonathan Meades, *The Times*

> … an impossibly hedonistic restaurant (eight courses, 350 wines on the list).
>
> Andrew Purvis – *The Observer Life.*

> … as well as a large international list… there's the most comprehensive and interesting range of American wines to be found in Britain.
>
> Charles Campion – *Evening Standard.*

The wine list is the size of a phone directory.

> Max Davidson – *Daily Mail*

The menus and wine list arrived less quickly.

> Matthew Fort – *The Guardian Weekend*.

I assume motoring correspondents do drive the vehicles they review. Is it too much to ask that restaurant critics apply the same level of attention to the restaurants they eat in? Wine is not tap water. A diner's bill is not just taken up by the cost of the food but more than burdened by the contribution the wine has made (plus service charge on top of the VAT automatically included). It is a reviewer's duty to pay equal attention to the wine as s(he) does the food. In a good restaurant the wine list must be reviewed. One last reviewer, the most wineless, the most witless, is also worth quoting: '... the cost of my two-night stay at the Vineyard was £1,300 for bed, breakfast and tea. I was perfectly happy. Make of that what you will.' I suspect most people, my dear Michael Winner, will know exactly what to make of that.

But what to make of *Charles Campion's London Restaurant Guide*? In spite of what Giles Coren of *The Times* has written of this Guide ('cannot be bettered') it is useless as an indicator to the wine on the lists of the 400 restaurants it covers. Does this man drink only mineral water? Or, greatly to his credit, strictly tap? Take Arbutus, the Michelin-starred and very reasonably priced restaurant in Soho. It is true that much of the wine list, as Mr Campion writes, is available in carafes, a terrific idea, but the list is only a third as thrilling as it could be. I want to know what Mr Campion drank there, what it cost, and how well it went with what he ate. He fails to enlighten us. I appreciate his publisher insists on a single restaurant entry per page and thus space is limited, but where a restaurant has gone out of its way to at least attempt to excel in wine I think we should know. In the entry for The Rivington Grill in

Shoreditch he only confuses the reader when he writes 'The wine list starts steadily and then skitters on through a handful of pricey bottles to Vosne-Romanée and the like.' Come again? I am totally in the dark as to whether this restaurant has a wine list of merit or not let alone what's worth drinking from it.[11]

21

OTHER RESTAURANT TRICKS

Do you know Monsieur Nez-Brun the famous chef? He had a TV show on BBC for aspiring restaurateurs. The restaurant/hotel he once supervised culinarily is famous.[12] People flock to it the world over and with a sense of someone going to visit the scene of a distant crime, I made my return visit a few years ago. I went there to do a live outside broadcast BBC breakfast TV show and speak about screwcaps. But of course, this being the HQ of a famous chef, there was a preamble involving Terence Conran, Pru Leith and an American called Larry Stone who was there to defend corks. Dapper fella, Larry: pressed suit, neat bow tie, slick hair, smile like the keyboard of a small accordion. Monsieur Nez-Brun poured himself all over old Sir Tel like double cream and then embraced Pru with similar clottedness.

But me? Me, he did not recognise – but then it was seven years since we had met when I took two people to lunch at his restaurant. The lunch opened with a perfect bottle of Alsatian pinot gris. The problems began when the wine which followed it was spoiled by its cork. It was a Mas de Daumas Gassac 1986. I informed the young waiter of the wine's unsuitability when it was served from the decanter into which it had been poured. He went off with a very nasty expression on his face.

The number one sommelier now appeared and tartly enquired what the matter was. I informed him that the wine was faulty and I would like another bottle. He disappeared with the decanter and I waited, my rabbit cooling on my plate; my guests like myself anxious for further vinous replenishment and for a replacement bottle to appear.

But appear it did not. Instead the sommelier returned and announced, to an audience that now included the whole transfixed, fascinated restaurant, that the wine had been tasted by certain individuals in the kitchen and pronounced perfect. I was, in effect, being told I was wrong to find fault and the restaurant knew better and that I should shut up and accept the faulty wine.

Now the wine's sin was not large. It was not undrinkable. The cork taint was subtle but it marred the pleasure of enjoying what is one of the richest reds in France. It was a tannic wine, that Gassac, but at ten years old (in 1997) the tannin had ameliorated but not completely softened and it was this, the sommelier opined, since I myself raised the matter, which was confusing Monsieur.

Monsieur, however, was not confused. He was struggling to keep his temper, and to save his guests further embarrassment he ordered a bottle of something else, a Vacqueyras (since the sommelier absolutely refused to bring another bottle of the Gassac). The Vacqueyras arrived, was fine to drink, and we soon got into glasses of it and into conversation and ignored the restaurant's appalling manners.

But the restaurant was in no mood to let les *chiens endormi* lie. The chef, Monsieur Nez-Brun himself, arrived and announced his dissatisfaction with the way the faulty wine had been treated by a paying customer.

'My nose,' said M. Nez-Brun,' can detect bad wine ten metres away, this nose found no fault with the wine you rejected.'

The restaurant fell as silent as M. Nez-Brun pontificated about his infallible olfactory powers and how I had committed blasphemy in arguing. I got rid of him by saying that if he put some of the Gassac into a sterilised bottle I would take it away and submit it to a laboratory. We agreed that if the wine was found to be corked he would stand me a free meal and if the wine was perfect then I would treat him to lunch.

However, the cost of submitting the sample of the wine to a lab, I subsequently discovered after making enquiries of Geoff Taylor at the Corkwise laboratory in Dorking Surrey, was between £300 and £500. It had cost me enough the lunch for three of us and I had no inclination to add to it by paying for laboratory vindication.

I had hoped I would be able to tell this story for the BBC cameras those years later when I again met Mr Nez-Brun, but no opportunity arose. The effusive Mr Stone spouted inanities about corks which I did my best to rebut; screwcaps won the debate from the telephone calls and emails I received afterwards. However, Monsieur Nez-Brun began this article and so he should finish it.

I reminded him on that second visit that we had last met seven years before and how he had refused to replace a faulty wine. He could recall nothing of the encounter.

'But, oh, Malcombe,' he oozed, 'you know, when I feel strongly about someting, bien, I must speak my mind.'

'You nearly ruined lunch. What you did was unforgiveable.'

He shrugged. Next time you send back a bottle of wine at his restaurant remember this story. Oh, by the way, the chef's real name is Raymond Blanc and Le Manoir aux Quat' Saisons the name of his disgraceful eatery. He may be a terrific chef but he is not in any position to tell anyone how to run a restaurant (as he did on his TV show).

Even more dramatic, though lacking any intervention of the chef, was the memorable meal Pied de Terre a bit less than a decade back. Having drunk three bottles satisfactorily amongst four people, the fourth, fifth and sixth were all rejected by me on various grounds and the sommelier lost his head and his temper and, like dear old muddle-headed Raymond, he got the attention of the restaurant. He was joined in his display of temper by the restaurant's manager. And it was not only my opinion that the three wines were not good enough but also that of one of my guests, an American with a Californian wine background.

'Oh, come on, Malcolm,' the manager said. 'You've had so much to drink you're not capable of telling whether a wine is corked.'

'I see. Well, I'm glad you've let the whole restaurant know that.

There are plenty of witnesses to your slander. I am a professional wine critic and I am far from drunk. If I say a wine is faulty I do not say it lightly. My lawyer will be in touch. And please give me my bill immediately.'

The bit about the lawyer was inspired. What blood there was in the manager's face drained and he dragged away the sommelier. I paid the bill and we left.

The restaurant's lawyer sent me a letter the next day. The notion that here was an actionable slander had been taken seriously when in fact I regard such actions are almost always morally dubious and I have never mounted one even when advised to do so. A little while later the restaurant offered a free meal to make up for its lapse in judgement and it was, as the food always has been at this restaurant, wonderful. Was I wrong to send 3 wines back? Only one was overtly corked. The other two, being wines of some age (I remember a decade-old Chinon but cannot recall the others), had merely badly aged as the cork had allowed too much air in.

But the real problem was the fact that the restaurant had purchased the wines itself. They were not supplied by a wine merchant to whom any faulty bottles could be returned and credited to the restaurant's account. The wine waiter, male, young, French, passionate, saw those wines as he would his own children. For me to reject them, and for the money to come out of his own budget, was too much. He found it unbearable. He was later replaced in his job at the restaurant by someone of a more temperate disposition.

Only once, for example, was I ever in a position to send back a wine at one of Nico Ladenis's legendary (and now sadly disappeared) London restaurants Chez Nico. Nico had an excellent English sommelier. I am pretty sure he always tasted any wine, behind the scenes, before bringing it to the customer to smell and taste confident that it was fine to drink. When I queried the condition of one white wine he whipped it away immediately and replaced it without demur and I later discovered that because the restaurant had been so over-run with custom he had failed to taste it before the waiter had brought it to me.

Such should be the norm at a top-class restaurant. No wine should be served unless it is in a condition fit to drink. But how many customers know this? How many customers will accept a wine which is less than good? How many sommeliers themselves know when a wine is not in perfect condition?

The answers to these questions plague the thoughtful eater out.

22

WINE WRITERS AND OTHER POSEURS

Uncovered: my own misdemeanours

Goodness me what a sinner I have been. It's a miracle I can walk the streets unstoned by outraged citizens disgusted by my own wine brand (Superplonk) I once had on sale at Tesco and appalled by my holding down the job, for eight years, of consultant wine editor of Sainsbury's magazine. Both these lucrative avenues, needless to say, upset particular wine snobs amongst the critical wine press who felt both compromised my impartiality.

However, both the *Guardian* newspaper, for which I wrote on wine weekly, and the BBC, for whom I was shooting a TV series, scrutinised the situation and felt it was not compromising. They were wrong. Both situations were compromising. My critics were right. It was amazing that not only did I manage to ride so many horses at the same time but was able also to commentate on the race.

The Superplonk wine was created by Tesco supplier Private Liquor Brands a dozen years ago. I supervised its blending in Spain and approved its design. The wines quickly became screwcapped and I viewed this as a major part of its appeal as I wanted to show drinkers that screwcaps had the support of a wine critic and were not, as they were widely seen in 1995, only found on the worst wines. The proceeds from its sale were intended to go to the newspaper which would further use the wine to promote itself in Tesco stores and drive up readership. The *Guardian* proved itself inept at this however, and also refused, to my surprise, to accept the royalties I had negotiated on its behalf. I had not got involved with the project for personal profit.

But I did personally profit once the paper turned down

receiving any income from Superplonk Red and White and so did the south London charity Kids Unlimited (to the tune of some £20,000) when I felt increasingly uncomfortable with the situation as a result of the *Times* and *Sunday Times* newspapers writing about my conflict of interest. However much theirs was ad hominem attack, I could not but admit the conflict. I had profited, before it became a charity project, for some years prior. *The Times* and the *Sunday Times* can both take credit for publicly shaming me, though of course in the true tradition of both these exploitative rags since becoming part of the Murdoch empire they went far beyond fair reportage and I was advised to sue both.

The *Guardian* had its feathers ruffled, and called me in for a frank discussion, because when asked by a Murdoch myrmidon over the phone about the Superplonk wine I retorted 'oh, yes, it's a conflict of interest I like conflicts of interest.'

The *Guardian* took the view that had I not said this the subsequent brouhaha would not have taken place. But of course it was a conflict of interest. A national newspaper critic cannot put his name to a wine, even if some of the proceeds do go to charity, no more than such a person can put his name to a wine competition or accept free tickets to cultural and sporting events which have nothing to do with wine. I always refused the latter, in fact, until I left the *Guardian* much later (except in one single instance when I attended a private piano recital given by the daughter of a Chilean wine producer). Superplonk wine was, for a few years, the number five best-selling brand in Tesco, notching up 100,000 6-pack cases a year excluding 3-litre wine box sales.

Sainsbury's Magazine was not so compromising an involvement, in practice, though it could be seen to be in spirit (when I asked other wine writers to contribute to the magazine none turned me down, including Jancis Robinson, though I never commissioned her in the end). When Delia Smith first telephoned me and offered me the job in 1992 I turned it down on the grounds that I could not work for a supermarket magazine. In spite of the fact that my bank was threatening to re-possess my house to repay the mortgage I owed them, and the monthly income from Delia's project would save the day, I could not see how the job would not compromise my impartiality. But when I was promised a free critical hand I caved in.

My family still had a roof over its head. I never once had my copy touched on the grounds it was unacceptable to Sainsbury's (even when I criticised its range of burgundies and said no-one should go near the beaujolais) and the only person whom I commissioned whose piece the editor, Delia's husband, refused to run was by Andrew Barr whose article criticised wine awards and Sainsbury's pride in winning them. Mr Barr, sadly, no longer writes about wine but his 1988 book *Wine Snobbery*, is a classic and the US edition can be picked for $1 via abebooks.com and it is worth twenty times the price. (I suspect I should have resigned when Andrew's piece, in spite of my championing it, was not allowed print space. But I didn't. Two children, a wife, and a large roof to maintain are powerful incentives to lassitude.)

Beware the romantics!

A wine writer is a wine's biographer who runs the danger of falling in love with the biographee. This is never taken to be a conflict of interest, however, because it is an invisible relationship. An obvious, visible, conflict of interest arises when a critic, whatever her or his field, is so involved with the object of criticism that an objective viewpoint is occluded, diluted, or even impossible. The precise nature of this conflict is often difficult to define since different critics enjoy or endure differing circumstances of involvement.

Were I a theatre or cinema critic, for example, I would find it difficult to have social relationships with actors or directors since I would regularly have to confront their work. A few years back I was entertained to discover when reading the obituary of a recently deceased prominent theatre critic, of the *Daily Mail*, that many public tributes were paid to him by impresarios and, further, that this critic was also involved in show business in a small way. How was it possible for him to be truly critical? If the producers of so many West End productions were also his friends, and possible collaborators, how he could possibly distance himself from these involvements when he reviewed their work? This, then, was a shadowy conflict of interest; the object of criticism and the critic's relationship with it were, from the reader's point of view, too murky to disentangle.

A true critic (such as I have tried and arguably miserably failed to be) must, then, have untainted, critical distance – otherwise (s)he is merely a publicist. At all times, the critic's readership must consider the critic free of prejudice, partiality and favouritism otherwise the opinions expressed, under the guise of criticism, are worthless. This is not to say that a critic might have personal partialities or favourites (I myself am peculiarly susceptible to draughts of German riesling) but there must be no suspicion that this is as a result of being in the pay of the German Wine Information Service or, at a smaller level, given to writing about a particular Moselle wine producer for no other reason than as a quid pro quo for hospitality received from the producer. But what of the German wine producers I call by their first names? Who invite me to stay in their homes? Who send me their wines on a regular basis?

I am, in these regards, no different from many other wine critics. How objective can we be in these circumstances? I have no doubt that where we find grounds to admire, or merely like, a wine producer we have already strayed into the area of conflict where ruthless untainted judgements are unlikely.

I wonder, for example, whether Hugh Johnson should write on Château Latour in *Decanter* when he is a director of the company. True, he admits to this but it renders his opinion on the wine of doubtful use. In the same way, if Mr John Radford were to review sherries in the same magazine, when he is, or was, a consultant to the PR company which numbers Gonzalez Byass amongst its clients, then his viewpoint on this category of wines is suspect. Mr

Johnson and Mr Radford have interests which conflict. In my view, no journal of any integrity should ask individuals with known conflicts to write on the areas of wine in which these conflicts are manifest. Should Hugh and John consider whether they should ever write on claret or sherry? A purist, like Robert Parker, might say that it would be better if they never wrote on wine whatsoever but this is surely going too far (it would be a tragedy in Hugh's case for his limpidity of expression is incomparable).

But are all these furious protestations on my part (a feeble stab at pretending to a purity of soul I will never possess) mere window dressing? I stopped being an independent wine critic the moment I warmed to Miguel Torres as a man or wine producer Patricia Atkinson in Bergerac as a woman. Oh yes, I could tell myself I liked their wines but didn't I admire them more warmly as people? If I did not find David and Jenny Jones of the Dalwhinnie vineyard in Victoria so wonderful as a family would I continue to trumpet their wines? If I didn't find brother and sister Abrie and Jeannette Bruwer of Springfield Estate in Robertson in South Africa so inspiring and worthy would I not find their wines less compelling?

It is the job of the shrewd producer to suborn the wine writer: to make a bad review less likely. All wine writers fall for the producer's wiles. How can we resist? Wine is a convivial liquid. It is not designed to be experienced, as Robert Parker the American wine critic would have it (sometimes), by oneself in a lonely hotel room surrounded by other samples. Wine is festive. Even if it is an everyday wine, it has an element of the merry crowd about it. That's what Bacchus is. We poor saps who claim to be independent wine critics are compromised before we even set lips to a tasting glass.

Free samples? As necessary as the ink in the critic's pen…
At the height of my weekly newspaper column I employed a part-time assistant, whose time I largely paid for personally except for that necessary for her to check the availability of each weekly column's wines by contacting each retailer. She had some 35,000

individual bottles on her data base that I had tasted in the recent past.

I could not possibly have bought this many, my newspaper would not have been keen to fund their acquisition, and I would, further, have required a second, full-time assistant to manage the ordering of the wines, and possibly a third full-time assistant to organise the tastings, log the wines, organise new bottles to replace those tainted by their corks, and, on top of all this, a tasting room would have been necessary either to hire or as an adjunct built on to my house.

When I first became a newspaper wine critic, I had not imagined anything like this. As I settled in to the job however I soon realised that if I didn't get the retailers to do certain things on my behalf I wouldn't be able to function. I know of no wine critic, in fact, who buys every single bottle he or she writes about. It is impossible to achieve.

On foreign trips, wine producers are sometimes insistent with their presentation of freebies, but it is important to refuse them as they are impossible to carry on aircraft. When there are times when I need to have several bottles of one wine, I buy these from the producer by credit card and have them shipped. I have done this in France, Germany and New Zealand.

Wine & junkets

I am trying to shine a little light into the murky world of the wine journalist not merely because I try to run my affairs openly but because I cannot attain the objectivity I need to do my job by operating in any other way. Some of my colleagues have so little ethical dimension to their personalities it is as if a part of their brains are missing.

I cannot ignore these charlatans when we sometimes meet on trips to foreign vineyards. This is another area where objectivity can be affected for the simple reason that such junkets are rarely funded by the wine writers themselves but by the vineyards they are visiting. This is an accepted part of the wine journalist's existence and the economic case is even greater than it is for the free samples. I used to take as many as five to eight short foreign trips a year (less than a week, some only two days), plus one long trip (three weeks or so); none cost me a penny in airfares or accommodation. Unless I had a specific newspaper or magazine assignment to write about the trip, I paid my own train and taxi fares and all my own film and development costs (which in a three week stint to New Zealand, say, can be considerable). I never billed my newspaper for any expenses incurred on these trips and it's too late now.

No newspaper or magazine would fund these trips and even if they did who would organise them? I would require a nigh full-time travel secretary to organise each vineyard visit. The involvement of a regional or national Wine Board is, therefore, crucial and, sometimes, an influential importer. Indeed, without the help and financing of others I would not be as free as I am to write what I like. I wouldn't have the time for it. You may say 'but those who pay the piper's expenses surely call the tune' but this piper likes to think he plays his own tune and I'm sure all the national newspaper wine journalists will claim the same.

Sometimes, it is true, this independence upsets those whose hospitality has been lavished on a journalist. I infuriated an important South African with what I wrote after my first visit to his country and he finds it difficult to speak to me again. The wine critic Oz Clarke was the subject of a banning order when he had a (justified) go at the champagne houses. Once they realised they had made a major PR blunder they were forced to rethink and concluded they had been stupid.

The most influential wine journalists may accept funded trips but they do not necessarily write partial copy as a result. It is possibly different with wine magazine journalists whose journals take lots of advertising from wine producers; indeed, I have been assured by one writer that he was fired by one wine magazine because his criticisms of a producer led to this company threatening to stop advertising unless he was dropped. But no national, or even local, newspaper is open to this kind of coercion.

Of course, a visit to a country predisposes you to write about it, that is inescapably true, but there is not a requirement to be craven and follow the party line. However, there is a way PR firms and trip organisers can reach the biddable journo's heart and to pretty well ensure the host country gets a write up. This is to offer not just free air flights and hotel accommodation to the journo but also to the journo's family. I have always refused this kind of lure, for dangerous lure it is, and I wish the wine trade would stop it.

It is, I feel, totally unacceptable for a journalist to claim objectivity if he or she accepts paid-for hospitality for a spouse or companion. Indeed, it is compromise of the worst kind because it is an open bribe. When I refuse, I also always make it clear why. *The Times* wine critic, Jane MacQuitty, was involved in an undignified spat with the people from Wines of California when she denied their allegation that she had once demanded business-class air tickets for her family as well as herself for a trip the Golden State. The matter, which involved *The Times* lawyers contacting the WoC people, never came to court so we must assume it was settled to everyone's satisfaction. The WoC director, John McLaren, was very discrete when I asked him about the affair.

As a winewriter, I have never tried to live like a monk. It is an impossible condition of sanctity to reach when wine is your livelihood. Wine is a business built on the reasons for its creation: celebration and socialising, food and companionship, the enjoyment of life. I am, then, a wine journalist, like every other wine journalist, whose operations are subsidised to some extent by the people whose products it is his job critically to review. Brutally frankly, it is a conflict of interest I cannot deny. But take away the conflict and you take away my job. I can only be judged, in the end, by my reviews, opinions, and my writings. My readers must judge me as they find me. No other arbiters are so disinterested or, more importantly, so vital to me. I certainly cannot accept in this role someone who is equally as 'subsidised', as human, as myself – even, some might say, more so. As Mannie Kant put it: '*Aus so krummem Holze, als woraus der Mensch gemacht ist, kann nichts ganz gerades gezimmert werden.*' Or: Out of the crooked timber of humanity no straight thing can ever be made. In the end, my readers give me living. I am happy, in return, to give them my liver.

oTHER FREEBIES

Does the truly independent wine writer exist?

It was Flaubert in a letter to his mother in 1850, who wrote that 'You may depict wine, love, women or glory as long as you are not a drunkard, a lover, a husband or a humble private.' It is not my brief to analyse the strange things the author of Madame Bovary scribbled to his mum but his notion that a writer cannot become closely involved in what s(he) wishes to depict is, though he was applying the stricture to the creation of literature, of more than passing interest to the wine critic.

The truly independent wine writer? Impossible.

What a difficult thing it is to keep distant from those influences which may fuzz one's judgement! I sit here, on my hill in north London, knowing I will be unable to resist descending to dinner at The Square with Jean-Claude Boisset or to accept Wine Australia's offer to fly me to Melbourne. I will tell myself I do all these things for my readers: that I will gain in knowledge and insight (and also in waistline, but some prices are worth paying).

Neither can I refuse all those bottles of free wine. I insist to myself each and every one is a necessary adjunct to my work. As a result of this there is no truly independent wine critic. We are all bought off.

The more blatant the more irresistible
We wine parasites, as writers on booze are familiarly known on the continent (though the Aussies continue, for some quaint reason, to refer to us as mates), are conditioned to receive, to accept or reject as we will, all manner of bribes but however blatant they may be there is always a degree of subtlety involved be it euphemistic,

civilised or just coyly seductive which makes you feel misanthropic when you say no. Now let us be clear here: a bribe is anything which mists the clarity of the objective viewpoint. Thus, the air ticket which takes you to a vineyard area you would be unable to fund the research for otherwise is a bribe. The free samples which arrive at your door, many unheralded, many, indeed, so mysterious in provenance, price and distribution, that they never get tasted or, as I have done in the past, get given away to rest homes, funeral parlours, and charity bonfire parties in order to assist others in their progress through this vale of tears called Life are bribes. A bribe is a lunch with a wine producer whose wines you admire or are anxious to discover more about. Such bribes as these are only different from the blandishments with barely any, even marginal, relationship with wine because they are disguised. These blandishments are out-and-out bribes.

In the recent past, in a moodily prim stab at pretending to be independent, I have refused tickets to Wimbledon, the Cup Final, the world rugby cup final, test cricket, Glyndebourne, the Albert Hall, to mention only a few. Those wine scribes who feel differently, some of whom, for instance, spectated at live Euro-2000 football matches in France under the guise of making vineyard research trips to the Midi, are to be congratulated on their nerve. My problem in accepting such hospitality, which has absolutely nothing to do with wine, is that the obligation I would feel under would render me not just a less than objective judge of the products of whatever wine producer, retailer or national wine board initiated the invitation in the first place, but a free-lance contributor to someone's PR effort.

The Australian wine writer, Tony Keys, on his website (The Key Report) in January 2008, revealed the problem thus: 'I have just received an invite to a tasting followed by supper followed by a seat at the quarter finals of the Australian Tennis Open. I have nothing against the company doing that, but as I already get their wines to review, there is little need for the tasting. Supper/lunch is standard practice following a tasting and I would happily get stuck into the tucker on offer, but I feel far too uncomfortable about accepting the invitation to the Open, as kindly meant as I know it is.'

He felt uncomfortable? He should have felt revulsion. He ought to have turned the invite down flat without bothering his readers with his troubled conscience. It is nothing more than a bribe. No human being can accept that level of hospitality and then fail to do what he is being asked to do: to write sympathetically of the wines and feel good about the company making them (unless the wines were truly awful, close to toxic). But poor Mr Keys is obviously a deeply troubled chap. In the next paragraph on his site he wrote this: 'I often question my ethics (a healthy thing to do) and did so when accepting a recent visit to Tasmania including airfares, accommodation and hospitability from Tamar Ridge. Add to that the two decades of friendship I have with CEO Dr Andrew Pirie and Anthony Woollams (Pirie Tasmania Brand Manager), and the fact that I find General Manager Will Adkins to be excellent company, and it screams of 'bias reporting'.'

I leave it to the reader to judge whether this Keys fellow can ever be called a wine writer or is not just the next best thing to (indeed, better than) a PR man. He often questions his ethics? Rather late, I would have thought, after twenty years 'friendship' with a wine producer. I do not think that anyone can maintain such close links with wine producers and be considered an independent wine writer. Even if Keys is more of an industry commentator than a bottle critic, his relationships make his views useless as objective reporting. It is healthy to question one's ethics, Mr Keys, but if you take no action you are merely being a hypocrite – especially when you broadcast the fact.

As another example of similar sporting seductions on offer, take the email I received in August 2007 from the Margaux Gourmet Day Tour Comittee.

'Please find attached information on how some of Margaux's most prestitigous chateaux are preparing for the Rugby World Cup this September. The Irish, Australian and Japanese matches will all be

held in Bordeaux, and the fine wine world is opening its doors. The
attached press releases cover

> 1) A one day gourmet tour of four Margaux chateaux,
> Château Rauzan Gassies, Château Prieuré-Lichine, Château
> La Tour de Bessan and Château Kirwan, accompanied by a
> sommelier who will match local food delicacies from terrine
> to chocolate with these famous wines. To run every day –
> except match days – during September.
> 2) And following the Medoc Marathon and the Margaux
> cycle tour, the world of Bordeaux fine wine is extending its
> link with sports via a three day ProAm Golf tournament to
> take place in the Medoc with visits and a gala dinner to
> Château Rauzan Gassies, Château Prieuré-Lichine and
> Château Kirwan.'

How difficult to turn all this down, even if one were indifferent to
rugby, running and cycling. But, being French, there was a degree
of elegance with this cunning bribe. Sometimes the bribe is an
invitation so crass, so deliciously adolescent, that in refusing it one
feels one has lost an opportunity to see just who would be witless
enough amongst one's colleagues to take it up. To wit, this email
received in 2006:

> I believe we sent you an invitation last week to attend the
> exclusive launch event for a new range of wines from South
> Australia called the Four Emus.... there will be lots of free
> wine to drink, goodie bags, interactive entertainment, and a
> bottle to take home. The event will be a lot of fun, feel free
> to bring a colleague, or if you are unable to attend please pass
> this on to anyone you may wish to send in your place. Feel
> free to call if you have any queries or require directions or
> travel arrangements. At the event, you will be able to discover
> your Emu personality and your inner Emu aura read by

psychic entertainers as well as an interactive wine tasting.

The venue for this desperate, gruesome-sounding event was a bar at a PR company in Soho Square. Presumably I could have got the PR totty who contacted me to organise a taxi there and a taxi home. I could hardly be expected to struggle back on my bicycle burdened with my goodie bag, my free Emu wine, my psychic aura printout, and with an impressive hangover building up, could I?

Some bribes are more creative. For two years running the PR executive at Marks & Spencer, Viv Jawett, sent me a silk shirt for Christmas. At receipt of the second, I had firmly to warn her I was considering banning the retailer from my newspaper column unless this practice was stopped. It did. She took me to dinner to meet Gordon Ramsay to say sorry. Tesco once sent me a Toblerone bar so large it was taller than my youngest son and retailed for forty quid. Said son was somewhat miffed when I donated it to the local church.

I once purchased a case of Chilean chardonnay as a gift for a friend from a branch of wine merchants Unwins where I was tasting a range of this retailer's wines. They were happy to deliver it but disinclined to later post me the invoice. Could they be hoping I would accept it as a gift? In the event, after two phone calls to the branch and two to head office – the last one containing the threat that if I did not receive the invoice within a week I would ban Unwins from my Guardian column and make public my reasons – the invoice arrived three days later. (Unwins has since gone out of business.)

Who gets rich writing on wine? The difference between a wine writer and a bum can be slight. It has to be admitted that wine writing is so wretchedly remunerated that it is no wonder that its practitioners are liable, indeed forced, to find other avenues of liquidity. Many are part time of course, but those who stick at it full time are not, for the most part, living the high life. The exceptions are few.

Hugh Johnson has carved out for himself a nice little earner in wine maps and his chairmanship of *The Sunday Times* Wine Club and his publishers claim he is 'the world's favourite wine author'. (A claim based on the annual sales of his wine guide, which he does not write a great deal of as it has at least two dozen contributors who do most of Hugh's work for him.) He is also a director of Château Latour, as mentioned earlier, and for a while he had a wine accessories shop off Piccadilly near Fortnum & Mason. Oz Clarke does okay, with his TV stuff and lending his name to wine guides (which, like Johnson's, can only be put together with the assistance of several contributors whose names do not appear on the front cover), and Jancis Robinson has several fingers in several pies and is assumed not to have to take in ironing to make ends meet. I did alright for a while with a £300,000 advance for my *Superplonk* books, £48,000 a year from Sainsbury's Magazine and £35,000 a year from the *Guardian* (the BBC's contribution, even the £30,000 fee for a six-part TV series, merely helped pay the income tax).

Many wine writers have a partner who works and so ameliorates single status poverty and can provide luxuries (Jane MacQuitty of *The Times*, Joanna Simon of *The Sunday Times*, Richard Erhlich of the *Independent* inter alia). But most wine writers struggle. Even so successful a wine dynamo as the Saturday *Daily Mail*'s Matthew Jukes said to me that he needs to continue his restaurant consultancy activities to make up for the short fall from his on-the-face-of-it successful annual wine guide *The Wine List* (which in 2007 ceased publication).

The most interesting revelation at a wine industry conference in 2005 was wine critic Andrew Jefford's announcement that his annual income for the tax year just ended was £31,000. With income tax levied, which I estimate to be £6650.20p, the poor blighter has to struggle on a yearly screw of £23,349.80p. As shocked delegates reeled, he piled on the agony further: for a 49-year-old bloke supposedly at the top of his profession, he said, his situation was depressing. I daresay there are checkout girls at Waitrose, for whom Andrew works part-time as a contributor to this retailer's magazine, who pull in more than the £468 a week he does (with overtime).

What incentive can there be for anyone to become a wine writer if the remuneration is so pitiful for one of its scintillants?

Wine writing is mainly an amateur pursuit. It is not necessary to have a single qualification in order to write on wine (otherwise I would have hardly got the job). Only literacy and a thirst for the subject are required. Likewise, wine merchanting and wine producing were amateur in many respects before the rise of the supermarket wine department and modern oenological methods and production techniques. The amateur approach to wine writing may not be hugely profitable for the writer but it can be rewarding for the reader. A writer who combines and connects in her writing many cultural activities is all the richer for it and those writers who can express this diversity are thereby the most enriching to read.

Style, insight, wit, wide knowledge, humanity – a wine writer with those attributes, even if s(he) is a dinosaur who considers screwcaps to be the invention of the devil and *terroir* to be the major determinant of wine style, will be far more worth reading than any po-faced professional prophet.

The mistake is to take oneself too seriously – wine after all is only alcoholised fruit juice – or to see wine writing as Mosaic prognostication. It is a privilege and joy to write on a subject one loves and those charms must remain, for many, its greatest rewards.

You can spray against any pest – except The Glassy-Eyed Wine Writer. Many a wine producer knows the truth of this.

24

THE MISERABLE WINE CRITIC

How to concoct a career out of a few-seconds sip

I do not believe there is such an individual as a wine expert. To be sure, there are those who claim to be and there are those who have some expertise in the area. There are expert wine makers and grape growers and within a defined region there are people who intimately know the vineyards and the vines.

But in terms of wine writing as we understand it in the UK, in the sense of implying familiarity with wines from just about everywhere and passing on judgement on all of them at any time, there is no-one who is truly expert. We are, at best, generalists, expert only at forming our opinions and eloquently reporting on what we find. We may be experienced. We may love the liquid we set out critically to acclaim or deride. We may have read widely, have visited thousands of vineyards all over the globe over many decades. We may know a thing or two that the average drinker, or even those who be considered knowledgeable, might not know. In English-speaking wine producing countries where export is crucial, Australia, New Zealand and South Africa, local journalists do acquire local expertise but whether their judgements are wholly impartial is open to question. One notable Aussie wine hack told me that if he overly criticises Aussie producers he will no longer receive samples to taste. He won't be able to do his job. This kind of threat makes objectivity fragile and compels some journalists in these countries to be no better than publicists.

When it comes to the crunch, when the judgement on a wine in a glass which is under our nose is called for, then few of us can be called an expert all of the time. We are at most a single experienced palate, passing an opinion on a moment or moments in time.

It is the fact that this fleeting experience is so different for each individual who partakes of it, and that wine changes over a very short period once its bottle is opened, which renders the designation of expert, to my mind, extremely dubious.

True, there are those who are magnificently expert at putting down their impressions of a wine on paper. Hugh Johnson, for example, is unmatched in his almost casual brilliance at depicting his drinking, or experience, of a wine. But literary skill is a different order of expertise than wine tasting, particularly that which is practised by those in the mainstream British press and media generally who depend upon being taken seriously in order to be considered a professional and make a living.

How does one become a wine writer? Where a newspaper is concerned it used to be first one who owned up to speaking passable French. In my case it was a wholly fortuitous (word chosen carefully) meeting with the new food and drink editor of the *Guardian*. It seemed he thought I could write and that having spent the past thirty years drinking wine that I knew something about it. I learned, am I happy to admit, a vast amount doing the job. One thing I did not need to learn was that I must not only maintain my independence but be seen to do so. I have never done any work for any wine producer and always refused to take their money. Once a wine writer has been paid by a producer or a wine region to speak or write on its behalf s(he) is no longer independent and every word they write thereafter is tainted.

Some critics, not mainstream, manage both roles and experience no qualms. Olly Smith, the ebullient British TV wine personality, has represented Tio Pepe sherry and wines from Chile and presented Tesco wines. Tim Atkin, the *Observer* newspaper wine man, wrote a book in the 1990s on the Languedoc which was little better than a display of copywriting for the region. (But then, to be

fair, with introductions by the chairman of the Union
Interprofessionnelle des Vins de Pays d'Oc and the chairman of the
Chamber of Agriculture for the Hérault, and the fact that it was
published by Gilbert & Gaillard, wine guide publishers and wine
retailers, it was hardly pretending to be otherwise.) Can the same be
said of the pamphlet Sopexa, the London based French wine and
food promoters, paid me anonymously to write in the early 1990s
on the wine regions of France? No. It did not mention individual
producers being a mere guide to regional characteristics.

One wine expert accepted money from a supermarket chain
(£50,000 is the figure alleged) to help in the production of a BBC-
TV series. Whispering to me in 1996, a BBC executive said that had
the Corporation known of this they might not have transmitted the
programmes. Wine writing, it must be said, is often so wretchedly
remunerated that it is not surprising those condemned to follow the
profession are forced to find other revenue streams. Many wine
writers haunt the nebulous area between criticism and public
relations. Charles Metcalfe has no qualms presenting wines in so-
called Master Classes to members of the Tesco Wine Club yet is co-
chairman of The International Wine Challenge. Joe Wadsack, who's
written on wine for his old employer at *Waitrose Magazine*, does
the same (and has also represented Gallo Brothers). Olly Smith, who
also writes for *GQ* and appears on TV food programmes as a wine
critic, also does work for Tesco's wine club.

I must declare that I am not entirely untainted by the existence
of this so-called Club. Unpaid, I wrote an article for it some while
back in the hope it would encourage its members to subscribe to
my website, superplonk.com. They didn't. The experience, however,
was salutary as my copy was monstrously changed without my
permission, to make it more cringingly soppy, and it was only at the
eleventh hour that I saw a proof and demanded my original words
be reinstated. They were. I realised I was experiencing what it was
like to be a Tesco supplier. I was treated with such hideous indifference I was shocked and had I not been vigilant words would have

appeared under my name I had nothing to do with. In the hope that this treatment was just an error, by a hapless PR at the Club magazine's design agency, I then developed the idea that I should present video downloads to Tesco customer members on a regular basis and teach them about wine tasting via their computers. Having renounced all newspaper wine journalism, I felt no conflict of interest. I had the broadcast facilities all set-up and so I proceeded to talk to Tesco. To say I was treated like a shit the second time is hyperbole but I certainly experienced what it was to swallow my dignity and push people to set up meetings, to be fobbed off with countless excuses and have emails ignored, and when after several conversations and meetings over several months I saw the two people who mattered one wanted to ensure the endeavour was funded wholly out of wine sales – i.e. I was going effectively to be a Tesco wine salesman and not a wine teacher – and the other executive left a little while later because he preferred to work for someone else. I don't blame him. I never heard from Tesco again and had I done so I had my reply to hand. I no longer wished to have anything to do with this retailer. My treatment by Waitrose and Sainsbury, on the other hand, when I have approached them with regard to wine education programmes, has been wholly different. They made themselves quickly available and were receptive, sympathetic and intelligent.

Hugh Johnson, ex-chairman of the Circle of Wine Writers, of which I was a bolshie and reluctant member before resigning in January 2008, is chairman of the *Sunday Times* Wine Club. So he is a retailer as well as a wine writer. (The Circle, which I fondly refer to as The Ellipsis of Idiots, is a flabbily un-amusing institution, the annual sub of which, at £50, is better spent on three or four exquisite bottles.)

A couple of CWW members have remarked to me that allowing so-called wine educators in as members is highly questionable, not to mention publishers of wine books and other individuals with dubious claims to be writers on wine, but I consider that so few wine writers can actually write that cavilling over members who never put pen to paper in the vinous cause is futile (and rather snotty). Besides, how many other specialist groupings can claim 100% purity of membership? I bet the Professional Footballers Association has more than one bod who's never scored a goal, or made a decent tackle, in his life and yet turns up at the annual Christmas bash, cracks a few jokes, and gets slapped on the back as a good ole boy.

The future of wine writing is bleak, it seems to me. The future is with the wine presenter, the dynamic TV-style individual who is really not a writer or a critic at all. S(he) will be so closely allied to certain wine regions or nations, or so intimately related to certain suppliers or retailers, that any bestowing of the title critic is farcically inaccurate. Wine writing, as impartial appraisal, will eventually be practised only by those who appeal to the 2% of drinkers interested in truly individual, complex, often demanding wines. By this I do not mean always expensive wines, merely those the mainstream retailers have little time to take any interest or see any profit in.

Anyone can be a wine critic – even a TV-cook

The *Guardian*'s news editor was desperate. Could I write 400 words by 6 pm (it was 2006, it was lunchtime) for the morrow's edition on Rick Stein, the cuddly restaurateur and ex-Oxonian who effects to be a peasant who waffles on about food on BBC television. Mr Stein was fine when he began his celebrity career, in Cornwall and with fish, but he has given a broader canvas now and he does not paint a pretty picture. The news editor wished me to comment on Mr Stein's grotesque attempt, via the BBC's listing magazine *Radio Times*, to drum up publicity for his latest TV series.

The man had uttered a series of extremely silly statements about French wine which coming, as they did, from someone who runs food businesses in the county with the dullest catering (and least sexy local wine) in England was interesting. The last time I ate at his restaurant in Padstow I had to send back my mussels because the chef had neglected to debeard them. Rick Stein is, then, in no position to besmirch the reputation of anything connected with French food, wine or culture.

'Wine lovers,' according to Mr Stein, 'can find a better choice in British supermarkets than in some of France's finest restaurants. You've only got to go into any UK supermarket to see how enthusiastically we have embraced all the different wines of the world. Meanwhile, the French stick doggedly to their own stuff, and while they still make the best, they're missing out on all those lovely Australians and New Zealands and Chileans they could be enjoying.' Well, you won't find much Aussie shiraz or Kiwi Sauvignon Blanc or South African pinotage in top Frog eateries, but you will find, mostly, a wide selection of the wines of the regions in which those restaurants are situated. Who could ask for more of a wine list? How could a country with 24% of its population concerned with agriculture be so insane as to start importing foreign products? That many New World wines are remarkable, and in many instances superior to French, goes without saying but if Mr Stein feels France needs foreign wines then why do a programme about France in the first place?

The Cornish klutz went further: 'I have to say that there is a lot of *vin very ordinaire* out there. The best French wines are still the best in the world – they have this real sense of belonging to the soil in which they were produced. But for every one really good French wine, there are 10 bad ones.'

Oh God. This is so much rubbish. Of course there is a lot of ordinary wine. The world is full of it. The best French wines are NOT the best in the world and soil has nothing to do with it. He is spouting patronising balderdash. The soil of a vineyard is far less relevant than the soul of the winemaker and there are two dozen countries which make wine as good, and as bad, as the French. You really must, Mr Stein, exercise discrimination on your barge (his TV series took place on French canals) and choose the many good French bottles. The true percentage of bad French wine to good is more like 50/50 than 10/90. Had this TV cook any real knowledge of French wine he could find precisely the opposite of what he claims to have found. It may, for all I know, be perfectly true that much wine made from vineyards adjacent to French canals is rubbish but that hardly justifies a call for French wine lists to offer Chilean Cabernet. Would you drink such a wine if you found it on a wine list in a local restaurant in France? You'd be utterly barmy to choose it and the restaurant even barmier to list it.

One further Stein inanity was a real stunner (and reveals that the man has no idea red wines can go with fish every bit as well as whites).

'Most of the wines on my own restaurant list,' he said, 'are no more than two years old, since whites are best drunk within a year or two of making.' Oh dear. What ignorance is displayed here. German rieslings, arguably the world's greatest white wines, taste and smell much more sensual after ten or fifteen years and even a Aussie semillon is best kept six or seven. White wine, in many instance more so than red, is sassier with bottle age. If the man who has passed the remarks quoted above is considered suitable by the BBC to front a programme about French food and wine culture, God help us. The only taste he has is for his own foot in his mouth.

Mr Stein gets his own back

When I met Mr Stein, he was, surprise surprise, indignant at my criticism of him. He said that he had in part been misquoted by the *Radio Times*. It was not, however, convenient for him to beat me up there and then (even with his brother, Professor John Stein, by his side) as we were all on duty at a charity auction evening at The Ivy restaurant.

At this evening a wealthy resident in Bath successfully bid £12,000 to have Rick Stein, Ivy chef Mark Hix, and myself put on a private dinner party/wine tasting. I wondered whether this bidder knew of the disaffection between two thirds of his prize and thus was eagerly contemplating the thought of the ripe exchanges as

Rick emerged from the kitchen with his *saumon en croûte aux truffes* and I came up from the wine cellar with bottles of 1990 Comtes Lafon Meursault Perrières or, more daringly, Hertz Pinot d'Alsace 1989, both wines capable of refuting the silly idea that white wines cannot age well and long, that red wines cannot accompany fish, and that French wines are largely rubbish.

But when the dinner took place at the winner's mansion outside Bath Rick Stein never cooked a damn thing and left me and others to do all the work. Mark Hix and a brilliant kitchen team from Scott's fish restaurant in Mayfair did all the cooking (and the clearing up) as I ferried the wine around, handed the canapés about, and organised the dancing afterwards. Mr Stein, dolled up in his immaculate white apron to look like a proper chef, sat there at table and hob-nobbed with the guests and any dreams that the host may have had about fisticuffs over the flapjacks or abuse with the anchovies vanished with exquisite champagne and magnums of Lafite and Latour. Crafty fellow, Stein. What I wouldn't give for an ounce of his beautifully disguised chutzpah.

Revelation: I'm the biggest phony of the lot

It was not even a few-seconds sip which started my career as a wine writer. It was writing an article on how to thicken *coq au vin* using the blood of a certain advertising agency's account executives (chickens to a man). Had not the newly appointed food and drink editor of the *Guardian* not read this tongue-in-cheek article in 1988 I would not have been asked to review food and drink books for the newspaper and, soon after this, been invited to write a wine column. I'm just a bloody amateur, dear reader.

(*Amateur*: non-professional, lover-of, volunteer, dilettante. Collins Robert French dictionary.)

Indeed, I can reveal that after I had been appointed Jancis Robinson protested to the *Guardian*'s food and drink editor, Matthew Fort, about my column and my existence as a wine critic. I was not, it seems, knowledgeable enough about what she

considered wine fit to write about. I was not, in other words, sufficiently snobbish. Even Tim Atkin, who started his own wine
column in the *Guardian* at the same time as I, protested at my
column's existence. Why? Because it had so many readers. Because,
unlike these puffed-up snobs who see wine only through the misty
pretention of being called a Master of Wine, I did not worship the
idea of *terroir*, I was open-minded about new world wines, and I
did not believe good wines were the exclusive retail preserve of
upmarket merchants.

'The reaction from established wine critics to your column,
Malcolm, 'Matthew has said to me, 'was vituperative. They said this
man knows nothing about wine. Where has he come from?'

Matthew pointed out to these protesters that had some of them,
toffee-nosed stick-in-the-muds to a woman, been doing their job
they would have spotted what I had seen writ large: that supermarkets had lots of interesting wines (far from the truth nowadays, alas)
and that readers were interested in value for money not ludicrously
expensive, obscure wines from merchants who it was necessary to
possess a 4x4 vehicle and an ordnance survey map to find.

These wine snobs have not gone away. Indeed, some have
followed Superplonk's lead and have discovered that supermarket
wines aren't so bad after all. Nowadays, major wine critics have to
take an interest in some of the leading supermarkets because their
readers do. Personally, I now find supermarkets less and less
interesting, as this book makes clear, and it galls me to ponder the
inescapable fact that my trumpeting of them, via my columns and
my books, has been a factor in turning them into brand purveyors
instead of being superb own-label brand leaders in their own right.
I have always kept an open mind. It is the only authentic stance a
wine critic can adopt (and it perfectly accompanies my open
mouth). But for the *Guardian*'s Matthew Fort the modern wine
revolution may never have got off the ground. He should, by rights,
now be sitting in the House of Lords. (I, as a republican, cannot of
course accept such honours.)

25

THE LANGUAGE OF WINE

The impossibility of truth in wine writing

Ratings lead an obscure life when they are confined to the Royal Navy but appended to wine bottles they cause controversy. Robert Parker's rating system is despised by several critics, Tim Atkin, wine critic at The *Observer* Sunday newspaper, most voluble amongst them in the UK, but even more than Mr Parker's 100-point scale, my 20-point system is doubted by dear Tim because it is based on value for money. My contention is that a rating system firmly nails down the critic's view of a wine. It is crucial information.

Perhaps critics opposed to rating systems have developed a superior system for letting their readers know how they truly feel about a wine? In a spirit of research I purchased the *Observer*. This is what I found (amongst other back-of-bottle style write-ups lack of space prevents me from exposing).

Domaine d'Angerville Volnay Premier Cru 2002, £32, Majestic. 2002 was a great vintage for red burgundy and this more than proves the point. It's got the delicate perfume of a great Volnay allied to silky, palate-caressing tannins and a core of sweet Pinot Noir fruit.

Now leaving aside the fact that the wine was only physically on sale in a single Majestic branch in St John's Wood in London W8, what purpose does this appraisal of a wine serve? Does the taster actually love the wine? What can the reader take from this curt review which is of any meaningful value? Even the two metaphors, 'great Volnay' and 'sweet Pinot Noir fruit' are empty because they refer to themselves and not to anything which unravels the mystery of how the wine performs.

Middleton Murry wrote that one is bound to be metaphorical if one attempts to be precise. This is at the heart of wine writing. However, metaphors only work if the reader comprehends the analogy. It is useless to say a Volnay smells like a Volnay or that it has pinot noir fruit. What else could it exhibit but such features? Who other than the critic and a few other know-alls understand it?

Mr Atkin believes rating systems are unrepeatable. That the scores given such wines one day would not be the same the next if the same wines were retasted. But this also applies to the metaphors, if the wines were to be so differing in performance. I readily concede it is wholly possible to arrive at differing ratings as wines do change from day to day (especially affected by low and high weather fronts, the mood of the taster, and because each bottle being sealed with a cork it is also an individual, perhaps unrepeatable, entity). A score is only a measure of the appraisal of a wine at a certain point in its life but if one wishes to communicate its value-for-money quotient, or its true critical worth, then a rating system is essential. A rating system transcends any metaphoric approach because it acts almost as a metonym or something like synecdoche. If I may be permitted the neologism, a rating system is a synecym. Mere metaphor is wholly transcended.

Is that Volnay Tim Atkin has chosen to write about so shallowly worth the money? The critic does the reader a major disservice by failing to rate it. Notwithstanding the uselessness of its metaphors, and the generalisation about the 2002 vintage, if it carried a rating then at least the reader would know how unambiguously the critic felt.

Shall we now see how two other critics approach such a wine? Robert Parker's notes for the same vintage Volnay are yet to be published but those for the 1996 have been. They read as follows:

Domaine Du Marquis D'Angerville Volnay Champans 1996. (89 to 92 points.)... has a creamy cherry-scented nose and an outstanding, sweet, medium-bodied and supple character packed with ripe black cherries and minerals. This lovely and well-focused wine should be at its peak from its release to 2003.

Another critic, who shall remain anonymous, has this to say:

Volnay Champans Domaine d'Angerville 2002 (12.5 points out of 20, £32, Majestic St John's Wood)… is too young to drink now… it needs at least 3/4 years more. It might rate 14, perhaps 14.5 in 2008/9 though £32 is a lot of money. It is not yet a sensual wine for it has a sere primness and somewhat arid finish, which needs some hours of decanting to eradicate though the tannic backbone is elegant. The 2002 crop has been touted as a fine vintage for the region but this only applies to certain wines from certain vineyards and I doubt if this is one of the great exceptions, though time will tell us more.

Now. I have no doubt that if readers were given a choice they would prefer its critic, soberly, to rate wines. By all means let Mr Atkin overcome his perceived failing in the ratings approach with a superior notion – I would hasten to ape his genius.

Can any wine writer ever write rational prose?
There is another reason why a rating system is unbeatable. It is because wine writers are the worst qualified of critical experts. This is largely, though not exclusively, because we are the most poorly equipped. The most important tool at our disposal is inadequate for the job. That tool is the English language.

How can language vividly convey what it is to experience the taste of a particular wine? Wine critics must conjure paragraphs from perfumes and contrive fantasies from flavours. It is the unmentionable in full pursuit of the ineffable. As the cultural commentator,

Alexis Bespaloff, has so succinctly put it 'taste and smell are the beggars of our senses for they have no accurate written language.'

The prose of wine writing, its struggle to depict abstract and highly personalised ideas, has given the world of wine writing two special languages. The first is used to announce the user's fluency with and command of his subject. Thus, a wine does not possess smell: it has a nose. A wine's flavour is its palate (further fragmented into mid-palate and back-palate). No lay person uses these terms for they are attempts, pretentious in the extreme, to give the person who uses them the belief s(he) is an expert. Crucially, the persons to whom such terms are addressed may also be kidded into believing in the expertise of the user. However, if we are to believe psychotherapist Adam Phillips in his book 'Terrors & Experts': 'Special languages, like sexual techniques, are cover-ups.' What are we wine writers trying to hide? Answer: our struggle to communicate.

Q: 'How many wine writers does it take to change a light bulb?'

A: 'None. They work in the dark.'

It is not very funny I agree. But working in the dark gives the wine scribe enormous powers. This is because the wine drinker is in the dark too but imagines, believes indeed, that the writer knows her way around. This belief is based solely upon language, but it is a different one from that cited above which comprises pseudo-technical terms. The second language of wine description has fewer rules and less of a pedigree.

Master of his craft

The language of this wine-speak has developed its own distinct credentials only since 1966 when Hugh Johnson wrote his book *Wine* and it dawned upon the booze hack that it was possible to acquire guru status, and drink for free, by handling words in particular ways. The very first paragraph of Hugh's book *Wine* is as vibrant and evocative now as it was when I first read it all those decades ago.

Think, for a moment, of an almost paper-white glass of liquid, just shot with greeny-gold, just tart on your tongue, full of wild-flower scents and spring-water freshness. And think of a burnt-amber liquid, as smooth as syrup in the glass, as fat as butter to smell and sea-deep with strange flavours. Both are wine.

These definitions of Moselle and old Tokay (if I have inferred correctly) are surely not over-embroidered but perfectly and elegantly stitched descriptions of the nigh-indescribable. I swallow them both with delight and complete understanding.

However, this small but elegant pebble precipitated the avalanche of prose which wine language developed in the latter half of the 20th century. This reached its apogee of expressiveness, some say its preposterousness, when performers on TV food and drink shows in the 1980s began to seem to lampoon wine, to treat it with metaphors of often barmy iconoclastic derision entirely fitting for a liquid which was no longer the status symbol of the middle classes but the beverage of anyone who had merely enjoyed a week's holiday in Benidorm (where wine was treated as if it grew on trees). Such language thumbed its nose at the traditions of wine; knocked off its stuffy pedestal.

However, in spite of wine nowadays being a truly down-to-earth experience, enjoyed by over 75% of Britons (whereas 50 years ago less than 4% of the nation drank it), wine writers flourish and continue to develop impenetrable wine-speak. We continue to deal in the crepuscular and the shadowy, the indistinct and the imprecise, in spite of the fact that wine drinkers show signs of being bored. Annual wine guides, written by a single individual tasting a great many bottles, have disappeared (*Superplonk* in 2005, Matthew Jukes's *The Wine List* in 2006). We critics are no longer widely considered as indispensable sentries, providing the code words, those stimulating shibboleths, which show the shining path out of the dark.

I always remind myself, in my high-flown moments, that I do not know as much as the next man and I know less than the woman next to him. Each of them knows what they like. I do not. How, then, can I communicate exactly what it is I have tasted? Who knows anything about taste except the person who experiences it? Taste is individual; translation nigh impossible.

Two rare animals

The problem of translating the experience of tasting a wine into words has led to an interesting development. Nowadays there are two kinds of wine writer, one more numerous than the other. Which kind of wine writer you are depends on which end of the bottle you start at; the linguistic approach to both is different because the two approaches are dissimilar. In splendid Lilliputian fashion, it seems to me, wine writers are either Top-Enders or Bottom-Enders.

The Bottom-Enders begin on the lees, amongst the bits and bobs of the liquid left over from the winemaking (miniscule of course and often fined and filtered out in reality). Such writers' focus is on the minutiae of the wine, the vineyard, the variety of the grapes, the philosophy (style or approach is insufficient to do justice to the depth of feeling considered appropriate here) of the wine grower. Such writers on wine are social animals before anything else: romantics, story tellers, fabulists; they have a great many friends in the world of wine. Their language depends less on metaphor and more on imagery. It has great influence, mostly amongst wine snobs, wine merchants, serious collectors, and other wine writers. Writers who start at the bottom of the bottle maintain the myths of wine and are idealists; without them Bordeaux would never be able to claim a 'vintage of the century', for example, and so purveyors of wine to the gentry adore them and massage their egos. (They speak the same language after all.)

The writer who starts from the business end of the bottle, the end the liquid flows from, has far fewer friends in the world of wine.

In a perfect world, as s(he) knows in her heart, s(he) would have no friends who grow and make wine just as no restaurant critic worthy of the status could hardly boast of an abundance of friendships amongst chefs. It is much harder, lonelier work being a wine critic rather than being a mere wine writer or commentator. Your pour out the wine. You regard its colour. You sniff around it. You agitate the glass to release the esters of the perfume and so better to appreciate the aromas, the nuances of the bouquet. You inhale these odiferous pleasantries, or unpleasantries, through the chimney of the taste, the nostrils (the only access to the brain open to the air) and then you taste. You swill the liquid around the mouth and breathe in air so that this liquid is aerated and experienced by all the mouth's taste buds. These are arranged in sectors of differently orientated cohesion (one designed to recognise salinity, another alkalinity, another sweetness and so on). They connect with the brain which in turn provides the sensory data, memory based, to form the critic's view of what s(he) is drinking. Some of the wine is permitted to contact the back of the throat, but only a small amount is allowed to proceed down the gullet, so that the finish of the wine can be studied. Then the wine is ejected and several seconds left to elapse whilst all these sensations are studied and written up as the impression the wine has left is mulled over.

As part of a working day, a critic like myself may taste over a hundred wines. I rarely think it wise to venture, critically, over 230 bottles in a single day not because I find my taste buds flagging but because I dry up – linguistically. The brain tires long before the taste buds. Metaphors shrivel and become repetitive and the dark becomes truly oppressive and clammy. Perhaps my recourse to a special language is indeed a cover-up.

What the hell are you talking about?
The problems wine writers have in describing abstract ideas has particular poignancy for any student of language and Professor Jean Aitchison, an eminent ex-Oxford linguistician, has referred to

examples of wine language in her work including the 1996 Reith Lectures and in her book Words in the Mind. She explains that around a hundred years ago there was no hard and fast vocabulary to describe word sounds, so the writing on language smacked of the same undisciplined and inconsistent use of metaphors which we see in wine writing, making accurate assessment and like-for-like comparison almost impossible. The science of phonetics has now got its act together but, she says, wine language is still in the dark ages.

We're back in the dark again. This is why we all grasp the easiest way out: the use of metaphors. The most common of these are fruit aromas and flavours because grapes do mimic many fruits, spices, vegetables and herbs as a result of the fermentation process and the more complex a wine the more of these things it might exhibit (though chemical elements like the acids and the tannins are hugely contributive here). However, metaphors, according to linguists, have to share minor characteristics with the words they are describing and not major ones. To describe life as a flight on Concorde is a better metaphor than likening marmalade to jam (and 'shall I compare thee to a summer's day' more telling than 'shall I compare you to my mum?').

This has led to an unfortunate development in my view: fruit metaphors and their precise detection and location in a wine bedevil the world of wine tutoring to the extent that far too many tutees consider themselves inadequate if they fail to unearth the exact fruits and/or vegetables and herbs the wine is said to exhibit. Texture is neglected, and that ineffable finish in the throat, and a febrile, and often fruitless, mental game is played called 'Find the Fruits.' This becomes a point-scoring exercise and too many people in the wine trade, and those who go on wine courses, graduate with the belief that this is the most important aspect of a wine. It is not. It has merely become received wisdom and in some instances actually prevents the drinker enjoying the wine for what it is.

Trust TV to dumb it down

Bewildered readers of wine columns or viewers of yesteryear's TV wine shows must wonder whether the wines being described actually taste of damsons, loganberries, or mangoes and so on. They must also marvel (which is the effect intended) at the wine tasters' brilliance at being so gifted as to find one or more of these things. The more alert viewer might muse over why the wine entertainer has not detected the aroma of grapes which one might have thought rather more likely to appear than, say, ugli-fruit. Even more odd, if the taster refers to the wine as 'grapey' this is to suggest something quite different and even, I suggest, ordinary as who wants a wine to merely taste of the berries it is made from? While many argue that the use of fruit analogies is extremely useful and gives consumers a very clear picture of the wine, others believe the fruit idea is heavily over-used.

When a word is over-used it can frequently become 'bleached' to use the linguistic term. In short it loses its meaning. 'Plummy' and 'blackcurrant' now have little impact as descriptors because these flavours are attributed to wines so often – even though I use both terms when these words, to my palate, precisely describe the taste sensation. Eventually words can cease to be metaphors and effectively become synonyms, or a shorthand which add little descriptive substance. Professor Aitchison once alleged that sauvignon blanc was so often described as 'gooseberry', that each had become almost to mean one and the same thing. She was, and is, right; but what I am I to do when the very next New Zealand sauvignon blanc or Sancerre I taste recalls gooseberries? I may have to record it as such, search as I might for other phrases to pin down the wine's sensation on the palate and nose.

In addition to its rather predictable use of fruit metaphors, wine language also appears to lack pairs of true opposites. Sweet and dry is the clearest example, but it is also one of the very few. What is more, it can only really be applied to white wines. When retailers introduce basic tasting codes for their wines, the whites can simply and clearly be indicated on a scale of sweet to dry, but the reds are harder to categorise. Most choose to classify them from full bodied to light bodied, but these are not opposite words but merely comparatives.

Another linguistic device that could be employed far more often in wine writing is the 'prototype'. In language, descriptions can be built on prototypes which act as 'central points' about which to define related ideas and objects. 'Within linguistics you set up a prototype and see deviations from it,' says Jean Aitchison, citing the description of birds as an off-the-cuff example. A bird can be said to have certain basic attributes such as a beak, feathers, thin sticky legs etc. With that in mind, one could establish a blackbird as a prototypical bird and describe other birds by simply relating to it. 'When people write about wine it would be very useful if they set up what would be their prototype,' she says. 'It would help to know what you regard as the centre point before you go on.'

Here at least the wine writer has some defence. Prototypes are used in wine writing, the most common relating to the established varietal character of a grape or the recognised style of a particularly well-known wine region. A pinot noir or chardonnay from the New World, for example, can be described as being burgundian in style. Jean Aitchison quotes an Oz Clarke tasting note in her book of the Reith Lectures, The Language Web, which provides an illustration: 'Wine of marvellous, minty, blackcurrant perfume with some of the cedar and cigar smoke spice of the great Médocs.' Here, Medoc serves as a prototype and Aitchison confesses that 'without the word Medoc there I would have been totally lost.' I would add that had Mr Clarke's wine had a rating, Professor Aitchison would have found herself even more enlightened.

One finds these allusions fairly frequently in wine reviews, and they can be effective – but only if the reader fully grasps the nature of the prototype. In order to be of maximum use from a linguistic standpoint, however, prototypes would have themselves to be defined somewhere – in a glossary or appendix – in order that they could function in the context of a write-up more or less as absolutes. Thus in defining them, one would unfortunately be back to square one. Or one could restrict one's writing, as many wine writers do, to addressing wine specialists exclusively (a narrowing of focus which, personally as a writer, I would find unacceptable.)

Another confusing factor is that the word Medoc works for Professor Aitchison because she is knowledgeable about old-world wine but in the past twenty five years a new generation of wine drinkers, weaned on new-world wines, has grown up to whom Medoc may, and in certain instances most decidedly is, an unknown quantity. In which case, the prototype is reader-selective and may not be appropriate. I myself use prototypes but only when I feel confident, as I did with my Guardian readership for instance, that it serves an essential role in defining the wine. I am a frequent user of such prototypes when the wine under review has definite characteristics which make it comparable with wines costing a great deal more. 'Burgundian', for instance, has already lost some of its protypicity because I use it to recall a style of burgundy of four or five decades ago but younger writers, who have tasted only those burgundies from the seventies vintages on, will have a different idea in mind when they say, as is far from uncommon, that a certain New Zealand pinot noir is burgundian in style. I would have to disagree with this writer's assessment and find the prototype misleading.

Therefore, using prototypes could never provide the whole answer because they are by definition literal. Describing a product such as wine, especially in the context of a newspaper or magazine review, will always require impressionistic, figurative and metaphorical garnishing. Further, notes on a wine do not restrict themselves to how it looks, smells and tastes.

The conscientious critic will not only write up notes offering this analysis, but also perhaps rate the wine (points out of one hundred or, as I prefer, twenty), and possibly provide ideas as to how each wine will perform with food – even which dishes for which it is best suited. This is, then, extremely concentrated analysis. It requires the taster, in arriving at a rating, rapidly (faster and more accurately than any computer) to run through similar performing wines at all price levels and thus arrive at a sensible value-for-money comparative judgement. It is often essential that metaphors and prototypes form part of the language of such a writer and this must go beyond merely stating that all cabernet sauvigon tastes of black-currants and all chardonnay of under-ripe melon and that all sauvignon blanc must taste like Sancerre to be exemplary. It is this 'going beyond' that gives us Top-Enders the licence to say anything we damn well please.

As a result, I have been taken to task more than once by bottom-end critics for describing a wine as having the texture of 'crushed light bulbs' and another for characterising a wine for its 'sweaty richness' which, tongue firmly in cheek, inspired the description that the wine was reminiscent 'of a sumo wrestler's jock-strap'.

Other tastes, more mundanely, such as chocolate, pepper and toffee are commonly found in wines and therefore also have obvious power as metaphors which can be further embroidered. Some have suggested (and count me in here) that fabrics make an extremely attractive metaphor system for wines. We already frequently hear wines described as silky and velvety, but what about corduroy or sauvignon blanc likened to drip-dry cotton or Côtes-du-Rhône described as leathery? The human body – hairy, fat, fleshy, thin, etcetera – can also provide an entry into an entire metaphorical system which is distanced from the product itself yet useful in providing part of the true image of a wine. (Though this context can produce knotty extremes which only the alert linguis-tician would wish to unravel. One particularly pretentious wine critic, Andrew Jefford, once said of Palo Cortado that it was a 'strange hermaphroditic sherry' with the idea, I guess, that this would convey what to his mind was the clichéd feminine/masculine gender mix of this sherry style. But the descriptor 'hermaphroditic' is so extravagant, since it means to be possessed of both male and female sex organs, that the normal reader is surely left utterly confused instead of enlightened – or encouraged to try a genuinely delicious sherry.)

The pressure to find more and more outlandish metaphors has been one of the defining factors in wine language. I myself relish reading my colleagues' more astonishing flights of fancy and I cannot, as I have said, resist becoming airborne at times myself. It becomes part of the individual wine writer's style and as long as the reader is left in no doubt of the writer's true opinion of the wine, then we can surely permit the indulgence.

For all these reasons, to provide that unequivocal opinion, I always employ my rating system. This gives the reader something which transcends the paucities and extravagancies of language. It offers an absolute, which language by itself cannot. To me, the rating is the most important symbol attached to any wine I describe.

Mostly, in true top-end critic style, I pay indifferent heed to the religion of the wine maker, the precise location of the grapes, the pH of the grapes at harvest, and what fabulous stories may be attached to the vineyard's or the wine grower's reputation. These things may be taken into account after the wine has hit the spittoon and indeed will have to be if the wine is a reputed colossus with an appropriate price tag since such a wine will have to have hit those hundreds of taste buds with some impact and complexity if this reputation is a worthy one and not simply a fable – as, so often, it is.

The rare few (who can write)

Wine writers in the UK who can actually write are rare and can be counted on the fingers of a single hand: Stephen Brook, Nicolas Faith, Neil Beckett, Hugh Johnson and, now and then, Jancis Robinson turns out a witty sentence. Mr Beckett, a trade magazine writer and editor of the hideously snobby *World of Fine Wine*, goes in for insidious subtlety. He once wrote a piece on the Vouvray estate Domaine Huet which was not just a finely sustained polemic on behalf of a magnificent (and organic) wine producer, but a brilliant apologia for the whole category that writers such as he are pleased to define as 'fine wine'. Now fine wine is a categorisation I dispute, but that is not the point I wish to touch on here and now. What thrilled me was the climax of Mr Beckett's piece. He finished with words paraphrased from the finish of sonnet 116 (or number 110 in some Shakespeare editions): 'If this be error and upon me prov'd, I never writ, nor no man ever drank fine wine for under £500 a bottle.'

Shakespeare, of course, did not write the last eight words. He wrote no man ever lov'd. How superb it was for a trade wine writer to so cleverly tell us exactly how he feels about wine. Let me remind you of the famous opening of the sonnet in question:

> Let me not to the marriage of true minds
> Admit impediments. Love is not love
> Which alters when it alteration finds,
> Or bends with the remover to remove.

In other words, if you love 'fine wine' you accept it as such, whatever the vagaries of a bad vintage, whatever the problems of bottle variation in older wines caused by the inane use of corks; if you love wine, especially wine from a craft producer like Noël Pinguet at Gaston Huet, you love it, accept it, unreservedly, warts and all, however expensive, whatever its lack of excitement when a duff bottle is opened.

Here we have arrived at the heart of what it is to worship *soi-disant* fine wine. It is to believe; even in the face of persistent mediocrity and high prices. It is to be a devotee; an unflinching believer. I, alas, am not made of this unbending stuff. I have no precious time at all to spend on it and certainly not the shekels. But anyone who can write about it as deliciously as Mr Beckett deserves applause.

The world of the wine buff in general, and the language employed, have also provided useful material for truly great fabulists.

Most notably, satirists; long before buffoons on TV food and drink shows made fools of themselves. The delicious combination of pompous snobbery and specialised phraseology makes it fertile ground for the lampooner. In Evelyn Waugh's *Brideshead Revisited* one of the many things Charles Ryder discovers through his relationship with Sebastian Flyte is a 'serious acquaintance' with wine.

> 'We warmed the glass slightly at a candle, filled it a third high, swirled the wine round, nursed it in our hands, held it to the light, breathed it, sipped it, filled our mouths with it, and rolled it over the tongue, ringing it on the palate like a coin on a counter, tilted our heads back and let it trickle down the throat…
>
> 'it is a little, shy wine like a gazelle.'
>
> 'Like a leprechaun.'
>
> 'Dappled, in a tapestry window.'
>
> 'Like a flute by still water.'
>
> '… and this is a wise old wine.'
>
> 'A prophet in a cave.'
>
> '… And this is a necklace of pearls on a white neck.'
>
> 'Like a swan.'
>
> 'Like the last unicorn.'

Rather than we wine critics shrinking from recognising ourselves in this brilliant send-up we would rather prefer to consider ourselves worthy of participation. Who would not like to be so Wildean as spontaneously to describe a young riesling as 'a necklace of pearls on a white neck'? Better yet, who would not like to taste such a wine?

26

WINE SHoWS

*How to sucker wine producers into coughing up
for medals of no value*

For years the co-called International Wine Competition annually pestered me to become a judge. I always refused. I regard it as a conflict of interest as a consumer wine journalist to be associated with such a dubious scheme. I abhor committee decisions where awards are concerned whether the product is wine, a book or a film. I wholly agree with Sinclair Lewis, the great US novelist, in this regard. 'All prizes, like all titles, are dangerous,' he wrote declining the Pulitzer prize in 1926, '… by accepting the prizes and approval of these vague institutions we are admitting their authority confirming them as the final judges of excellence.' Not that Lewis maintained this maverick stance for long. Four years later he accepted the Nobel Prize.

The IWC is a wonderful money-making scheme and though it may be undeniable that some splendid wines win medals, many do not, and many wine producers do not bother to enter. It is not, then, a contest which involves all the players. The Federers and the Nadals of the wine world do not concern themselves with the IWC. Regularly, I taste wines commended by this competition and find them not especially interesting.

Of course, the judges themselves make a fuss about their roles in the exhibition. Jancis Robinson will plug it on her website, and discuss her role as a judge, and several prominent wine critics will follow suit. The wine critic of the *Observer*, Tim Atkin, is even a co-chairman of the IWC. He is paid for the job.

These chairmen (there are three others apart from Atkin) taste the wines to which the various tasting committees of the competition have given medals, golds, silvers, bronzes (not difficult to win an award when the catchment area is so large). In 2007, 9,358 wines (which includes, would you believe, a number of sakés) from 35 different countries were assembled for 400 judges to slobber over. 260 wines picked up gold medals (2.8% of the field), 1,129 wines won silver medals (12.1%), and 1,839 wines managed to get bronze medals (19.7%) and a proportion of wines got Commended. That is say that 34.6% of entries got a gong. Is this not an utterly fatuous, one is almost tempted to say fraudulent, state of affairs? Why not give 75% of entries medals? Indeed, why not give a medal to every bottle entered?

No wonder so many retailers and a good few gullible producers love the IWC. It provides them with abundant scope to publicise their wines. In an industry so bereft of imagination, wit, and creativity, and thus any great advertising and marketing flair, the IWC offers retailers and producers an irresistibly simple opportunity publicly to exhibit their prowess. It does not require them to think. They pay a basic £94 a bottle to enter (£82.25p if entered on-line) and hope to pick up a prize (however insignificant does not matter, though a gold, or even better a trophy, obviously means the trumpet can be more strenuously blown). So the IWC, for the 2007 show, had a maximum income of just under £800,000 from the entries alone. The hundreds of judges (I nearly wrote drudges) work for free. Indeed, I know of some keen poor saps, desperate to rub shoulders with Oz Clarke and Jancis Robinson *et al*, who feel compelled to travel, by air, at their own expense, from lands thousands of miles away. Some state on their business cards and websites that they are an IWC judge as if it were some kind of professional endorsement or qualification.

Expensive nights out

Can you wonder I have always refused to go near such a scam? It is true I have attended two of the IWC awards dinners, as guest of a retailer or wine board. I went purely out of curiosity, to confirm my suspicions. Twice was enough and I have declined all further invitations to attend. It costs £150 a ticket, by the way, or £1250 for a table of ten. So there's a nice little earner for the organisers there. Then there are the stickers you have to buy to affix to your bottles. These cost, for all levels of award, £40 for a thousand-sticker roll with discounts of up to 40% if you order over 200 rolls (these are ex-vat prices by the way).

All in all, then, I estimate that the income the IWC trousers from its activities is probably around £1.3million to £1.6million annually. Small wonder the publishing giant William Reed, as owner of the IWC, is so happy to operate it alongside its International Spirit Challenge and International Beer Challenge. No doubt someone is working on the International Soft Drink Challenge and International Tap & Mineral Water Challenge. Go for it fellas! It's that word Challenge, which does it. Brilliant stuff!

The IWC is not alone.

There is, confusingly, the IWSC. This stands for the International Wine & Spirit Competition and claims to be the premier competition of its kind. It's been going since 1969, some way ahead of the IWC which started in a hobbyist sort of way in 1983 with fewer entries than Chelsea F.C. has footballers on its books. The chairman of the IWSC judges has said that 'The IWSC boasts the most highly qualified group of international judges of any wine and spirit competition in the world. We are inundated with applications from people who want to judge for the Competition, and have to turn people away every year.' It is owned and run by Nexus Business Media which also publishes the trade magazine *Harpers Wine & Spirit* for which I write a monthly column.

In 2006, the IWSC received 5778 entries and its 250 judges generously found 72% of them deserving of medals: Gold Best In Class 4%, Gold 7%, Silver Best in Class 14%, Silver 15%, and Bronze 32%. 289 gold medals were awarded and 2,900 seals of approval. How difficult is it not to a pick up a gong here!? I am most admiring of the saké scam that the 2007 competition introduced.

There were 228 entries and 130 were awarded medals. Fabulous idea! Rich pickings for the organisers here. Most sakés suck with food, to my mind, and I have tasted, with and without food, what are reputed to be some of the world's finest (some at over £150 a bottle). I found that even with Japanese food, wine in every instance was a more agreeable companion than any saké. But, of course, when it comes to enticing entry money, such niceties go out of the window. And, presumably, the UK consumer in this context is irrelevant as few Britons consider saké a palatable, let alone affordable, liquid.

It costs £141 per wine to enter, bottle stickers a cost of £55 per 1,000 (discount for large orders), and point of sale material is also on sale. When asked, the IWSC said to me: 'We offer digital material free of charge to retailers, and make a charge of £155 to producers (this is currently under review, as we may provide material free of charge in future years).'

I am happy reveal that the IWSC has never once approached me, certainly not in the mildly aggressive way the IWC annually used to, to become a judge.

The virus has spread

The latest wheeze in wine competitions, started by Robert Joseph who was a big cheese at IWC until they gave him the boot, to add to his events in Singapore, Russia, China and Japan is the India Wine Challenge. This latter organisation claims (and I sure no-one can contradict it) to be India's 'major independent and truly influential wine competition' which will 'recognise excellence in wines from India and around the world.' Entry fee per bottle is US$160. It is run in conjunction with the magazine to which I contribute a monthly column, *Harpers*, and its wildly generous proprietors offer all entrants a 3-months free subscription to its website. (It is interesting, in this regard, to note that I when I wrote a column, highly critical of wine competitions for the July 2007 issue of this magazine its editor, Richard Siddle, refused to publish it. I concede he had several legitimate grounds for doing this, reasons unconnected with wine comps, but I do now wonder if my views were considered too embarrassing.)

In July 2008, I was invited to become part of yet another awards scheme, designed to extract money from gullible retailers. The so-called Own Label Awards, created by wine critic Matthew Jukes, invited me, for a fee of £500, to join its panel of judges. Naturally, I turned down the chance to swig yet more of the largely revoltingly indifferent gunge to which supermarkets append their own labels (when once it was an area replete with splendid bargains) not because the money was a joke but because the competition is. Only Sainsbury and Majestic, from what I gather, felt as I did and turned down the chance to participate.

Personally, I find all decisions reached by awards juries worthless. (Indeed, in the single instance I was foreman of a major criminal trial jury, the verdict we came to was rubbish also – as it transpired after we let the villain off.) And I do not say this having never judged a wine competition. I have judged two in fact, both in Australia, so I am intimately acquainted with their shortcomings and fraudulencies.

I accepted judging in Australia because I could see no conflict with my being a UK consumer journalist. The results had relevance only in Australia, not in the UK. My antipathy to judging in my home country has developed over several years, from when I first became a wine critic in 1989. My objections form an inelegant sextet.

1. Readers occasionally wrote to me saying the vintage of an award winning wine was different to the one on sale in the shop.
2. Readers occasionally wrote to me asking me to try an award-winner as they found it unexciting. In every instance, I concurred with the readers.
3. I felt that in putting my name to such an event by agreeing

to be a judge, I endorsed it wholly, every awarded wine, every fellow judge. In 2007, for example, the IWC awarded 21 medals to English wines. I struggle to think of as many as half-a-dozen English wines which are worth recommending. But if, as a judge, it is incumbent upon you to find medal winners in a category you will find them. This completely contradicts the role of the independent critic whose palate (and, one hopes, her sense of what is value for money) must be her only guide in relation to all other similar wines not just those grouped in a geographic category which cannot fail to find award winners.

4. Several senior judges who were indiscrete in conversation to me remarked how ill-equipped certain other judges were, either by virtue of their lack of experience, fitness to judge a particular section, or ability to be sufficiently discriminatory. As Jancis Robinson, herself an IWC judge, had the honesty to remark on her website: 'One has to wonder whether every one of the 400 individuals who judged the IWC 2007, from a total of 19 different countries, truly are experts in their fields.'

5. Very few, very few, of the world's great wine producers enter their wines in such competitions. Their voluntary exclusion (on the grounds of indifference or cost) renders the results dubious to put it mildly. I personally doubt that any gold medal winner in any UK competition, if put into a blind tasting with the very greatest of its class (similar grape or whatever), would come out top. Many, I suspect, would not even get close. Only wines from producers interested in commercial exploitation or from retailers anxious to have their good taste endorsed bother (or can afford) to enter. I read somewhere an official promulgation from the IWC that it is 'a competition that has established itself as the pre-eminent arbiter of wine quality' which is a pompous, wholly outrageous lie. It arbitrates, if subjective judging can be said

to be such (another thing open to argument here), only of the 10,000 wines entered. What of the tens of thousands of wines, which includes the world's greatest, which do not enter?

6. The very nature of consensus judging makes me want to vomit. The organisers of competitions believe that committees are 'vigorous and democratic.' I say they find a common denominator of second-rateness. Charles Metcalfe, one of the head-honchos of the International Wine Challenge, a dear delightful man whose company, in all other respects, I find extremely congenial, has said this: 'We are a competition that believes in discussion and consensus. The IWC judges discuss the wines every step of the way. By the time a wine has been awarded a Seal of Approval or been rejected, it has been tasted at least twice (once by the first round panel, checked by a Co-Chairman). And, by the time it wins a medal, at least three times (first round panel, plus second round panel, plus Co-Chairman checking). By the time it wins a Trophy, at least five times. I know of no other competition that judges so thoroughly and even-handedly.'

When I investigated the matter, along the lines of the evidence and statistical data above, I could never rid myself of the feeling that if I agreed to be a judge I would be allowing others to take advantage of my name, and to profit by it (at no profit to myself or, more importantly, my readers).

It may well be that I am being a little pious in putting the matter like this, but there it is. I respect Charles Metcalfe as a human being of great decency and humour, but if I were to stand alongside him and others judging a vast swathe of commercial wines, I know I would end up agreeing to acknowledge wines I would never in normal circumstances rate highly let alone drink myself. For the same reasons, I would not be a judge on the Man Booker literary competition and where I have had power of veto I have not wanted any book I have written to be submitted for an award. (Some of my books have been submitted for awards, I know, but I respect the wishes of a publisher who may want her team to be recognised and in such instances I have specified that the publisher can pick up the award not me. When I was an advertising copywriter I won many awards, in competitions where I did not personally enter, and was a judge at two competitions. I came to the realisation that they were self-serving egotistical affairs, and, worse, that certain jury members had no critical powers worth a light. Is it any different in the world of wine? I see no reason to doubt it.)

Conflict of interest

Unambiguously, I am against the idea that any consumer wine writer, commentator, or media performer, can profit by a wine competition, either my receiving fees for judging or supervising judging, and be considered impartial. In the summer of 2007 the wine correspondent of the *Observer* Sunday newspaper, Tim Atkin, writing to the *Guardian*, protested at my views in his capacity as co-chairman of the International Wine Challenge. Among other things, I had been taking serious issue with the idea that English sparkling wine as a whole was the equal of champagne.

I responded to his letter with the riposte that he must feel obliged to defend English wines because English vineyards entered so many wines in the IWC. It was an extraordinarily compromising situation for Mr Atkin and it reinforced my conviction that getting involved with wine competitions undermines a wine writer's independence and critical distance. It is important to add here that I have tasted many English wines, especially bubblies, and have only ever found two I would cheerfully drink more than a glass of. I find almost all English reds cabbagey and the majority of the white spineless (there are exceptions). I am always ready to accept that wine judgements are subjective, and each taster's palate is individual, and I also accept that English wine has improved greatly in the past decade (thanks to global warming). But the idea that English sparkling wine, one or two rare specimens apart, can be spoken of in the same breath as champagne is utter balderdash, piffle and poppycock.

To be a party to promulgating the idea that England is comparable to Champagne is, then, deception. It is hyperbole at best; a lie, at worst. For a wine writer to lend credence to either interpretation, to support it whilst in the pay of a wine competition which profits from English vineyards' slavish devotion to awards (which in my view are largely undeserving) is the substance of my charge that it is a conflict of interest.

In September 2007, a certain Rudolfo Carrion emailed me, via wine writer Tom Stevenson, and then subsequently telephoned at my invitation asking if I would be a judge at Iberwine in Madrid. He said (sic): 'It would certainly be a pleasure for us to welcome you in Madrid, where you can taste the wines that most interest you and to decide which of these are the best of them. The wine taste trial will be composed by international taste-judges from the United Kingdom, Spain, Portugal and Southamerica (Uruguay and Brazil) we will take charge the flight tickets, two hotel nights. Additionally, we are glad to offer 250 Euro per day as travel expenses to help you to getting a better stay in Madrid.' I had no option but to refuse. I assume Senor Carrion will find his UK judges without trouble (especially at £174 a day 'expenses'). My only regret is that I did not think to say to him that as I was unwilling to take part he could always try Tim Atkin.

One other wine competition is the Decanter World Wine Awards, run by *Decanter* wine magazine. This is a dreary affair, profiting a tediously fawning magazine. 5,500 wines entered the 2005 competition which gave eight English wines awards some of which I tasted and found truly awful. It is of course easy to find winners when you have an English Wine Category. Finding winners is inevitable. You do not judge the wines against good wines from other countries — in the way a consumer would to decide which s(he) wanted to buy. The judges merely decide from the entries which English wine is the best, the second-best and so on. Such an approach has no integrity whatsoever. It is competition solely to benefit the entrants, not the consumers who might buy the product. On this basis, I have not investigated this competition in any further depth as it is patently another profit-orientated enterprise. It costs £195 a head to attend the awards dinner which is, in a superficial attempt to lend gravitas, black tie. Frankly, the whole charade is beneath contempt.

Wine shows in Oz

This is very much my view, the one expressed latterly above, of one of the major Aussie shows at which I was once invited to judge. I had already done one Aussie show, McLaren Vale, and here I could readily see how the proliferation of such events in all regions of Australia had led to a nation-wide raising of standards over many years. But the Sydney 100 International wine show is unique. It is the only one where one chews as one gargles. Yes, food was matched to every flight of winess. The Sydney 100 International is the only wine show on earth where the judges go home heavier than when they arrived.

When the invitation first popped up on my computer I laughed and binned it. But then I thought, why pass up such an experience? If you don't do it, I reasoned, you will never know what it's like to judge wines alongside food. After all, I scolded myself, isn't wine designed to go with food? It is surely not designed to be tasted and spat out into a spittoon and pontificated upon by individuals many of whom may have no idea what food it could accompany (when in fact most consumers are as interested in this aspect of a wine as they are in its price).

So I reconsidered. Said yes. Flew out to Sydney. The chairman of the judges was an Aussie wine hack called Huon Hooke. He had been chairman of judges of this competition five times before. He was a tall, thin man with sad eyes and a way of looking at you like a traffic cop.

The judges were partnered. My partner was a dapper Kiwi called Ivan Donaldson. He looked like a pre-war army colonel though he was in fact a neurology professor and proprietor of a vineyard near Christchurch in New Zealand. I spent a most agreeable day tasting in his company happy to note that if I had sudden motor neurone failure he would know what to do.

Ivan and I tasted 36 semillons, 60 chardonnays, 31 cabernet/merlots, and 49 shirazes on the first day. At this stage we did not taste any food. The first and second day's sessions were a weeding out process to find the real humdingers: the ones which would advance to the finals, when we would taste the selected wines with nosh. The other ten judges were also paired off and tasted similar amounts of wine to us.

On day two Ivan and I tasted 29 sparkling wines (including shirazes), 35 pinot noirs, 27 cabernet blends, 35 other reds, and 20 other cabernet sauvignons. When I went through our selections with Warren Mason who runs the show (owns it indeed, as his sole source of income), he remarked that wine number so-and-co hadn't been chosen and I said 'interesting you should bring that up because I thought it was pretty marvellous but Chairman Huon thought otherwise and since we must restrict ourselves to passing only 15% of wines to the semi-final stages we agreed to drop it.' Warren crossed it through with a yellow felt tip to indicate its acceptance. 'You didn't see me do that,' he says. 'Indeed I didn't,' I respond. 'Crazy a wine like that not getting through,' he says. I squint at his list. I see the word Yalumba. How can a major sponsor of the show not have a wine through to the finals? Never mind what the chairman of judges thinks. It is going forward.

On the third day, we were fed as we slobbered. We 12 judges and one chairman, Huon, are given flights of various wines in categories from aromatic white to full bodied red, including fortified and sparkling. The judging pairs face one another across a table and each judge tastes his or her own wines and gives them points out of 20. When the pairs have finished each flight they discuss their respective ratings and come to a joint decision over the wines they have especially liked. In tasting, say, 60 chardonnays, only 7 or 8 can be semi-finalists. This is harsh on many wines because many are excellent. If I had felt dubious yesterday, when the organiser passed a wine rejected by his chairman, I felt doubly so today.

Ivan and myself and ten other judges, two of whom are feeling rather crook, now go through a range of aromatic whites (with Jerusalem artichoke terrine, mussels and artichokes), medium bodied dry whites (with blue swimmer crab terrine, Tabasco sauce and parmesan), lighter bodied dry reds (with confit of duck, pumpkin, spiced sauce), rosés (with smoked salmon and leeks) and pinot noirs plus one sparkling shiraz I campaigned to go through to the semis (with pesto risotto and quail). Huon remarks to Ivan that the artichoke terrine went with none of the wines in its flight (which made me wonder how he can bear being chairman of such an event). The amazing thing was that eight of the judges went out to dinner after that. I was not one of them.

On the fourth day I realised that what had began as a seemingly civilised idea had turned into a purgatorial chore. I am quite certain several of the wines Ivan and I had excluded were perfectly legitimate medal specimens. I feel bad about this.

The next day of judging my palate was to be assaulted by 39 lighter bodied dry whites with a cheese and asparagus soufflé, 45 fuller bodied dry whites with whiting fillets with scallop mousseline and a crab beurre blanc, several dozen medium bodied dry reds with a rabbit casserole, a dozen or so dessert wines with rice pudding with fruit compote, and eight fortified wines with chocolate truffles.

Of course we take pauses for breath during each flight of these wines (though spitting out is more colourful than usual as we have to digest most of the food). What we do after we have tasted each flight and made our marks on paper is record our impressions of each wine into personal Sony recorders. Were a visitor to witness one of these sessions, twelve seemingly normal people in white aprons, madly muttering into little black boxes the size of fag packets, each taking up a discrete private space in Warren's garden, or lavatory, or bedroom, or one of the side-rooms, might suppose he had wandered into the precincts of a bijou loony bin. The visitor would also be aware of, and have carefully to step around, Carla the rottweiler's shit, some of it days old, which litters the path. Downwind, the septic tank adds a further fragrance.

Mercifully, the fifth day is a half-day: some sparkling wines with some amuses bouches and then four dozen fuller bodied dry reds with kangaroo pie (I swear I have not made any of this up). I manage the bubblies but baulk at the reds with that steaming marsupial. I have lost my appetite. I bring an appetite to what I do and if it is absent then I am useless.

I felt abused and used. The Sydney 100 show is an absurd lottery. All wine shows are to a greater or lesser extent, but this one takes the biscuit (not to mention the whiting fillet, kangaroo pie and Jerusalem artichoke terrine). I now feel its medals are worthless (as so many good wines pass unrecognised), its judging procedures dubious, and its organiser a manipulator. I also wondered that, since the competition requires entrants to submit six bottles of each wine, what happens to all the unopened bottles? An unscrupulous organiser could sell them off or keep the best ones for his own cellar. I am quite sure Warren Mason does neither.

However, does anyone go to all the trouble of organising a wine competition if s(he) is not going to be handsomely remunerated? Judges, chairpersons apart, often work for nothing and are eager to take part. The only wine shows I shall take part in future, if I am ever again invited (extremely unlikely), will be regional Australian ones where almost all the local producers enter, no-one is in it to make a large profit, and the taking part gives the inquisitive judge valuable insights into a discrete area's grape growing abilities and wine making skills. No reader can deny that this is well worth the time of any critic to explore.

The Sydney 100, however, I shall never judge again even if I were to be invited (more than extremely unlikely). And I have not even revealed to you the most embarrassing part of the show: the post-competition dinner, where judges are expected to dress in black tie. (Though this was rescinded the year I judged as I refused to attend if I had to doll myself up in empire uniform). At this dinner a fat wad of Aussie dollars exchanges hands for each ticket and consumers can rub shoulders with the famous judges. It is a gruesome evening and my table was only bearable because I sat opposite a gorgeous housewife who told me stories of her eight Rottweilers, acquired because she had once had her washing purloined off the line by a passing tramp who swore at her when she remonstrated with him. She felt her person and her clean damp underwear needed protection. (I have to say, if I could be promised evening entertainment like her every show, I might reconsider my embargo.)

27

GODZILLA VS QUEEN KONG

Why you should rely on your own judgement

'I don't want to develop expensive tastes and be like people who can only drink the best wine!'

Iris Murdoch putting her own philosophy
into the mouth of a character, Gerard Hernshaw,
in *The Book & The Brotherhood*

A very illuminating disagreement in 2006 between two eminent wine critics demonstrates the truth of the maxim Have Faith in Your Own Judgement. A wiser way of putting this would be to say Always Keep Critics at a Distance.

In so many ways, this book is an appeal to the reader to be so empowered. I may be the only wine critic who rates wines on a value-for-money basis, but this approach was not made purely for pecuniary motives but because approaching wine like this leads to the eventual development of discernment by the interested reader.

With discernment – which I take to be the ability to judge between several things and accurately opine which is the best to your own mind and why it is – comes an appreciation of cost. If money is irrelevant you do not develop discernment because your choice is so unrestricted you simply perceive excellence as being related to scarcity of acquisition and if not always high cost then certainly never inexpensive. Though this may permit the acquisition of a set of principles related to personal preference, being so well endowed with financial resources creates a less than robust intellect and a lack of critical nous. It is to many such drinkers that Mr Robert Parker and Ms Jancis Robinson appeal so powerfully (particularly the former as he is seen as a prophet, devotedly to be listened to in the same way that the acolytes and followers of Indian mystics hang on to the utterances of their guru).

This appeal leads to reliance. It is a reliance which, certainly with regard to the much more powerful Parker, has been fostered by certain wine producers and wine merchants. These commercial interests, devoid of imagination and creativity, see the advantage of exploiting as a promotional weapon a high Parker-score (points out of 100) or a decent Robinson-rating (points out of 20). She has only rated wines in this way since 2001, in fact. Doubtless she was inspired to follow the Superplonk 20-point system which I introduced in 1989 (though as mine is the only one based on value-for-money it is not comparable to hers in analytic terms).

Wine is seen as such a thorny path that a guide is considered essential and a map indispensible. Certain wine critics therefore are seen as the one and their prognostications the other. But what happens when two guides, both hugely experienced, proffer two different routes and two wildly divergent maps?

This is when it is crucial to appreciate the difference between taking a critic's words as gospel and seeing them merely as yet another, albeit worthy, opinion of one wine often, but not always, tasted at one particular time. Robert Parker is fatuously touted (not by himself it must be said) as the world's most influential wine critic. This is fatuous for many reasons, but one cogent one has to be that the vast majority of the world's wine drinkers have never heard of him. Because she is a woman and English Jancis Robinson is less of a guru but her comments are nevertheless hugely respected by the UK wine trade and a dedicated band of knowledgeable drinkers.

Personally, I would always be fascinated to hear what either of these individuals had to say about any wine just as I would lend an ear to what a published author said of someone else's novel or what a professional musician remarked of another performer or a piece of music. But it does not follow from this that I would slavishly accept their views or that I would be chary of profoundly disagreeing with the opinions they expressed.

The opinions of those who have set themselves up as experts or have become expert by no personal ambition always teaches one something. But wine, with so many thorns attendant upon its every rose-stem, is not fiction or a collection of musical notes. True, many wine critics like to cherish and polish the thorns (that's why such toffee-nosed charlatans love corks and admire *terroir*) but with Parker and Robinson there is a degree of concentration of what is in the glass not always in what surrounds it. Nevertheless, they are hardly apostates and both have high regard for the idea of *terroir*. They are, then, formalists not iconoclasts and, as such, to be regarded as proponents of some things I deride.

Their eminence lent their spat much spice, like two meaty, well-matched heavyweight prelates arguing over the sex of angels, and made the entertainment more amusing to the lookers-on. It concerned a wine made in the area of Bordeaux called St Émilion and it related to a single vintage, the 2003, famous — one might say notorious — for being the hottest in France for many decades. The vineyard in question is called Château Pavie which is owned by a man called Gérard Perse.

With such heat, and the type of grapes favoured by Pavie, it was inevitable (it seems to me) that the wine of this chateau in that year would tend towards the alcoholic and richly fruity, unsubtle and intensely forward. The key to the character of such a wine is how solid were its tannins. I have not, however, tasted Pavie 2003 as my attempts to buy it were deterred by its UK price of £1280 a case at Farr Vintners (£2082.86 — outrageously! — at every-wine.com, and £174 a bottle at Berry Bros & Rudd). Tannin is an antioxidant developed in the skins of berries by a vine as protection for its fruit (which is the enticement, via sugar, ensuring the future of its progeny, via seeds). In hot years sugar levels also increase and if the alcohol which results swamps the tannins the result is an unbalanced wine.

The minimum alcohol required by French wine laws for a St

Émilion to legally call itself St Émilion is 11% abv (alcohol by volume). This would be easily achieved but even at 12%, in a very cool year, the wine would seem insubstantial and at most, if not all, chateaux sugar would be added to the must, what is called chaptalisation, in order to reach 12.5% or 13% or beyond. In a hot year, like 2003, 13% would be easily achievable and no chaptalisation would be necessary. With the Pavie of that vintage there is, it seems, some confusion as to its actual alcohol. From Ms Robinson's and other critic's descriptions of their (unfavourable) reactions to the wine, especially the prevalence of the key descriptor porty, it had to be at least 14% if not higher it seems to me. The label is not a precise guide here even though it is required by law for all wine labels to state the alcohol level of the liquid inside. On the Berry Brothers and Rudd website the wine was described as 12.5% and other sources reported 13.5%. This puzzled me, as I cannot believe a critic whose palate has led so dazzingly experienced a life as Ms Robinson's would find a St Émilion at 13.5% alcohol porty and at 12.5% she would definitely not. When I asked BB&R to investigate the matter for me they examined bottles in its possession and told me its website was in error and the abv on the Pavie label was given at 14%. It may be higher, perhaps nudging 14.2% or even 14.4%. This would explain the hostility of UK tasters to the wine's structure and texture as this is high for a merlot-dominated bordeaux.

Château Pavie's blend of merlot, cabernet sauvignon and cabernet franc grapes would be nicely quaffable at 12.5% but at 14% certainly not. This alcohol level is high but not as uncongenially monstrous as some Aussie and Californian wines where levels above 16% are achieved. I have never tasted a wine with this level of alcohol that I have enjoyed. Mr Parker, however, is not deterred by such alcoholic Himalayas whereas Ms Robinson is more delicately inclined and, unless a rare weight of compensating tannins caused such a wine to be in balance, would, I suspect, find 16% too much.

In February 2006, for example, in the Clare Valley in south

Australia, winemaker Kevin Mitchell showed me some of his Kilikanoon wines. Whilst I thrilled to his local semillons and rieslings, I had some difficulty squelching my way through certain of his reds. These were made from Barossa grapes and on two specimens the alcohol was far too prominent, superficial and vulgar, it being over 15%. A barrel sample of a Kilikanoon Reserve Shiraz, Mr Mitchell proudly announced, was rated 98 points out of 100 by Mr Parker. To me, it was unfriendly, uncouth and, crassest of all, undrinkable. I hesitate to apply such terms to a wine I have not drunk, but I wonder if I would not say the same of the Turley Moore Vineyard Zinfandel 1997? Mr Parker rated this Californian red very highly, giving it 94/96 points, and it was 17.1% alcohol.

As for Pavie, which I never particularly rated highly as a red wine let alone an outstanding St Émilion, before Monsieur Perse, who made his pile in supermarketing, got his hands on the estate in 1997, it is difficult for me explicitly to say as I have not tasted any since vintages of the early 1990s. Regarding the vintage in question, the 2003, I am not prepared to cough up £100+ for a wine rating 96 Parker points or, for that matter, somewhat more of my own money for the Pavie 2000 which achieved a maximum Parker rating of 100 points (see further on for my own rating of this wine).

Does this mean I have no time for Mr Parker's views and his ratings? Not at all. In some cases, our tastes coincide.

For example, to put the Parker palate into context, let me refer to another Bordeaux the man rates 100 points, Château Haut-Brion 1989. I also gave this a perfect score of 20 out of 20 (even at its price of £500 a bottle). I described it as awesome and profound, as he has done but the crucial difference between his approach and mine is that I only rated one out of the four bottles I tasted as perfect. The three others were each affected by their corks in various ways which rendered them less than 20 point wines. One rated 16 and two others 13.5. (Remember, I take the cost of a wine into account when I arrive at a rating and at £500 a bottle I expect perfection or very close to it.)

It is such a caveat which makes all ratings on mature wines, and young wines designed to be drunk in a fairly distant future, utterly useless as a guide to absolute performance. I considered one bottle of the Haut-Brion 1989 drunk in 2006 in the class of a 1959 Haut-Brion drunk in 1974 and in the same league as a Château Cheval Blanc and Château Margaux, both 1947, drunk in 1966. But I would only apply the rating to the bottle I drank. In the case of the Haut Brion 1989 the three less compelling bottles had all had their tannins, to varying degrees, dissipated by over-eager corks whereas the single great bottle had a cork as hard as wood. It had, like a screwcap, sealed the tannins in and allowed them to develop beautifully without air getting in and the wine was as a result supreme, magical, invigorating, life-affirming and perfect. Just as its maker would have hoped for every bottle.

Of the Château Pavie 2003, Mr Parker wrote: 'An off the chart effort, it is a wine of sublime richness, minerality, delineation, and nobleness. It traverses the palate with extraordinary richness as well as remarkable freshness and definition. The finish is tannic, but the wine's low acidity and higher than normal alcohol (13.5%) suggests it will be approachable in 4–5 years. Anticipated maturity: 2011–2040. A brilliant effort, it, along with Ausone and Pétrus, is one of the three greatest offerings of the right bank in 2003, 96–100 pts.'

Apart from the misapprehension Mr Parker was under regarding the true alcohol level, this is a description of a very great wine of balance, cohesion and huge promise. Nobility is a rare attribute in any wine. There is no suggestion here that the wine's fruit has overpowered the tannins. Quite the contrary. As one would expect in a barrel sample (I assume) of a wine so young, the reference to the tannic finish suggests a delicious future.

Ms Robinson was not so swept away. She found it: 'Completely unappetising overripe aromas. Why? Porty sweet. Port is best from the Douro not St Émilion. Ridiculous wine more reminiscent of a late-harvest Zinfandel than a red Bordeaux with its unappetising green notes. 12 points out of 20.'

Now the first thing to be said about this, which as far as I can ascertain no other commentator has seen fit to point out, is that these two people were not tasting from the same bottle or the same cask sample. Bearing in mind my own experience with four bottles of Haut-Brion, admittedly a mature wine with much wider scope for variation between bottles, this is no minor consideration. Ms Robinson's words are damning and seem impossible to ascribe to the wine Mr Parker tasted. But then it was not the wine Mr Parker tasted. It was from a different bottle, at a different time, on a different day. Yet even if the weather pressures were dissimilar on the two occasions these two people tasted a wine of the same name from the same vintage, which would affect aroma and finish, it is hard to see how two people with such gifted palates could diverge so widely.

This divergence in the two critic's opinions caused feathers to fly. It was said by Mr Parker that Ms Robinson might have been lying in her tasting notes. 'Her comments,' Parker wrote, 'are very much in keeping with her nasty swipes at all the Pavies made by Gérard Perse…'

'Am I not allowed to have my own opinion?' Ms Robinson quite reasonably pointed out. 'Only so long as it agrees with Monsieur Parker's it seems…'[13]

Other wine critics entered the debate. The most chuckle-worthy comment came from the British writer Clive Coates who wrote of the Pavie: 'Anyone who thinks this is a good wine needs a brain and palate transplant. This wine will be scored simply as undrinkable.' He refused to rate the wine on this basis. Who can blame him? If the wine was as Ms Robinson described, it sounds a most unfriendly liquid. But, gosh, consider this. Will Robert Parker follow Mr Coates's advice and check into one of those high-tech Californian plastic surgery clinics and get a transplant? One presumes, however, it would require a donor. Who might it be? One thing we can be sure of is that it would not be Jancis Robinson.

Perhaps Michael Broadbent, possibly the most respected UK wine palate when it comes to bordeaux reds, will offer his. Mr

Broadbent, a Christie's wine auctioneer, tells us: 'Parker is looking for concentration, opulence, impressiveness. He should be looking for a wine that is civilized, that is for drinking with food.'

Ms Robinson has written 'Robert Parker, however much he may write that he values subtlety, he has continued to reward sheer size ... (and) what they (bordeaux producers) seek above all is a high score from Parker.'

So. What does 2003 Château Pavie taste like? Is it worth the money? Should you splurge? The answers are: who cares, no it is not, and absolutely not. I have tasted, in 2008, the Pavie 2000 (£360 a bottle), which Parker rated perfect and awarded 100 points, and I found it marvellous (considerably sexier than the '85 Lafite I tasted it alongside at £445 a bottle). However, I would regard its true price, as an object of value for money, at around £25, and so can only rate it 14 points out of 20 (remember, I tasted it many years after Mr Parker did). What does this suggest? It suggests that there is an imperative placed upon intelligent civilised people not to jump on bandwagons, to be sceptical of experts, and to ignore all events which are, at bottom, superficial. And the argument about a single wine estate in France is just that. A row about fermented grape juice is not important.

Or rather it is, only inasmuch as it helps support the theme of this book. Mr Parker and Ms Robinson are not con artists. I would certainly not demand they cancel their palates, hold their tongues, and retire (to a monastery and nunnery respectively) so we may no longer read their thoughts on Bordeaux reds before such wines are released for public sale.

The scandal is in the stupidity of those who slavishly follow what they write, exercising no critical judgements of their own, and in the cupidity of the merchants who exploit their promulgations for their own commercial ends (and who also exercise no critical judgements of their own). All wine writers relish the celebrity attendant upon their words being used by those selling wine to publicise it. My own ratings and descriptions of wines I have greatly admired have extensively been used, with my blessing, by UK retailers. I have only had occasion to abhor this is when the retailer, either through sloppiness or a desire to deliberately misrepresent, applied my words to a wine different to the one I had rated because it was a follow-on vintage.

Mr Parker and Ms Robinson will continue their work in supreme indifference to anything I may say and if they think anything at all it will be that their success only makes others jealous. This is undoubtedly true. I believe that many UK wine critics hate Robert Parker's dominance, arrived at by a level of dedication and intellectual application to which they could not in a million years aspire, and that Mr Parker, in his turn, has a deal of suspicion regarding what he sees as the compromising positions of some UK wine critics who see nothing wrong in combining their roles as commentators with other interests which make them less than impartial.

Ms Robinson has no such interests but she does, for example, places MW after her name, meaning Master of Wine. This is a UK wine trade qualification, though some overseas wine people have the qualification, and is mostly seen as useful for those within the wine trade itself. Less than half-a-dozen wine writers have been so ambitious as to go through the MW examination process. I myself would certainly not, as I do not regard myself a member of the wine trade. Ms Robinson does see herself as a member of the wine trade, however, and lends it her support.

Mr Parker, on the other hand, sees any wine trade as irrelevant to his activities. In the book *Questions of Taste – The Philosophy of Wine* Gloria Origgi wrote: 'Parker is supposedly incorruptible, he sees himself as a self appointed consumer's advocate, a crusader whose mission is to free the world of wine from hypocrisy and bad faith. His publication does not accept advertising; does not speculate on the wine market, and he prefers to taste alone at home, without the pressure of social occasions. His detachment is a guarantee of trustworthiness. He also shows a total disregard of the lore of the hierarchies of wine. He is not a snob as he claims are his British competitors, too sensitive to the lineage of wine. As his admirers claim, he brings a democratic breeze into the wine industry by detaching the evaluation of wines from the reputation of their location and history.'

If Godzilla and Queen Kong might be criticised it is only if it is a fact that they enjoy power and the wielding of it. Power makes me personally uneasy. I do not like it and, hard though it may be for you to believe this, I was troubled when I realised it had been given to me within a few months of my first column appearing in March 1989. I developed a fierce loyalty to my readers as a result and felt I must never let them down. I am glad to have relinquished a great deal of this power since giving up the column, my annual wine guide, and my wine rating website. Many UK wine critics, however, who openly bask in their influence, feel differently and have no qualms about taking pride in their egos, their ambitions and, however minor, their celebrity. This is not to say they do not love wine and have highly developed, scrupulous palates. It is not to say that they do not speak their minds and report as they find.

It is only to say that all wine writers, when it comes to their views on a wine, must be taken with the pinch of salt they are unable to apply at the time. The great South African winemaker, Abrie Bruwer of Springfield Estate of Robertson, has often been asked to be a judge in wine competitions and he has always refused. 'Absolutely not,' he was reported as saying. 'To judge someone's wine I want to spend the time to know it from the tip of the neck to the bottom of the bottle.'

In passing a judgement on a wine, many a critic will spend only a few seconds, rarely more than a few minutes, on what is in her glass. In some cases, the wine may be re-tasted several times. I would be surprised if Mr Parker and Ms Robinson have not sampled Pavie 2003 a few more times since they first tasted it. I do not know what their current views on the wine are, and whether they have changed their minds since first publishing their thoughts. But when they both tasted the wine for the first time it is for sure they were not following the Abrie Bruwer school of thought and consuming and reflecting upon a whole bottle over many hours.

It is possible for a wine writer to con herself. I have. I have more than once tasted an uninteresting wine, in the less-than-a-minute time-frame allotted to it, only to discover much later, at another time, with a different bottle, experienced over an hour or more, that the wine was more complex than I could ever have imagined. This may make me a mediocre taster, but, that aside and far more crucially, it should make you a much more critical appraiser of any taster's notes and opinions.

To develop your own palate and critical intelligence is to be protected from swallowing any commentator's views wholesale. With such power on your side, you can apply to any expert's writings a degree of distance, scepticism, and objectivity. Critics, remember, do not make the world go round. We are only opinionated spectators who catch a brief glimpse of it as we open our mouths as it revolves around us.

28

CELEBRITY WINE

A recipe for crap?

Why is the wine attached to a celebrated person almost invariably lacking in all the attributes s(he) brought to the calling for which they are known? Even celebs in wine cannot escape this stricture. (I leave out my own Tesco-branded Superplonk as I do not consider myself a celebrity as covered by the terms of this chapter.) The marvellous British TV-star Gilly Goolden, who set the standard for wine-in-the-glass gobbledegook in gushing lampoon style somewhere between Joyce Grenfell and Joanna Lumley, was not able to transfer her flowery brilliance across into the South African range of wines which bore her name (circa 2005/6) before it vanished from the shelves almost as quickly as it arrived. Why did the range fail?

Because there was a credibility gap between the personality of the person and the taste, provenance, style, and presentation of the wines. For a start, the wines were not, in my view, good value for money. I was sent them to taste and gave them below average scores. Second, the UK wholesaler and importer who handled the project, a company called Western Wines (now subsumed into the giant Constellation wine conglomerate), lacked the management genius to take advantage of the Goolden imprimatur and so pack design was uninspiring and marketing lacklustre. Third, the choice of South Africa as the source of the liquid was not compatible at the price point (well over a fiver a bottle). Consumers were not prepared to overspend on wines which had so little relation to Gilly's hearty personality.

Or, as with some critics I spoke to, drinkers simply saw the Goolden range as a cynical, last-ditch attempt to take advantage of stuttering TV wine career before it finally ceased. The wines should have succeeded. Gilly ought now to be a TV-star again, in her own commercials for her own range of wines. She could, like TV food-presenter Lloyd Grossman, be seen grinning at us from the supermarket shelves as shining and as proud as any middle-aged celeb given plastic surgery via a fresh lease of life on the box.

Mr Grossman has in fact been trying to get a range of his wines off the ground. But, at time of writing, no retailer has taken the bait. The ad agency and brand development company, Bryt, has been trying to entice supermarkets to stock Lloyd Grossman wines but according to the wine trade magazine *The Drinks Business* (August 2007) 'Bryt has… repeatedly been told by the trade that celebrity wines don't work.'

But this is nonsense. They do work. Drinkers, it is true, do need to be highly sceptical of celebrity wines but if the name is right and the wine has charm – an attribute which has nothing to do with its quality as a liquid – then it can succeed.

But we must make a distinction here between the true celebrity wine and a wine produced by a celebrity. I find Cliff Richard's past two vintages (I refer to his Portuguese red) as I do his songs, sentimental gush. On his TV show in 2006 the chef Gordon Ramsay invited the singer to taste some wines blind. One specimen Cliff dismissed as uninteresting was revealed to be his very own wine, so he and I agree on that at least. Yet Waitrose couldn't get enough of the stuff and it sold out very quickly. This is because the wine, Vida Nova, was not a cynical brand project but the genuine product of a genuine wine lover who happens to be an iconic British singer and who owns a vineyard in Portugal. Only the Cliff Richard fan will buy the wine. No wine lover will show the remotest interest.

In the same way, vineyard owners Gerard Depardieu, Carole Bouchet, Sam Neill, Francis Ford Coppolla, Fess Parker, all film and TV stars (though the latter you will only recall if you owned a black and white TV set in the 1950s and liked westerns), try to make decent wine. I have sampled Depardieu's and Coppolla's, but was not much struck by them, though the former's had, like the man, a certain craggy charm whereas Coppolla's were very thick and jammy. Carole Bouchet (Mrs Depardieu) has her vines not in France like her husband, who owns Château de Tigné in Anjou and also has a joint-venture project with French winemaker Bernard Magrez, but on the Sicilian island of Pantelleria renowned for rich sweet moscatos. Sam Neill's Two Paddock's vineyard in Otago is a serious commitment for the Jurassic Park star and he is a serious pinot noir grower. (I've had dinner with him and had him pick my brains and sat opposite him at a pinot noir conference as he picked other people's. How serious can you get?) Danny DeVito has his own drink but it isn't a wine, being a limoncello liqueur sourced via fruit from the Sorrentine coast and it's as strong as bourbon.

Grease-star Olivia Newton-John, the Australian songstress, has her Koala Blue range of Aussie wines, which first got off the ground in 1983. There was a further range launched called 'Olivia' which was said to be 'Olivia's deluxe signature series of wines'. Koala Blue is a division of Great Stone wine company which has a winery in Penola in Coonwarra which I have visited several times. I must have driven past it or near Miss Newton-John's bottling line a good few times, but no-one in the town has ever mentioned the existence of the wine. You'd think they'd be proud of it. When I go back, I'll make sure I taste some and see if the wine is as sweet as she is.

In 2005, the pop group Simply Red's Mick Hucknall launched his own Sicilian wine in Rome. Called Il Cantante (The Singer), it is made by winemaker Salvo Foti near Etna and was sold via internet auction (in its first release 2001 vintage). I have not tasted the wine, but there is no doubting Mr Hucknall's serious interest in wine and abiding fascination with Etna. Doubtless, he will invest further in the area and its vines and expand the range. If it were a crass exploitation venture it would, no doubt, be called Simply Red with Simply White and Simply Rosé in the wings. Mr Hucknall is somewhat more adventurously motivated (it is good to report).

Barry Manilow also has his own wine range. The velvet-voiced Las Vegas crooner has a cabernet sauvignon, a merlot and a zinfandel, a chardonnay and a pinot grigio, all from various California wineries, on offer on-line, bearing his name from $20 to $25 dollars a bottle. I have not had the pleasure of sampling any but I assume each has an exquisite nose.

In 2006 even Bob Dylan got into the act with a wine called Planet Waves (after his 1974 album of the same name). An amalgam of montepulciano and merlot grapes its retail price in the UK was around £35. Surprisingly, no-one was much interested. I suspect drinkers only got as far as examining the signature of the singer on the label before they replaced it on the shelves. It was made by a hardcore Dylan fan, a wine grower from Ancona in Italy called Antonio Terni. The guardian.co.uk website reported Mr Terni as remarking that "I tried to make a wine that reflects both sides of his (Bob Dylan's) character. Angular, difficult and unpredictable like Montepulciano, yet generous and friendly like Merlot.' Did Dylan and Terni really think people would fall for bullshit like that?

Golfers seem particularly heavily into wine. The South African golfer Ernie Els has a vineyard in the Cape. I've driven past it. I've tasted the wine. It didn't make as big an impression on me as I assume Mr Els has on a golf course.

Greg Norman, golfer, has vineyards in California and Australia. Never tasted the wines. Somehow, wines which offer autographs of sports stars on the label don't really appeal.

Arnold Palmer, golfer, is a shrewd manipulator of his famous name and in 2005, with Mike Moone of Luna Vineyards in California, the Palmer range was launched. It comprised a cabernet sauvignon and a chardonnay. I assume the geriatric golfer and lazy golf widow are its target markets.

Mike Weir, a golfer new to me, farms grapes in Niagara in Canada where in 1969 I was offered one of the most wretched wines in my entire life. But Niagara Rosé 1969 bears, I suspect, little relation to this man's ambitious ice wine, chardonnay and sauvignon blanc, though I have yet to taste them.

Nick Faldo, the Welwyn Garden City golfer, launched wines under his own name in 2000 in cahoots with the excellent Katnook Estate in Coonawarra which has produced some of the sassiest cabs created in this region. I did not get to taste the Faldo wines, even though I have visited the estate and enjoyed winemaker Wayne Stehben's wines more than once. In 2007, a UK wine sales website had this to say: 'To Celebrate Nick Faldo's 50th Birthday on the 18th July – we have put together this special case to include a bottle of each of Nick's wines made with the ledengery Master of Wine Wayne Stehbens and a bottle of each from the Founders Block and Premium Estate Range. Price: £115.50 (Including: VAT at 17.5%)'

Ledengery eh? Better than being a cebelrity I suppose.

The family of David Frost, international South African golfer, has farmed wine grapes for decades and Mr Frost says it was the family vineyard where he first hit golf balls. The first wine under his name was produced in 1997 and sells in the Cape. They are well regarded, but I have never tasted them (just as I had never heard of their eponym until I did the research for this chapter).

FW de Klerk, the ex-president of South Africa, with his wife Elita are rumoured to be producing their own wine. There was no sign of this wine when I visited Paarl, some 60kms outside Cape Town where the de Klerks have a farm, in 2006, but I am sure, like so much else where this remarkable man is concerned, he will deliver on his promises. Paarl has some of the world's nattiest winemakers and some beautifully sited vines so there is no excuse for less than thrilling liquids.

Mario Andretti, the ex-racing driver, has his own winery in the Napa Valley, California, and sells wine under his own name. He is a serious enthusiast. I have not tasted the wines.

In 2001, the Botham Merrill Willis range of Australian wines was launched. The first and last named are English cricketers, the man in the middle being one of Oz's most flamboyant winemakers. It was offered exclusively through Tesco, around £8 a bottle, and the first vintage offering was mediocre, the second better, and third even more of an improvement. The cabernet was on sale, in 2007, at tesco.com for £51.19 a six-pack case. It can appeal only to dyed-in-the-wool cricket fans. It was, and is, not your average let's-make-a-quick-buck celebrity wine projects as both Botham and Willis are genuinely interested in wine and Merrill is a dynamo. It may stay the course. After 5 years, if a celebrity wine is still going it must have something and this example of the genre may last a few vintages more.

The rumours about Brad Pitt and Angelina Jolie buying a vineyard have been rife in the wine industry for some time. The Luberon and Barolo have both been mentioned as possible sites, but movie stars like these have only to go out for a drink for an extravagant rumour to be hatched. Mr Pitt likes his wine. But does he like it as much as his fellow Hollywood thespian, Johnny Depp, does? Mr Depp once paid over £11,000 for a bottle of burgundy in the London restaurant Mirabelle. How much might such an actor pay for a vineyard? And how much would his fans be happy to pay to drink it?

In 2006 a prominent member of the UK whispered to me that he might be able to get me involved in project with Mr and Mrs David Beckham. 'They want to know about wine,' he said. 'But they'll need help. Maybe get a Beckham range off the ground?'

'Why not Victoria wine?' I riposted. 'Or has that already been done?'

Can any celebrity, however slight, however fleeting, get into wine? Yes. Paul Burrell, once one of Queen Elizabeth's footmen who became Princess Diana's butler, has launched his own range of wines. As far as I can ascertain, they are only available in New Mexico and Georgia in the US as Mr Burrell's website states that his wines are 'available through the renowned importer National Distributing Company inc' which is not national at all, but I believe it can distribute in nineteen other states. Mr Burrell's whole enterprise, with its ghastly royal butler logo, is tacky, exploitative, and designed to appeal to impressionable Americans who will assume a man who has poured for a princess will know something about wine.

The notorious American socialite Paris Hilton, in 2007, introduced her own Italian sparkling wine called Rich Prosecco. It is a brilliant concept, one which I would have thought would have had Prosecco makers, always in the shadow of champagne (let alone cava and other bubblies), celebrating, delighted that such an international celebrity will encourage lots of her fans, young women I assume, to try a wine they have never heard of. I believe Rich Prosecco will succeed brilliantly but are the Prosecco makers happy? Not a bit of it. Fulvio Brunetta, president of the wine growers association of Treviso in the Veneto region where a good deal of Prosecco comes from protested to Reuters that 'Hilton hotels are a sign of quality. Paris Hilton is sensationalism. It's not good. It's not adequate for Prosecco.'

What a silly old fart. (I assume he is old. No young president would have reacted like that.) Apparently, Miss Hilton features in her Prosecco's advertising naked covered in gold paint. It gets more and more delicious this story. How can anyone protest? If it is genuine Prosecco, it is one of the few celebrity endorsements which is exciting, relevant and will work and I think it will persuade men to try Prosecco. I wish I had been invited to the launch of this product. Maybe a sample is in the post. Ms Hilton is welcome to call at my house with a sample anytime, with or without gold paint.

Perhaps the dumbest celebrity wine range I've so far encountered was that of the Chinese chef Ken Hom. Out of curiosity, I actually attended the launch of his range of wines, some years ago now, which was designed to go with his ranges of chopsticks and cook-in Cantonese sauces as well as, for all I know, his martial arts exercises, Feng Shui herbs, and moxibustion cups.

The event was staged at a Thai restaurant in Putney. I must confess it was the worst wine tasting I have glumly sat through since Cornwall's (1984), Moravia's (1988), and Crete's (1998). Mr Hom's

range, which as far as I know is no longer with us, was called Spicy
Varietals which had the dubious advantage of sounding like a lap
dancing club somewhere off London's North Circular road but the
disadvantage that no-one, outside the membership of the Circle of
Wine Wankers, knows what a varietal is or cares. With the wines in
question, it really didn't matter anyway. They were mediocre
examples not just of individual grape varieties but of wine generally
and, a further fatuity, they failed to accompany with any wit any of
the dishes chosen. The wines comprised a chasan, a roussanne, a
grenache and a mourvèdre. When Mr Hom asked me what I
thought I gave him my view of their mediocrity and so he waffled
(he is patently an expert on the waffle as well as egg fried rice) and
he said 'well, these wines are not aimed at the European taste but at
Asian people' but this was flatly contradicted by Hom's PR woman
who told me the range had undergone research in the UK for sale
to UK drinkers.

When you consider purchasing a wine with a celebrity name
attached you must differentiate between the celebrity who is a
genuine wine lover, is keen to learn and get his or her hands dirty,
and someone who merely puts his/her name on a bottle in the
hope of making quick and easy bucks. It is the latter projects I urge
you to ignore. The wine trade in the UK is desperate to find points
of difference, especially along a crowded supermarket shelf with lots
of similar products jostling for your attention. There is no doubt, for
example, that if you idle by the pasta sauce shelves of any large
supermarket you will see shoppers, mainly women, stop and check
out the Lloyd Grossman range simply because he has some TV
celebrity. They do not necessarily buy but they take note. Maybe
they'll buy next time or the time after that.

This is all that the marketeers of celebrity products can hope for,
unless they also invest in TV advertising as did the licence owners
of the Lloyd Grossman brand, Premier Foods of St Albans (one of
the UK's mightiest food giants), when it launched the range. The
range is now a £50 million brand. Premier therefore views the

Grossman sauces as dispassionately as it does its Batchelors Super Noodles, Birds custard, Bisto gravy mix, Branston pickles, Cadbury's cakes (made under licence from Cadbury Schweppes), Campbells soups, Crosse and Blackwell, Frank Cooper's jams, Fray Bentos meat pies, Gales honey, Hovis bread, Mother's Pride bread, Mr Kipling cakes, Oxo stockcubes, Paxo stuffing, Robertson's jams, Sarson's vinegar, Saxa salt and Sharwood's oriental sauces. Each of these is a Premier Foods profit centre. No more, no less. Each has a brand manager. I have no doubt that if Premier had any wine expertise, or interest in the area, we would already have a Lloyd Grossman wine range on the shelves. If only Gilly Goolden had gone to the wine equivalent of Premier Foods she would now be in clover, pulling in a few hundred grand a year in royalties and able to charge £25,000 a time to open local supermarkets.

Such is celebrity. Such is the loss of it. Where wine is concerned avoid it at all costs, unless the celebrity concerned is widely cultured, owns the vines, and is not out to rip you off.

29

RIP

The wine merchants supermarkets have eaten

I accuse the supermarkets metaphorically. (Unlike the wine merchant who wrote to my publisher in the early 1990s holding my supermarket wine column responsible for being instrumental in causing the destruction of his business. He threatened to have me assassinated.)

Tesco and Sainsbury have not physically taken over any wine merchants, though both examined Oddbins' books at Companies House a decade ago when the wine chain was for the umpteenth time up for sale. They have, as my putative assassin was surely right to observe, created conditions in which many old style wine businesses simply could no longer compete. Why should anyone purchase wines from an old fogey who had little buying skill, perhaps a dodgy palate, was hoity-toity when it came to accepting returned bottles, and charged high prices? Such a merchant's dusty charms (and bottles), which were genuine, might appeal to those only a few months away from their *Times* obituaries but the new breed of wine consumer prefers the dumbness of the supermarket wine aisles and the fact that s(he) does not need one syllable of a foreign tongue to acquire an otherwise verbally tongue-tangling liquid. (It was part of the Aussies' appeal, of course, that the tongue was English. Even Barramundi Chardonnay was friendlier, and the fruit likewise, than any bottle of tricky-to-call Puligny-Montrachet.)

So it was that the supermarkets took over. And it was not just the old brigade who were overwhelmed, many of the newer merchants vanished too. Remember Victoria Wine? KwikSave? Littlewoods? William Low? Safeway? Wine Cellar? Cellar-5? Davisons? Fullers?

Safeway? Unwins? In the summer of 2008, Somerfield also disappeared, swallowed up by the Co-op (an acquisition of which I thoroughly approve, I might add.) These retailers are now history. All alive twenty years ago, all dead and buried now.

Take Unwins. It was not just the buying power of the super-markets which made a wine chain such as Unwins uncompetitive. It could not even compete with its rival high street off-licences. The last wine tasting I attended at this retailer was the most remarkable I attended all year (perhaps all-career, so the retailer's achievement is all the more impressive). It was held at the White Horse pub in Fulham which I reached after 55 minutes in the saddle from Finsbury the other side of London (having cycled there from Hampstead to first attend a Budgens tasting). I mention the amount of cycling involved because I wondered, after I'd mouthed my way through the Unwins whites, if perhaps I wasn't a little saddle sore and my judgement awry. However, after consulting the only other wine taster in the room whom I knew had a respectable palate my views were confirmed: these wines were wretchedly dull, though some merit was conferred by their coming in glass bottles and having the labels stuck on straight. Tasting was not assisted by two members of Unwins staff chattering with ribald humour only a few feet away. Perhaps they were trying deliberately to distract the studious taster? These wines, after all, did not reward close scrutiny. Who in his or her right mind would want to drink Palandri Riesling 2002, Drouhin La Foret Bourgogne Blanc Chardonnay 2001, Babich Gimblett Gravels Chardonnay 2000, or Bourgogne Vieilles Vignes Chardonnay 2002, all at prices far from bargain-basement?

It had been, I must also admit, an unconfident tasting upon first entering it. Behind the bar of the upstairs tasting room at the White Horse, an excellent public house in all other respects, stood three wide-eyed PR women. They could not offer clipboards to hold the tasting sheets but they could, in little bowls set by the wines, provide fresh coffee beans. I enquired at the existence of these caffeine-charged nodules and was told by the leggiest PR totty that 'I discovered this in France. If your nose gets clogged up with so much tasting you just smell a coffee bean and, um, *et voila*!'

I smelled one of the pots. Very pleasant. I then nosed one more of the reds (I was on to the reds by then). This was not so congenial an experience and indeed the consistency of the reds' dullness was only interrupted by a lively Villiera Shiraz from South Africa and a tasty Oyster Bay Merlot from New Zealand. Two wines I could like! Two out of a hundred! Thin pickings and obviously Unwins customers, as thin on the ground as the fruit in an Unwins red, felt the same.

Unwins, as I had been forced to do in my tasting glass, bit the dust. Can you blame the Tescos and Sainsburys of this world if wine drinkers prefer their offerings to those of inept wine chains?

The only note of disquiet is that the supermarkets are always going on about choice. So where is the choice if there are fewer and fewer national retailers at which it is possible to buy interesting wines?

The only truly vibrant major high street chain is the independently owned Majestic. Oddbins, until recently owned by the French company Castel, which also operates the Nicolas chain in France and the UK, had its individuality stifled and its chutzpah crushed. It lost money for Castel and in August 2008 was sold to private individuals. In 2006 it was £8.6 million in the red (pre-tax). Thresher is staffed by people who largely do not know about wine in depth and is involved in a number of franchise operated outlets. Such is the pressure these two retailers are under that there was talk, in late 2007, of a merger between the two. It would have been a disaster. One retail analyst remarked of the suggested merger that 'I can't see why people need off-licences.' We are left, then, only with high-end wine merchants on the high street who charge a lot and do not necessarily match that with first class wines.

Of the British supermarkets Waitrose is tops, with Sainsbury's and the Co-op a close second, with Tesco hovering on the edge of second place. Morrisons has too many brands and its own labels are mediocre. But things are better at Asda which still develops own labels, though its £3 and under wine are poor and bad value. Budgens is brand-led and so most other large chains. Only Aldi has a small selection of interesting wines exclusive to it (under the La Forge label).

After this, where can you shop in Britain? The bigger independents of course, which do have some splendid wines amidst a degree of overpriced dross. These include Lay & Wheeler, Corney & Barrow, Yapp Brothers, Berry Brothers & Rudd, as well as e-tailers and a several smaller merchants in major cities. As with everything else when it comes to choosing a wine, it is your palate you should rely on and not any merchant's blather. And if the wine is not right take it back and complain (nicely but firmly).

30

THE WINE SUBSIDY SCAM

When visiting wine producers in Europe over the past ten years I have attempted to tell my hosts a joke. We have in Britain, I say, come up with a terrific way to keep the UK motor industry alive and its tens of thousands of workers fully employed. We will maintain the factories by continuing to turn out vehicles which no-one wants to buy. But as each car comes off the assembly line, maintained via huge EU subsidies, it will be taken away, and the body and passenger compartment recycled into refrigerators, kitchen utensils, plastic toys and leather goods and the engine broken up and sold as scrap. Thus, the UK motor industry is saved! After a few seconds reflection on this marvellous scenario, the irony of which a German twigs in a nano-second but which goes completely over the head of the average Frenchman, the EU citizen I have addressed nods and says, in all profundity, *c'est absurde*!

I can't think why you say that, I respond, isn't that exactly what is happening in Europe with wine? That this is so be in no doubt. EU subsidies maintain many growers and their vineyards, their wine and its production, but the wine is never drunk. It is taken away and recycled, by distillation, into industrial alcohol.

Since 1999 Brussels has gone through over two and one half billion Euros subsidising Europe's vineyards in the name of modernisation, reconstruction, renovation; money spent trying to improve competitiveness against New World wines. I do not say that all this money has gone to keep afloat vineyards the products of which are recycled; I do not say that some of these vineyards do not deserve assistance; my beef is directed, firstly, at those vineyards we can do without, which do not merit subsidy, and which should be ploughed up and other things grown there and, secondly and more crucially, at all those generic and regional wine committees which use money no more imaginatively than if they had half-yearly bonfires of the stuff.

How much of that two and one half billion Euros has been money burned I have been unable to determine, but one thing is clear: Europe is struggling to compete with Australia, South Africa and the Americas and it is we, the EU tax payers, who are expected to maintain this uncompetitiveness by keeping second-rate producers in business and funding mediocre wine committees.

In 2007, the European Commission announced the allocation of 450 million Euro to what was called 'Europe's struggling wine producers.' Spain got the lion's share of 159 million, France 111 million, and Italy 100 million Euro, leaving 80 million for the application of first aid to the stricken producers of 11 other EU nations. I doubt that anyone tasted the wines of any of these vineyards, took note of their viticultural practices, looked at the ambitions and talent of the producers and said, yes, these guys deserve our help. Why not, for a start, insist that no producer dependent on EU aid may spend the money on chemicals? Let's turn all of them into organic producers. Let's force the blighters to farm in the best interests of Europe and its peoples.

Agriculture commissioner Mariann Fischer Boel made clear the point of the 450 million Euro spending exercise. Part of her statement read: 'Improving the quality of the wine we produce is a top priority if we are to fend off the challenge posed by New World wine producers.' To achieve this ambition, the proposals from the European Commission called for: 'an end to all subsidised distillation; an ambitious grubbing-up programme to reduce vineyard capacity, including resettlement grants for farmers who give up wine growing; relaxation of the present rules on the labelling of European wines; an extension to the current ban on new plantings; the abolition of subsidies for the use of grape must to enrich wine; a ban on the use of sucrose for enrichment; and a campaign to promote sales on EU wine outside the Community.'

In July 2007, confirming that the situation was being recognised for the Lewis Carroll–cum–Kafka farce it was (and one given an added fatuity because some of the proposals will be resisted fiercely by wine producers), the House of Lords European Union Committee published its findings. This Committee had just finished a six-months inquiry into the EU wine industry and was commenting on the European Commission's proposals for reform. This parliamentary Committee was in no doubt that some of these proposals were much needed, others less so. The press release (August 2007) from the Committee said, amongst other things, that the

EUROPEAN WINE MARKET IS IN CRISIS, PROFOUND REFORM IS NEEDED TO RESTORE ITS HEALTH.

In the Committee's view, the present regime is unsustainable. Despite subsidies from EU taxpayers totalling nearly £1 billion a year, the industry is producing substantial quantities of wine for which there is no market. It is also steadily losing market share to 'New World' wine producers who are more in touch with what consumers want and who are not hampered by EU regulations. Imports from the New World have risen sharply in recent years and the European Union is in danger of becoming a net importer of wine.

The committee is content with the broad thrust of the Commission's proposals, and is especially supportive of the proposal to end all distillation subsidies. Without this change, says the committee, reform stands little chance of success. But it is also critical of some of the other proposals. There is no need, says the committee, for a ban on new plantings once subsidised distillation is abolished: such a ban would simply serve to keep enterprising winegrowers out of the industry. The ban on the use of sucrose, which is cheaper than its alternative (grape must), will unnecessarily increase production costs as well as putting the EU at a competitive disadvantage with New World producers. And the committee has also sounded a warning note over the proposed campaign to promote European wines. Advertising alone, it says, will not do the trick. There is a need to connect the EU wine producer with the market and to establish proactive marketing networks.

Lord Sewel, chairman of the inquiry, remarked that 'The Commission's proposals are long overdue. The present pattern of subsidies is not just a burden on the EU taxpayer: it is also damaging the industry by deflecting attention from the real problem, which is lack of competitiveness.'

In October the same year, the Committee published what it called its final report. Only one of its recommendations sent a chill through me. This was when it said that 'Europe should be looking to secure greater scale of production, whether from cooperative or corporate farming.'

Whilst it is true that certain large co-ops in Europe, particularly in Champagne, Alsace, Languedoc and Moselle, are guardians of high standards in wine making and grape growing, the idea of large corporate wine farms with all the mass production techniques this implies, especially chemicals in the vineyards, is wholly against the interests of Europe as a trading block and EU citizens as consumers. It is these large producers who are so against any reform of the EU wine laws with regard to sugar enrichment. In my view, sugar will continue to play a major part in wine production because there are too many vested interests which on economic grounds structure their whole wine manufacturing basis around sugaring. Who needs sun when it can shine (cheaply) out of a sack?

Raise your glass to a disunited Europe
There is a more delicious irony to this than the one highlighted at

the start of this section. It is that every time a UK drinker has satis-factorily downed another bottle of Aussie shiraz or South African chardonnay, another two European vineyards have felt the cold and the drinking of those two wines has cost the drinker more than their actual retail outlay. Part of the problem is the UK's inability to see itself as part of Europe, where wine consumption is concerned, for we see all wines as imported (leaving aside the mostly humdrum and miniscule production which is not, i.e. that from English & Welsh vineyards).

If we thirsty Brits were more inclined to think of ourselves as Europeans, we might then consider wines from EU countries as home grown. However, not only is our own Exchequer a major stumbling block to this perception because duty rates as so high and out of kilter with everyone else in the EU so we Brits can only see ourselves as foreigners in Europe, but we feel an especial affection for wines from the New World because they speak our language and in the instances of the USA, Australia, New Zealand and South Africa were once British crown territory. (Not that this affection counted for much politically once Britain joined the EU and ended the so-called Imperial Preference on colonial imports. Now wines from such places pay a per-case EU wine tax in order to go on sale in European member states and doubtless this income helps to fund the subsidies the success of such wines makes so necessary and, largely, so futile.) There are several further factors which enhance the British Isles' status as Europe's odd bod, and the most cogent is the fact we insist on our own currency.

I am wholly in agreement with subsidies to help producers change the varieties of the grapes they grow, to relocate and expand vineyards where appropriate, and to improve techniques. As I said above, and so important is it I'll say it again, one way to facilitate this would be for the EU to assist growers to go organic. This would have the double effect of not only improving European soils and wildlife but make the wines more competitive because well-made organic wine is a hugely marketable commodity if the price isn't obscene. I also concur with the wise and cautionary words from the House of Lords regarding advertising. The practitioners in advertising and consultants of marketing who advise almost everybody in wine lack imagination and creativity and this is aggravated by their often having to deal with committees. The only way to promote wines where EU subsidies are concerned is to advertise wines people can buy and invariably this is lacking from generic campaigns which is why this is yet more money thrown on the fire. The ad agency execs and marketing gurus laugh all the way to their Michelin-starred lunch-time restaurants, to their Ferraris in their staff car parks, and to their banks. The EU should issue a directive that only marketing of specific wines is to be tolerated where subsidies are involved, not the promotion of a general area or a wine style which no-one can buy.

Yet generic advertising and marketing campaigns are beloved of bodies representing wine producers. Such advertising is not built around something you can purchase but something it wants you to believe. This may work with politics, because the advertising enters our head immediately, but it does not work with something you can only experience by visiting a shop at a later date and then taking home (or visiting a restaurant or wine bar).

A casual glance at some of the campaigns mounted by European producers confirms their idiocy and, where EU subsidies have been involved, offers a profligate picture of the monumental waste of tax payers money.

It is a fact widely known in adland that any ad agency's creative department will collectively decamp to the nearest pub when a brief for a generic campaign is being touted along the corridors.

It is impossible to write and art-direct an exciting campaign on a generic subject; a campaign which has a coherent and meaningful strategy which can be translated into anything dramatic, original, compelling, meaningful to the consumer.

Do you recall the slogan of the Bordeaux producers advertising in the early part of the new century? Of course you don't. No-one

remembers it. (Not even the producers probably.) 'Be Bordeaux –
Experience a World of Finesse' it trumpeted via extravagant full
colour ads. What in God's name could such gobbledegook mean?
I'll tell you. It meant no single talent or creative team wrote it. It was
research-lingo assembled, like pieces of metaphysical Lego, by the
degenerate minds of a conglomerate group desperate to fly to the
moon using feathers.

The Portuguese poster campaign, which I was forced to
confront on London underground tube stations (and indeed
opposite my own column), was no less fatuously flighty. It showed
celebs without celebrity (Karen Brady, Tony Parsons, Mark Fuller,
Alastair Little, Jean Christophe Novelli) as, and I quote, Portuguese
Wine Explorers. Few people knew who these people were and no-
one cared. The Portuguese wine institute, or whomever or whatever
instigated and approved the campaign, would have better spent their
funds, as with Bordeaux, advertising something you can buy. Both
campaigns were flatulent strategically and flabby tactically and a
waste of money.

The only way to change any drinker's mind about a drink is to
stick a bottle in front of her. This never happens with generic
campaigns because internal politics prevents any wines getting
preference. Hence meretricious bathos is the result. When I aired
some of these views in a magazine article at the time, Bordeaux's
below-the-line agency, Summit Sales Promotion, protested and said
that there had been a 7% volume growth in Bordeaux off-trade sales
in 2001. This was, the agency said, 'no happy coincidence' but a
result of the generic campaign's effects.

This was codswallop (a dish with which claret is perfectly
suited). Bordeaux's improved performance was wholly the result of
supermarkets and wine chains finding decent around-a-fiver clarets
to peddle. The generic campaign had no effect on consumers
whatsoever. Of course the agency would be able to cite research
evidence to contradict this. They no doubt stuffed its client with
pie-charts and stats. But was there a single Briton who saw that

generic advertising or below-the-line activity in 2001 and was inspired immediately to go into an off-licence and buy a bottle of bordeaux? If you believe that you find equal credibility in the existence of flying saucers.

Generic campaigns are a waste of money in terms of exciting the people they are aimed at. Michael Paul, once one of the leading figures in the UK wine industry when he was managing director of Orbital Wines, wrote in the industry's leading wine trade magazine, *Harpers* (September 7th 2007) that 'generic wine promotion has almost entirely failed... in engaging the consumer.' The EU must legislate to prevent its subsidies being employed in generic advertising. Bordeaux and Portugal, or any other wine region or country, cannot be advertised.

I can readily appreciate that a generic campaign committee might serve some purpose in uniting disparate producers to a common cause. But subsidies should not be required for that. The producers should pay every penny out of their own (unsubsidised) pockets.

How our money is thrown away

Once a EU wine subsidy is in place how it is spent? Over 2006/7 Austria, Cyprus, the Czech Republic, France, Germany, Greece, Hungary, Italy, Luxembourg, Malta, Portugal, Slovakia, Slovenia and Spain all received money. But let us take one example. In northern Portugal there is a region called Vinho Verde, consisting of some 147,000 acres of vines (according to the *Oxford Companion to Wine* encyclopedia) or 87,000 acres (if, possibly more plausibly, the Comissão de Viticultura dos Vinhos Verdes is to be believed). They make a wine here called Vinho Verde, green wine, and many a holidaymaker to the Algarve and other tourist hotspots in Portugal will have quaffed, with no small degree of satisfaction, one of the spikier specimens, white, well chilled, around 8.5/11% alcohol, delicious in torrid weather and perfect with grilled sardines and the suchlike. Is not such a wine perfect for modern health-conscious Europe?

Certainly the UK is developing and marketing lower alcohol wines, but what more natural than these should emanate from the Vinho Verde region. But do they? Well, the latest figures I have been able to obtain reveal that 542,337 litres of vinho verde were exported to the UK, the 6th biggest market for the wine, in 2005. That's around 60,000 cases. It's a drop in the ocean. It's not even close to a single major brand annual sales figure through a single large supermarket chain. Perhaps it was this the EU commissioners bore in mind when they handed the CVRVV the piddling sum of 2 million Euro in 2007 to promote its region's wines in the UK, Portugal itself, Spain, France, Germany and Belgium.

4300 Euro went on a single wine tasting for professionals (i.e. old soaks and hacks like me) in Barcelona and the rest has been earmarked for similar events. In July 2007, the CVRVV hosted wine tastings for 180 trade professionals in Los Angeles (at the Murana restaurant) and San Francisco (venue the Prés-a-Vi restaurant). This latter hostelry has been described by a food critic as a place where 'the wines are picked for maximum aficionado amusement', so one assumes it is jolly expensive, and the events included, in the CVRVV words a 'formative seminary by the wine specialist and critic Anthony Dias Blue' also an expensive hiring I would guess as his website describes him as a 'life-style consultant'. Mr Blue also organises wine competitions in the USA which one would have thought required him always to be seen as neutral and unsupportive of an individual region but that is another question.

The sum allocated to the UK market will not, though, stretch to many fancy restaurants. Just 150,000 Euro is to be spent over the next three years on a seminar, more wine tastings, something called a 'wine-buffet' in Birmingham and London and of course they'll be throwing money at the usual old soaks and hacks by jetting them off to Vinho Verde for lots of lunches and dinners with glasses of the wine. The advertising department of Decanter wine magazine will prick up its ears and perhaps some wine hack will be despatched, at EU subsidised expense (via the hospitality of the CVRVV), on a jolly to Portugal so congenial journalese can be published to entice an ad spend. The quarterly journal of the UK's Circle of Wine Writers will publish the notes of one of its members who will also go on one of the freebie trips but few will feel any benefit apart from the discrete circulation of the journal. What is the point of it all? I grant you that getting people to taste the product is a good idea, but it must be related to a wine they can buy, promoted alongside the tasting, in major retailers. I don't want my tax money going to feed parasites and support lousy ad agencies and do pointless marketing exercises. You may say but 2 million Euro is not a lot, but when you multiply it by all the other regions in the Community holding out their begging bowls you can readily see how the 450 million Euro total subsidy easily gets gobbled up.

The Portuguese are masters at exploiting EU subsidies. Given EU money to improve viable vineyards and grub up useless ones, it was revealed by *Harpers* magazine in October 2007 that EU officials were very unhappy with the way the money had (or had not) been spent. 'We have seen shortcomings in the way the Portuguese checked that the money was going to the right people... This is not necessarily fraud it could just be bad management.' a EU spokesperson was quoted as saying.

But which half?

A chairman of Unilever many moons ago once remarked that 'I know half my advertising spend is wasted, but I don't know which half.' When it comes to the EU wine subsidies scam we can, surely, be much more precise. All that which is earmarked for generic advertising and promotion is suspect and all subsidies which help maintain cheap UK supermarket retail prices is an unacceptable waste of resources (see below). Perhaps an ombudsman, one with wide commercial and marketing experience, should be appointed ruthlessly to examine all funding schemes and with the executive power to recommend the withholding of monies if their suggested employment s(he) considers unwise. But what am I saying?!

Recommending appointing another pig, a really big one, to get her/his snout in the trough!? But what is the answer?

To do away with all agricultural subsidies? No. I am a firm believer in subsidy (transport, health, education), but where food and wine is concerned I do believe that it is crucial that subsidies are kept to a level low enough to not overburden the EU taxpayer yet high enough to stimulate innovation rather than maintain frowsty and anachronistic traditions. What should the Vinho Verde producers do? Create their own brand (or brands) and sell them through small wine merchants and restaurants and bars in the UK.

The reason the VV area requires subsidy and its wines perform so relatively poorly in the UK market is because most sales of the product in the UK go through major multiples who just see it as another cheap line. Sainsbury's has an own-label Vinho Verde, selling at 492 stores, priced at £2.99. Tesco has a similar product, same price. Waitrose has a pricier, and much finer, specimen, Quinta Azevado at £5.49 (and at 13% not low in alcohol). When I put it to these three supermarkets that surely they had an opportunity to create a new market for Vinho Verde, as a fresh, naturally lower-alcohol white wine, in tune with today's drinking habits, the only sign of life was registered by Tesco's wine product development manager James Grisewood. He emailed me: 'We sell one Vinho Verde which is a Tesco label wine. I have been looking at the possibility of further developments in this area for exactly the reason you point out (lower natural alcohol). Nothing has been confirmed so far however, so I am unable to give any specific details.'

But isn't it far smarter for the producers of this wine, as I point out above, to use their EU subsidy to create their own range of products instead of waiting for a UK supermarket buyer to descend on them who will demand a 30% margin and a £2.99 sales price tag? This is using subsidy properly. At the moment, a £2.99 Vinho Verde is subsidised to the benefit of supermarket shareholders. The UK taxpayer, who drinks the stuff, is actually contributing to subsidising her own tipple. How much better, smarter, and more long-lasting it would be to subsidise not producers to turn out cheap supermarket wines but good value wines whose fortunes they manage themselves. At the moment subsidies merely maintain the status quo. There is no dynamic in the way the money is managed to compel the recipients to eventually come off the subsidy and stand on their own feet.

How subsidies help sustain obscene salaries for UK bosses

I am not an economist or business strategist, but it seems obvious that subsidies as they are currently organised are a con, for they help maintain a low UK price as much as they prop up the producers. It is an insane waste of money and human resources and the problem begs an urgent solution. That solution requires lateral thinking, imagination, and creative application. True, the EU shows scant evidence of any of these attributes but may I make a plea that someone in government or politics in the UK reads what is written here and acts in the way an intelligent and liberal conscience ought to. Why should I see my tax money benefit the shareholders of Tesco and Sainsbury and all those partners at Waitrose? I want to see the producers flourishing, in control of their own markets and their own destinies. To hell with supermarket shareholders. The chairman of Tesco, Terry Leahy, picked up along with his annual bonus around £3.75 million salary last time I looked. That's 5.4 million Euro, enough for him personally to have out-matched the EU Vinho Verde subsidy by some way. How much of that Leahy income is as a result of the buoyant profits enjoyed by his chain of shops whose turnover in wine is, with circa 400 million bottles sold annually, around £50 billion? It is wholly the result. Which begs a further enquiry: how much of that £50-billion Tesco wine turnover accrues from subsidised European wine?

What a wheeze! European tax-payers give money to wine producers who are then enabled to sell their wares at minimal profit to a UK supermarket which makes huge profits. A wine selling at £2.99 at Tesco returns to the producer a mere 0.46 Euro, or 34p, out of which he has to pay freight, bottling (plus cork or screwcap), labelling, insurance and oh yes how could I forget? the liquid itself. The producer is a mouse in the claws of the supermarket cat, to be played with until something livelier or more pliant comes along.

There is a further delicious scam which relates to recycling wine which has received a subsidy to be destroyed (as briefly touched on elsewhere in this book). Known as EU Intervention Wine this is wine which the producer does not actually pour away but takes EU subsidy to destroy and then in secret sells it, dirt cheap, to someone prepared to turn it into a bottled product for sale.

One UK wine importer I tackled on this subject said he was surprised that the supermarkets turned a blind eye to such malpractice and he had harsh words also for the UK's Wine & Spirit Association which, he alleged, turned an even quicker and blinder eye.

And we EU tax contributors, silently unprotestingly unwittingly, underpin the whole scam. Somewhere in the Greek pantheon there is a god (minor but with a huge sense of humour) of scams, and the European Union subsidy programme as it applies to wine – and doubtless a good many other agricultural areas as well – keeps him alive and merrily chuckling year after year.

(He must, for example, be in fits of glee over the EU subsidies given to the Portuguese cork industry to help in its losing battle against the increasing popularity of plastic closures and screwcaps. Some of that money has gone to fund wasteful advertising campaigns, which in the UK featured, ludicrously, the ex-Chelsea football club manager Jose Mourinho, and to fly Antipodean wine people on freebie business class return flights from Sydney/ Melbourne/ Adelaide/ Perth/ Auckland to Lisbon ostensibly to tour the cork forests but which in reality the recipients of the largesse cheerfully exploit as a cheap gateway to the rest of Europe. One canny Aussie critic I spoke to said 'I've always wanted to visit the Prado and the Louvre, and from Lisbon the air taxi to both cities costs peanuts. When I get to London shall we have lunch?' I myself was on more than one occasion begged by cork-industry PR slickers to experience at their client's expense the delights of touring oak plantations and eating the feral pigs which exist on the acorns but I felt unable to accept.

31

WINE CLUBS AND E-TAILERS SLIPPERY CUSTOMERS

What is the difference between the *Sunday Times* Wine Club and an octopus? That's right. An octopus has only eight arms. As we shall discover in a moment, this is only one of several colourful metaphors which can be laid at the door of this mail order wine merchant which in the ordinary course of events would remain only at the periphery of my purview as a consumer wine critic. However, I have gone to the odd Club press tasting, to exchange *bon mots* with chairman Hugh Johnson as he puffs around the wines smiling like Thomas the Tank Engine and Laithwaites, who run the Club on the newspaper's behalf, occasionally send me samples. (I also once interviewed Tony Laithwaite at his business in Reading and was astonished to be told that I was the first wine critic ever to have taken the trouble to visit.) More pertinently, I am now and then accosted by readers of my column who have strayed into the orbit of the STWC and, rather like we are led to believe will happen to any astronaut falling into a black hole, found themselves in the grip of a gravity they found it difficult to shake off. Others found the wines not to their liking.

The STWC operates on a simple basis, taking advantage of the unique fact that it is able to utilise millions of pounds worth of free or subsidised advertising space in the newspaper itself. It is well known by the cunning minds which put this sensational paper together that its readership is aspirational and insecure and in need of coaxing and easy-to-digest newsbites and the Club's advertising exploits these tendencies posited around one simple tactic:

It offers an introductory case at such a price that not even the shrewdest cost analyst at Asda or Tesco can devise competition. Someone in the trade told me it was a loss leader but I personally doubt this, believing that though the case is an enticement it probably breaks even. The trick is having got the sucker to order the introductory case and become a member a trained Laithwaites sales team, on behalf of the STWC, goes to work to ensure as many introductory-case customers as possible re-order. It is in the re-ordering that the profit lies. The Club targets the uncertain drinker, the one-bottle a week fellow, who is promised 'if you ever find a wine you don't like, for any reason, we'll refund you in full. We'll even come and collect the bottle.'

The language of the introductory offer offers no subtleties and is much like the paper's own presentation of news. For example, here is one wine from the Club's so-called 4 Seasons offer in autumn 2007. A case of 15 bottles of wine, excluding £5.99 delivery, for a ludicrously low £39.99 and for early responders a free corkscrew. Imagine! The whole world of wine is turning to screwcaps and the Club wants to giveaway a relic of the past. The 4-Seasons offer is so-called because it hopes the customer will be naive enough to be so dazzled by that introductory offer that he also buys the '12-bottle case reserved' for him 'every three months'. But of course there is no obligation, the brochure makes clear, to buy these further cases. Let us look at this one wine in particular, for it is instructive.

'From a Bordeaux-trained winemaker and the multi-award winning Vina Tarapaca Estate in Chile, comes a sumptuous Merlot it's enough to give Bordeaux chateau owners sleepless nights.' A sumptuous merlot for £2.66 must be quite something and I can assure the *Sunday Times* that no Bordeaux chateau owner will suffer a sleepless night because of it. The only sleepless night might accrue from the purchaser who finds it perhaps corked, not to his liking, gives him a headache, or is not remotely sumptuous. Wines ordered mail order and sealed with a cork do run the risk of being less than 100% and it requires a special kind of mail order merchant to handle massive complaints.

My own experience is exceptional: having ordered a case of

Brézème, a Côtes du Rhône Villages red, from Yapp Brothers I found nine of the twelve tainted by their corks. However, when I rang Robin Yapp, because I knew him personally, he organised delivery of a whole new case, all the bottles of which were in health, two days later. All mail order merchants claim to offer refunds or replacements but few, I suspect, would be as trusting and sympathetic as Mr Yapp. And he was not remotely interested in coming and picking up the nine diseased bottles. (I suspect that the *Sunday Times* Wine Club saying it will pick up any bottle or bottles not to a customer's liking is designed to deter complaints. There is no point in collecting disappointing bottles unless the customer's beef is a serious one which can be laboratory analysed.)

Sunday Times Wine Club customers have contacted me in the past, but the most eloquent and detailed is someone whose identity I shall protect by calling him Mr Vokoban. Mr Vokoban first contacted me in 2004 regarding, as he put it, 'my attempts to unstick myself from the octopus-like grip of The Sunday Times Wine Club.' He went on.

'I was bought an introductory case as a present and so continued to buy. Eventually I came to feel that their increasingly frequent mailings to me were becoming irksome. Each time I bought a case, whether of Rhône, Chilean or Aussie red, or New Zealand white, this was evidently fed into their database and seemed to generate further targeted mailings. I was then enrolled without asking in their Charter Plus scheme which generated further mailings to the point where they were almost weekly. This culminated in an unsolicited phone call from a salesman to offer me a 'special deal of a mixed case of New Zealand white at a special price due to low stocks'. I accepted and received this purchase (nothing wrong with the wine or the mail order service incidentally), only to discover the same case was still on offer from their website and the price I had been charged was not a reduction on any previous price since there was ample supply. I was enormously angered at being suckered in that way and they admitted a 'human error' with profuse apologies, sending a bottle of Pomerol to shut me up. When I then received a demand for a membership subscription for the club in general, and another for their Charter Plus 'service', informing me these would be charged to my credit card I finally realised that they wanted me to pay them for the privilege of continuing to be a sitting target for their intrusive marketing.'

Mr Vokoban wondered whether ringing the Club's managing director at 2 am might bring relief. I wondered if I might slip him chairman Hugh Johnson's phone number but couldn't find it. Mr Vokoban reported he had resigned his membership. However, the octopus did not cease writhing. The mailings did not cease. He found he was still on the Club's computer and demanded a promise that his file would deleted. 'I asked why there was still a file for me and was told it is policy only to note the cancellation... but not to expunge the record. I said this was unacceptable... I asked that my file would be totally expunged. They (said) no-one there knew whether this is possible, because it has never been raised before, allegedly. They would need to consult head office and let me know in due course. The sad thing is that the wines are perfectly acceptable and the delivery service is excellent. Pity the same can't be said about their selling practices as it seems to me they are underhand and manipulative in a way which cries out for some investigative journalist to take a peek.'

I replied that I was ceasing my column in the *Guardian* and could not investigate for some time. Mr Vokoban, however, got in touch again.

'Despite my forceful telephone conversation with them I have today received yet another unwanted mailing from the *Sunday Times* Wine Club... after I made it crystal clear I wanted nothing more to do with them, and had demanded in the clearest possible terms that I wished to have my details removed from their files. Totally unacceptable, and surely also illegal? Just what do I have to do to escape from their clutches? Complain to the Data Protection Registrar?'

I responded that I would get back to him. Three years later, in researching this book, I did so. Mr Vokoban was in much chirpier spirits and reported that a 'lot of wine has been drunk and enjoyed since' we had last corresponded but that 'none of it (was) from the *Sunday Times* Wine Club. He went on.

'I am very pleased to say that the *Sunday Times* WC ceased their merciless pursuit of me and my credit card soon after we corresponded... On reading through the emails again I do recall with a shudder the feeling of helplessness engendered by being seemingly in the grasp of a determined and unscrupulous entity which had decreed I must buy my wine from them or else, and when I did not reply to their written blandishments were not above ringing me to sell down the phone using blatant and easily discoverable falsehoods as part of their patter.'

He now, he said, patronises Oddbins and Sainsbury but best of all is 'the Majestic website. You browse to your heart's content, make your selection, fail to buy online (who remembers passwords? I don't), phone the local branch, pay with your card, and they deliver free unfailingly within 24 hours. That seems to me an unbeatable model, and no pressure.'

The only other mail order merchant I received a serious complaint about was Avery's of Bristol, which had, in an ad in the *Guardian*, offered a case of wine which upon being purchased by a reader was found to contain different vintages, for three of the wines, from the ones advertised. This does happen, when a stated vintage runs out, though one vintage of a wine is not the same as another one. They should be treated as different wines. I have also received a complaint about this merchant that it delivered wines different from the ones advertised but, in its words 'of the same quality'.

My own view of certain of these wine merchants who advertise cheap intro cases, or bargain offers, is that they target the unschooled light drinker who enjoys wine but does not, unlike Mr Vokoban, aspire to the confidence required to shop at Majestic. To some of the more unscrupulous merchants such customers are merely sheep to be shorn and their timorousness means they rarely complain or if they do they are not, unlike our Mr Vokoban, prepared to go to great lengths to make their point.

If you live where access to wine merchants or supermarkets is not easy, or if you hate the idea of visiting either emporia, then mail order is an obvious route to the ready bottle. It is easy to take a bottle back to a supermarket and get a refund or a replacement, but with mail order you have to use the phone and have a conversation. I suspect that many mail order customers, those not 100% happy with every wine they buy, simply accept their disappointment as part of the price they have to pay for shopping in this way.

But nothing excuses bad wines and there a lot of examples out there and mail order merchants have their fair share of them. When it comes to risibly cheap introductory offers, that share may be considerable. Whatever wine merchants who specialise in home delivery may say about how they deal in 'small special parcels' or wines which 'beat the big brands hollow' or are acquired as the result of assiduously searching for the 'little known but wonderful producer' who the supermarkets and other major merchants have overlooked, never forget that in the end some of them depend on consumer apathy and the national British disease of having an eye for a seeming bargain in order to run a profitable and largely hassle-free business.

An example of the kind of dubious claiming and ludicrous pricing appeared in an ad in the *Times* of 10th November 2007 by Virgin wines.com (whose wines I have, over the years, only found a small proportion of I was prepared ever to recommend). It offered a 'limited offer – only 150 cases available' of what was, wickedly, called a 'majestic, Rioja-beating grand reserva' for £3.83 the bottle (£39.99 the 12-bottle case, plus £5.99 delivery). Perhaps it was deliberately intended to mislead by using the words majestic and Rioja but, unambiguously, other claims in the text were misleading. To wit: 'when you buy Gran Reserva you know you are getting a wine made from the finest quality grapes' '50 year-old vines wines made from old vines are richer, smoother and just altogether more scrumptious' '2000 vintage – a great year and perfect for drinking now' and there was also a load of waffle from Virgin's chief wine buyer about his job which was to find wines better 'than you can get at your supermarket'. However, Virgin's ad left a nasty taste in my mouth. Can you believe that the wine's makers, according to this ad, 'are too busy making great wines to bother with the big boys'? I just hope Times' readers saw through such hokum.

If I wanted to set up as a mail order wine merchant dealing in cheap mediocre wines I could do so tomorrow as easily as turning over in bed and switching on the night light. There is no magic required, just chutzpah, ambition, a website, a decent-sized garage, a liquor licence, and a delivery company. If I was asked to do it with only terrific high-rating wines unavailable anywhere else, always at fair prices, with assured intelligent delivery drivers and customer access to informed pleasant wine experts to handle all questions, I would rather put my money on a greyhound and keep my fingers crossed.

32

WINE WRITING AWARDS

First qualification – no writing skills required

The first thing to be said is that those who win want desperately to win. All those cajoled into entering want to win. This is the first suspect sign in my opinion, as awards are only truly worth having (and so very few are) if they are made without the slavish participation of the entrants. I plead guilty to being amongst these poor saps when I was first published as a wine hack, in 1989. It was required of me by my food and drink editor, Matthew Fort. How could I refuse? He placed huge store by winning awards. It irked me I had to go to so much trouble to enter and I remarked to Mr Fort that surely my readership was reward enough (though an increase in my paltry weekly fee might have acknowledged this more tangibly).

Soon, the truth dawned on me (I am slow. It took 3 years). I realised that for so many wine and food writers – a hideously jealous, competitive bunch all squabbling over a tiny patch of influence, and income, let it be said – it was winning awards that was more important than writing what was in the best interests of the reader. Award-hungry writers would seek opportunities to pen articles which would sit well with the judges above any considera-tion of relevance to the person at which it was putatively aimed. Some writers used utterly meaningless language techniques designed to appeal to mutton-headed judges.

I gave up entering wine writing competitions once I realised they were media circuses of no relevance to my readers and were mere ego-exercises for the entrants. Further, I took leave to doubt whether some judges on those juries knew what a paragraph was. If the Glenfiddich award is devalued by being sponsored by a second-rate malt (to use one recent winner's own phrase) then the

Roederer (or Lanson as it used to be before that sponsor pulled out) is total self-parody. All attempts to inveigle me on board as a judge of the latter have failed. How can I judge a competition I despise and do not enter? For the same reason when I was asked if I would be a candidate for the Wine & Spirit Communicator of the Year award I declined. I did once enter this, early on in my career, but only because I was given the impression that I had already won it and that my putting myself forward would merely endorse a decision already taken. I have since declined a further invitation to put myself forward.

I regularly peruse wine and food books, and have reviewed them on my (now defunct) website superplonk.com, and the ones which strike me as having any pretence to style and integrity hardly ever win prizes. This is not to say that the conceit of my own opinion is so all-powerful I cannot recognise that others might make legitimate claims for books or publications I find uncongenial but some Glenfiddich winners have taken prizes for work in which sentences appear of no rhythm, little originality, and very scant regard for the reader's patience and intelligence. Now I cannot claim to read all other wine writer's work but on the odd occasions I did read the constipated effusions of one particular year's winner I found he couldn't write for toffee (or any other hard candy for that matter).

This is the nub of the problem, don't you think? Winners have to be found. The sponsors demand it. Can you imagine a Glenfiddich jury, composed of the wine industry in-crowd, reporting back that no-one has won because the standard of writing was so low? Winners must be found. Their worth is irrelevant. The sponsor demands a winner.

Just as certain wines are made to stand out in competitions, yet are of little value to any drinker, so wine writers compose certain of their columns so that they will appeal to wine awards judges. I know this to be a fact with food writers, though I am on my honour not to reveal names, and it is surely no different with wine writers.

What is bad writing which impresses judges? Like the showy wine it is rich, fervid, melodramatic, ambitious, opportunistic, clumsy, overwrought. Splendid examples abound in the work of wine writer Andrew Jefford. I came across the following specimen in a merchant's catalogue. I do not know if it formed part of a prize winning package but it has all the hallmarks of the kind of sentence which would be considered outstanding by a wine writing judge (whose qualifications for the role may be negligible if not dubious): 'Pure fruit perfumes lick from Florent Viale's wines like flames from a bonfire, while the wines themselves are vivid and quenching.'

One's breath is taken away. Can a perfume lick? It is like a shoe on the wrong foot. It is mightily uncomfortable. Can wines which are described as hot be quenching? Or is this paradox an attempt at oxymoronality? Worst of all, the phrase 'while the wines themselves' is not only redundant as the wines are already under review, but positively crippling. Its freight sinks the ship.

Yet this writer, who picks up writing awards like some of us pick up cold viruses, is addicted to the inept flashy metaphor. Mr Jefford once wrote of a Moulin à Vent that 'the fruit comes helicoptering into the mouth' which to me suggests such an intemperate rush of crazed windiness that I am repelled. In the wine snob magazine *The World of Fine Wine*, the same writer said of Château Latour 2004 that 'it is a kind of velvet fruit bomb quietly ticking. Inside it, curled like nascent ferns, lie the densely packed black fruits…' Well, if it is quietly ticking it cannot be nascent which means it about to be born or, if a bomb, primed soon to explode and surely if it is so potentially explosive it is not ferns which will emerge but something nastier and not as leafily soft.

Now I am hammering away at this poor, deluded, neurotically ambitious writer because of an important point I wish to make.

All the clues one needs in order to decide whether a wine writer (or any other kind of writer for that matter from poet to polemical journalist) is worth following is contained not in his or her tasting abilities (Mr Jefford's may be superb for all I know, perhaps he is the greatest wine taster on the planet), but in their style of delivery of words which is a most useful indication of their state of mind.

The examples of over-ripeness I have quoted from this wine writer's work all come from the book *Questions of Taste: The Philosophy of Wine* (2007), and to provide an example of a subtler, richer mind at work I wish to quote one other from this source. All indulgent scribes can learn something from it as it obviously comes from an uncluttered well-ordered mind wholly in control of its feelings and its pen. The writer not only offers a simile which creates a vivid impression in the mind, and provides the pleasure of reading it and musing on it, but it serves the purpose of communicating with deadly accuracy a genuine feel of the wine as it is. The 1945 Château Pétrus, Jancis Robinson is quoted as penning, is 'Like velvet. But with a pattern on it.'

Superb! Simple, elegant, purposeful, delicious, mature, authoritative: doubtless like the wine itself. When such a taster exposes her mind like this, we can only wish to experience the wine as she has done. If only all writers on wine could offer us such laconic limpidity, and such writers won all the awards going, then I would warmly applaud.

The only writer on wine who in my opinion is worthy of any writing award in recent years is one who never even thinks of himself as a wine writer: Adam Brett-Smith of merchants Corney & Barrow. He not only wields an incisive and witty pen but he flaunts, throughout his biased prose (he is, after all, trying to flog wines), a wonderful subcutaneous authority without piety or forced metaphoric self-indulgence. (A flavour of some of this man's originality and wit is to be tasted on p 101). Compared to the blowsy metaphors and unmusical ploddings of several so-called wine writers, some of whom carry off the prizes, we find ourselves in the company of a writer whose sleek control only Hugh Johnson can match.

Mr Johnson writes regularly in *The World of Fine Wine* magazine and only he could write so endearingly as the examples below demonstrate. Yes, they are faintly absurd (but genteel), parodic even (as Lewis Carroll might have had a wine writer think), but they are gorgeous *and they reveal something of the true nature of the wines.* We want to share a glass with this writer. I do not want to be anywhere near someone whose fruit comes helicoptering into the mouth and neither would Mr Johnson, I am sure.

> Léoville-Las-Cases is always austere in a donnish way and is never more spectacles-on-nose than in this grown-up vintage. Fragrant, firm, pitched perilously on your crease, just outside the off-stump. A whiff of embrocation, even.
>
> Another favourite of the vintage, Château Poujeaux, from that haven for the sane and unsnobbish, the mid-Médoc Moulis-Listrac zone, is wearing its dress off one shoulder now, breathing deeply, lips just apart. It met a lamb casserole the other night, and consummation was immediate.

It takes chances, such prose, it risks derision and is easily lampooned; it is unremittingly masculine and old-fogeyish. But it is real writing. A real man is putting his engaging mind to work and sharing its contents with us. We delight in his company and wish we could experience such wines in the way he does. A wine writer who does this is performing the most civilising of influences and is true to his craft, faithful to his own style, at ease with his predilections and opinions.

33

THE DEATH OF THE WINE GUIDE

As author of the most successful UK wine guide for many years, *Superplonk* (1991-2006), I was witness to the astonishing rise in the popularity of such publications, and their eventual decline. A bookseller remarked to me it was exactly the same after Peter Mayle had written *A Year in Provence* and, more recently, Lynn Truss authored *Eats, Shoots & Leaves*. The publishing business is so risk averse and unimaginative that when a new gap in the market opens up scores of writers are commissioned or self-motivatedly rush to fill it and the inevitable result is eventual public boredom with such a torrent of me-too mediocrity. *A Year with My Dog in Aix* and *The History of the Apostrophe* — certainly somesuch titles — proliferated, and so it was when it was noticed *Superplonk* was top of the *Sunday Times* best sellers list for many years. Superplonk was copied by several wine writers.

The Grapevine (by Anthony Rose and Tim Atkin), and, most outrageously, *Superbooze* (by Tom Stevenson), were rushed into print and almost as quickly out of it. British TV wine presenter Oz Clarke followed in 1992, but his was not remotely like mine as I was always its sole author. The 2008 Oz Clarke guide has Mr Clarke's name on its cover above the blurb 'Britain's Favourite Wine Writer' but close inspection reveals that nineteen other writers, none of whom might be considered to be Britain's favourite, had a hand in it. This is, then, not a wine guide as *Superplonk* was; as a guide to wines on sale, at UK retailers, it is not overwhelmingly helpful. Even the author's stab at providing a list of favourites, to convey the impression this is one person's guide, is useless as it does not provide vintages. It is not, in my terms, a wine guide of any profundity or great utility. The same can be said of Hugh Johnson's annual guide. Indeed, Mr Johnson, through gritted teeth, once congratulated me on *Superplonk* when we met at an official dinner and said 'Dear boy, you really must have a word with your publisher. Is it really necessary to price each wine and list its retailer? Lot of work isn't it?'

It was a lot of work, yes. No other wine writer went to such trouble to compile such a guide. I was the only one who tasted almost all the supermarkets wines, the good the bad and the downright ugly, and in order to pull it off, I would, for example, go to multiple tastings to which no other writer was invited. I remember one year Tesco had around 1200 wines and I visited this retailer's head office in Cheshunt six times in a few months to achieve this work rate. And I maintained this regime over April, May, June, July and some of August each year thus always being able to boast that *Superplonk* was the most up-to-date guide of all.

Small wonder my imitators, who never tasted so many wines and had finished tasting weeks before I had done, were insubstantial in comparison. Only Matthew Jukes, with his annual *The Wine List* guide, got close to the single-minded, sole-author intimacy of *Superplonk* but even here there is no user-friendly division by retailer or strict rating of each wine and the coverage is scant compared with *Superplonk*. Matthew, who ceased publishing his guide in 2007, is now being copied in his turn, as I was by the same author in 1992, by Oz Clarke who in 2006 published the first edition of his *250 Best Wines* guide.

The only other individual who put his name to a personal wine guide has been the Australian wine waiter Matt Skinner. However, as he himself admitted in an interview with *Harpers* magazine in January 2008, the wines he lists in his *The Juice* book are not his favourites. 'The bottles I put in *The Juice* aren't my real passion. Leflaive, Domaine Romanée Conti and Ramonet are favourites, but if they went in, no one would buy the book.' So. Another phoney unmasked, another closet wine snob whose real passion is

France and its most illustrious (and most cripplingly expensive) wines, puts his name to a demotic wine guide hoping to be taken as a man of the people.

Why then am I so pleased to be no longer compiling and writing a genuine wine guide? After 15 years I got bored, sales were declining, the publisher had no idea how to manage what had become a brand in its own right, and I believed, erroneously, that the internet, with superplonk.com, was the new way forward. But above all I was getting heartily sick of all the brands supermarkets were stocking, their own-label wines were increasingly being manufactured to a price point with no clear aspiration to quality (unless that quality was sweet gunge), and I felt it was time to do something else with my drinking and writing time. I was not, like Mr Clarke, prepared to put my name to a guide of which I was not the sole author.

Closer has been the *Which? Wine Guide*, but this is a multi-author effort also and in many respects, though containing much useful information about a great many retailers (far more than *Superplonk* covered), was not structured in the same as my own. The 2005 edition, the last one I saw, only confirmed why I regard wine writing awards with such distain. On its front cover the Guide announced, amongst an abundance of turbulently ugly typography, that it was winner of the La Prix du Champagne Lanson 2003 award for Annual Wine Guide of the Year. It also claimed on its cover to be Independent, Reliable, Unbiased, all of which is undermined by the reference to that past award because the weight of the type is such that it suggests to the wine-bookshelf browser, to whom the guide is aimed, that the award is current.

Indeed, the *Which? Wine Guide 2005* could not have claimed to have been independent when it carried on its front cover what was nothing more than a banner advertisement for a lousy value champagne (which also made a mockery of the guide's claim to be reliable, as if its misjudged and snobbish attack on under-a-fiver wines hadn't done enough damage to its fragile credibility and bolstered its general user-unfriendliness). Looking at the *Which? Wine Guide* and accepting as fact that a wine jury gave it an award only hardens my belief that wine writing competitions serve only three purposes (all of which are valueless to consumers): they tickle the vanity of the winners, they give the sponsors much-needed credibility, and they permit the members of the jury to feel puffed-up with importance. That a Guide as ponderous as *Which? Wine Guide* should ever be singled out for commendation is evidence of the total lack of imagination of wine writing awards juries.

I do not know if the *Which? Wine Guide* will continue to be a two-yearly (not annual) publication but I can say that wine guide sales are in a slump. In the mid-1990s I forecast this, recognising that more and more users of wine guides, and followers of newspaper wine columns, were beginning to feel they knew their own minds, that much of what wine writers wrote was patronising and prejudiced, and that it was time to exercise their own judgements. This situation today has only got healthier (though not if you are a wine guide compiler); wine drinkers feel advice from outside is only required in special circumstances and so wine guides are now bought by a very small base of readers. Such guides are less and less relevant, more and more out-of-date when published and are no longer motivating (or profitable) for a single author to write. The manic concentration required to write mine each year for 15 years will not, you will doubtless be pleased to learn, be seen again in our lifetimes. None but the dyed-in-the-wool wine nerd needs one and very soon blogs and wine websites will take him over.

I rejoice in this possible future scenario. I am pleased to have been a part of the revolution but now it is time to write a book like this which is, in my far-from-humble opinion, a more valuable guide to wine than any I have previously published.

Appendices

1. 2003 Burgundy tasting notes
The dangers of the blanket verdict or barrel-only prognostication

Of the wines below only some are listed by shipper, others by *domaine*. Unless otherwise stated, prices are as they were at the time of tasting (in bond, duty unpaid, excluding Vat) in Spring 2005. Points are out of 20 and no wine scoring less than 14 is listed here. 14 is good, 15 on the edge of very good, 16 very good, 17 exceptional, 18 outstanding, 19 sublime, 20 to die for. Where appropriate I have given a score reflecting how the wine tastes now and how I expect it to perform at a given date in the future (which is a variable, depending as it does upon storing conditions and, vitally, each wine's cork which always ensures variability however healthy). In all cases where a barrel-sample has been tasted, the rating is provisional and any recommendation given does not apply to the finished bottled wine which may be different. Men often fall in love in light so bad they wouldn't choose a suit by it, as Maurice Chevalier remarked, and so it is with getting too excited by a barrel sample. You have to see it in its true light, bottled, before being sure.

Goedhuis & Company / www.goedhuis.com

Whites
Meursault Le Meix Sous Le Château, Jean Philippe Fichet. £198. 15 points (16.6 points in 18-months). You can to some extent mimic the effect of cellar aging by wholly decanting this finely textured wine and letting it go for a walk in the air and stretch its aromatic legs. It has slight tannins making it nicely chewy yet far from over-ripe. It is a most elegant white wine.

Meursault Le Tesson, Jean Philippe Fichet. £275. 14.5 points (maybe maybe 16 in 2007/8). Loosely knit, which time can never repair, but this is the house style and what makes me like it as a potential solid ager is the hints of old-fashioned gaminess it will display if cellared. It is not as fine as the wine above from the same grower.

Reds
Gevrey-Chambertin Vieilles Vignes, Domaine Christian Serafin. £295. 16.5 points. Organic, unfiltered and lots of new wood (hence the expense of the wine, or a major contributing factor at any rate). This is really fine with craggy tannins of weight and

wit. 'Tough when first tasted back in November,' the shipper told me in Spring 2004 but the wood/fruit/alcohol balance is superb. It will age to possibly 17.5 over the next 3 to 5 years but I would drink it now as well.

Morey St Denis 1er Cru, Domaine Christian Sérafin. £349. 16 points. Even better for immediate drinking. It has superb colour, acids and tannins and some beguiling touches to its perfume. It is impressively svelte yet full of character and should develop that characteristic gamy, wild mushroom undertone certain Morey producers revel in.

Gevrey Chambertin Vieilles Vignes, Domaine Géantet Pansiot. £225. 17 points. This was one of my favourite reds from this shipper, the one (of two) I would buy myself if I could afford it. This tasting, tannin-wise and with Gevreys, just got raunchier and raunchier. Stunningly crunchy tannins and a touch of licorice Might rate 18.5 in a couple of years, or it might not. I love it young. Under £20 a bottle ex-Bond is pretty good for a grower so bold and principled (by which I mean he is obviously not trying to make show wines, but real wines).

Chambolle Musigny Vieilles Vignes, Domaine Géantet Pansiot. £225. 16 points. Even a sign of chocolate in the fruit of this beauty.

Côte de Nuits Villages Clos du Chapeau, Domaine de l'Arlot. £139. 15 points now, 17 (?) in 2008/9. Interesting price for such sturdy tannins. Has an agreeable fatness to its pluminess. Being a barrel sample, I would not like to bet my house on any prediction made here; however, this is a meticulous estate, trying for minimum interference and I would guess fining is light so I might bet a window box if not the house.

Volnay Vieilles Vignes, Nicolas Potel. £159. Great price! 16 points now. Possibly 17 around 2008/10, thanks to its tight tannins).

Pommard 1er Pezerolles, Nicolas Potel. £259. 16.5 points now. 18.5 points 2008/12. Had to retaste this one several times as it is one of my favourites for aging (and for buying and drinking now, i.e. in 2005). Has an immensely impressive structure and texture, almost arrogant in its confident classiness.

Chambolle Musigny 1er Cru les Fuées, Nicolas Potel. £275. 16 points. Elegant yet rugged, bursting with style yet has tender finesse, great tannins and a finely extruded fruit finish.

Bonnes Mares Grand Cru, Nicolas Potel. £425 (x case of 6). 17 points. High class price but high class act. Tight tannins as finely rippled as a young Baryshnikov's buttocks. It is a pity that any fining may remove character.

Observations: I did not like the alcohol levels on Château de Chorey wines, as a matter of interest (routinely, Beaunes at 14%). There was one other, good-value red wine of interest here, Mercurey 1er Cru, Domaine Brintet (16 points, £110) which had a most attractive tannic suppleness and therefore interesting maturation potential for the 2 years at least. Indeed, I suspect the less known areas, those not in demand from the foolish international drink-the-label market, may turn out to be the star buys of the 2003s.

Montrachet Fine Wine Merchants / www.montrachetwine.com

Whites

Domaine Thibert Pouilly Vinzelles Les Longeays. 14 points. £95. A lot of creamy wood.

Domaine Billaud-Simon Chablis 1er Cru Les Vaillons. 14.5 points. £130. More darned creamy wood. Chablis? Not as I know it.

Domaine Alain Chavy Puligny Montrachet Les Charmes. 13 points. £184. I know. It rates too low for inclusion, but I thought I would include it. Too much wood for my liking. (In 2003, growers may have been persuaded to put more wine in new wood to allow greater oxygenation of the liquid and to reduce any excessive enthusiasm of the wine due to its extraordinarily hot vintage birth.) I felt the same about Domaine Yves Boyer-Martenot's Meursault 1er Cru Perrières and Domaine Michel Bouzeareau et Fils' Meursault Les Grands Charrons.

Domaine Jean-Marc Pillot Chassagne-Montrachet 1er Cru Les Chevenottes. 16 points. £261. At last, here, some class and potential to reach 17.5 points, and go gamy and burned-hay-like, in a few years (or maybe months).

Reds

Domaine Jean-Jacques Girard.

Savigny Les Beaune 1er Cru Les Fourneaux. 14 points. £123.

Savigny Les Beaune 1er Cru Les Serpentieres. 16.5 points. £133. Restrained sumptuousness, very fine and dry.

Savigny Les Beaune 1er Cru Les Peuillets. 16 points. £144. Bright cherry fruit. Good drinking now.

Savigny Les Beaune 1er Cru Les Laviéres. 16 points. £148. As above, but with more plumminess to the finish.

Domaine Chandon de Brialles

Pernand Vergelesses 1er Cru Île de Vergelesses. 15 points. £184. Good tannins with acid iffy. Good drinking now.

Corton Les Bressandes. 16 points. £322. Bitter almond and cherry, wholly atypical, but cheerful, New World undertone (heresy!), enjoy now.

Domaine Rossignol-Trapet

Beaune 1er Cru Teurons. 17 points. £179. Calm, classy, possible rating two points higher given time, if the tannins remain intact and the fruit is faithful (in 2/3 years in 2008). I really like this wine, but find it impossible accurately to assess its future (maddening!). Buy it and invite me around to taste it with you.

Gevrey-Chambertin 1er Cru Petite-Chapelle. 17 points. £240. Lovely perfume! Grand design. Classy. Fruit unguent, with those craggy tannins to give it depth and complexity. Not pinot as we know it, but that goes for every wine here doesn't it?

Domaine Daniel Rion

Nuits St Georges Les Grands Vignes. 16 points. £200. Huge tannins appeal to me, crisp acidified fruit. Hmm. Drink now. Gosh, what a conundrum! Let me add that of all the world's wines, I believe red burgundies are the most tricky to estimate when they will reach their apogee of tastefulness and rich perfectability (well, few do this in any vintage, but bear with me). I sometimes find that after 5 years a burgundy seems over-the-hill only for it stage a recovery and 2 years later to be fine. But often only fine for a few months, infuriatingly, as if it mocks the drinker with its capriciousness and moodiness. I waited for six years for a Leroy Pommard 1998 to come good only for it to be that way for 3 months only and then only one bottle per dozen was at that peak because the cork conferred such variability, and so there was another factor adding to the caprice. You wonder why I love screwcaps? Interestingly, following years of screwcapping of 'museum' wines by such Burgundy co-ops as Buxy (so it was possible to analyse the cellared wine later without cork interference or taint), the Nuits St Georges *négociants*, Moillard, are introducing a range of screwcapped burgundies. It is reported the range is aimed at 'younger French consumers' whatever that might mean and UK supermarkets are a target. Boisset, another large Burgundy business, is also screwcapping some of its high-end products.

Nuits St Georges 1er Cru Les Vignes Ronds. 17 points. £286. Incredible concentration and longevity potential (if the fruit lasts with charm and does not go foxy or paranoid). Encrusted with tannins and a possible perfect 20-point score, perhaps for 480 hours only, in 2008. Or there again, who the hell knows? Not even the producer.

Vosne Romanée 1er Cru Les Chaumes. 16.5 points. £286. Almost as good as the wine above. Has, though, slightly more bravado on its finish and will, as a consequence, drink solidly much earlier.

Domaine Jacques Cacheux et Fils

Vosne Romanée. 17 points. £169. Immense tannic power. Even a hint of chocolate. My God, what were the grapes going through to be spoonfed Green & Black's?

Vosne Romanée 1er Cru Les Suchots. 17.5 points. £391. Chewy, rich, very big and stolid with promise. To be given now to heart patients and angina sufferers.

Echézeaux. 17 points now, possibly 19 in 2010. What a gamble! Possibly a gem though. Will go gamy, if the fruit holds out, if the acids don't detach themselves. Tannically nigh-perfect, alcohol balance excellent. Please! Buy it and invite me for a drink on New Year's Eve 2009 so I can swallow my words (or choke on them).

Domaine Amiot-Servelle

Chambolle-Musigny 1er Cru Les Charmes. 16 points. £299. Tannins, yes, but fining and filtering yet to come – who knows? This was a barrel sample. Might be wonderful. Might be a dog in 2 years.

Domaine Lucien Boillot et Fils
Gevrey Chambertin Les Évocelles. 16.5 points. £187. Potently tannicity, berried-up-to-its-neck richness. Hmm. Good potential surely here.

Louis Boillot et Fils
Vosne Romanée Vieilles Vignes. 16 points. £189. Catches the teeth, the tannins, but does the fruit get the point? The point is will the fruit last alongside the tannins, not fade? Drink now and avoid the question.

Vincent Girardin
Marsannay. 16 points. £102. Bargain price. Best Marsannay I've ever tasted. Drink now.
Chambolle Musigny Vieilles Vignes. 14 points. £187. A little too fruity? Rather obvious, certainly.
Corton. 16 points. £238. Lots of sweet fruit.
Volnay 1er Cru Les Santenots. 16.5 points. £199. Richly textured fruit, most attractive. Big tannins. Finely judged by its maker.

Domaine Marquis d'Angerville
Volnay 1er Cru Champans. 16 points. £352. Better than the 2001, 2002 from this producer which had some critics – not me – slavering.
Volnay 1er Cru Clos des Ducs. 16 points. £493. Crunchy, rich, very complete.

Bertrand Ambroise / www.genesiswines.com
Nuits St Georges 1er Cru Clos des Argillières. 16.5 points. £281. So typical of the 2003 vintage with its gorgeous tannins (or rather, if typicity is the key here, its tannins gorgeous or otherwise). This is nicely drinkable and fine, with texture, and chocolate to go with the gamy cherries (though these are subtle and would be brought out over time, if the acids and tannins permit).
Clos Vougeot. 14 points. £465. Just goes to show how not all 2003 show great tannins. This is sweet, rather forward, somewhat too fruity for me.

Whites
Maison Deux Montille
Meursault Les Grand Charrons. 14 points. £197. Rather thick and creamy (wood), and rather obvious. In 3/5 years? 16 points? I really don't know. Hmm. Best avoid.
Meursault Les Rougeots. 15 points. £231. Much better acid structure.
Puligny 1er Cru Les Champs Gains. 13.5 points. £315. 1st bottle, corked. 2nd, okay, some acid charm.

Corton Charlemagne Grand Cru. 16 points, drink soon. £498. Lot of money, only marginally a lot of wine. Oh, I am being mean. But it should develop excitingly (perhaps, given impeccable corks – which hardly exist of course).

Domaine Hubert & Olivier Lamy
Puligny Montrachet Les Tremblots. 15 points, drink soon. Lovely plump texture not overcooked. Very fine future before it, given the usual caveats.
Other whites, from Jean-Phillippe Fichet, Guy Amiot, Bernard Morey, Cordier, I was not remotely struck by.

Reds
Domaine de Montille, Maison Deux Montille, Domaine Gouges, not struck by. Domaine de Courcel had a good Pommard 1er Cru Les Rugiens. 16 points, drink soon.
Domaine Bize
Savigny es Beaune Aux Grands Liards. 16.5 points. £175. Not a bad price for such a little cracker. Beautifully structured and finely paced tannins, acids and fruit.
I was not forcibly so impressed by the same producer's Aux Veregelesses Savigny les Beaune, 14 points.
In the COte de Nuits, Domaine Lignier Michelot had a decent Morey St Denis en la Rue de Vergy, 16 points, £180.
A curate's egg also from Domaine Engel, whose wines I have for years admired for their spiciness and bulk (an untypicality of almost iconoclastic proportions) in some years. Réne Engel's Echezeaux and Clos Vougeot, both so-called grand crus, were not as resiliently fine – too juicy for me – as his Vosne Romanée at half the price. René Engel Vosne Romanée. 16 points. I would buy this wine if I had the room in the house. And if I had the money.

Domaine Confuron-Cotetidot
Good tannins throughout here, though the wine is easily passed off as 'the jury must still be out.' This producer's 2000 Clos du Vougeot was, though, a magnificent 18.5 pointer (drunk in the summer of 2007).

Domaine Robert Chevillon
Nuits St Georges 1er Cru Les Chaignots. 16 points. £241. Love these tannins, squire! Just love 'em.
Nuits St Georges 1er Cru Les Cailles. 15 points. £309.

I did not taste *Domaine Leflaive* from Corney and Barrow (though to read the purple prose accompanying these wines would bring a blush to any Feste's cheek). Neither did I get to taste any of the producers' wines sold by the combative Winchester-based merchant Stone, Vine & Sun. Simon Taylor from here strikes me, on the evidence of his prose, as a sensible, unhurried fellow and his discrete set of producers, Grivot, Fourrier, Arlaud, Digioia-Royer, Cathiard, Lequin-Colin, Chofflet-Valdenaire, and Dureuil-Janthial, is interesting. The list, if still available, is worth perusal: www.stonevine.co.uk.

2. UK Labelling Deceptions

At various retailer tastings in 2007, I found the following deceptions (and there are thousands more examples).

Torronero Sauvignon Blanc 2006 from Spain (Tesco, £6.99) has 10% verdejo added. Nepenthe Tryst Sauvignon Blanc 2006 from Australia (Tesco, £8.99) has 11.6% semillon and 2.4% other unspecified grapes added. Excelsior Paddock Sauvignon Blanc 2006 from South Africa (Tesco £5.99) includes 10% viognier. Flagstone Free Run Sauvignon Blanc 2006 from South Africa (Tesco, £9.99) is only 85% sauvignon, the remaining 15% is semillon. Kendall-Jackson Vintners Reserve Sauvignon Blanc 2006 from California (Tesco, £8.99) has 5.2% semillon and sauvignon musque added. Tesco Finest Sonoma Chardonnay from California (£7.99) contains 2.5% muscat. Grove Mill Pinot Gris 2006 from New Zealand (Tesco, £8.99) is hardly pure pinot gris with 5% gewürztraminer and 8% pinot blanc in the recipe. Kendall-Jackson Vintners Reserve Pinot Noir 2005 from California (Tesco, £8.99) dares to include 9% syrah, 6% merlot and 4% zinfandel. A pinot noir? Hardly. It's a blend and its label is a bald-faced lie. Marquesa de la Cruz Old Vines Garnacha 2006 from Spain (Tesco, £5.49) has 12% shiraz the age of which vines is not revealed. Napa Family Vineyards Cabernet Sauvignon 2005 from California (Tesco, £10.99) has 5% merlot. Trinity Hill Gimblett Road Cabernet Sauvignon/Merlot 2000 from New Zealand (Tesco, £14.99) does not feel the need to include on its front label the fact that 15% is also cabernet franc. Tesco Finest Napa Merlot 2004 from California (£7.99) is only 95% as advertised. 5% is cabernet sauvignon. Ragged Point Syrah 2006 from California (Tesco, £6.99) sneaks, would you believe, 3% muscat into the wine. Who would buy a Syrah/Muscat? Perhaps no-one. Syrah sounds so much purer by its lonesome.

But at least Tesco makes it clears to wine tasters, on its tasting notes where I gleaned the above information, what the constituent grapes are in wines otherwise called by a single varietal labelling. Sainsbury is not so open minded, providing no such insights in its tasting booklets and wine lists.

At Oddbins, a feeble shadow of the once ballsy retailer it once was, there is more clues as to the grapes in its wines. Lourensford Three Peaks Chardonnay 2006 from the Cape (£6.99) has 5.5% viognier added whilst Lourensford Three Peaks Merlot 2006 (£6.99) has all of 15% shiraz. Pepperwood Grove Syrah 2005 from California (£7.49) has 2% petite syrah. A small crime perhap. But it makes its labelling untruthful. De Martino Legado Carmenere 2005 from Chile (£7.99) is only 90% carmenere. The other 10% is cabernet sauvignon. The prize at this retailer, however, must go to Anakena Ona Pinot Noir/Merlot 2005 from Chile (£8.99) a bizarre sounding marriage which is even bizarrer, a genuine menage a quatre forsooth, when one learns that it also adds 3% syrah and 3% viognier to its unlikely relationship.

Morrisons has some nicely misleading labels. The Dreaming Tree Verdejo 2006 from Spain (£4.99) is not solely verdejo but 15% viura. Why not say so? Who in God's name shopping at this witless retailer, which was once so virile before it swallowed Safeway, is going to seek out 100% verdejo? Morrisons The Best Australian Chardonnay nv (£7.49) includes 9% semillon. Hardly the best let alone any kind of chardonnay is it? First Sighting Sauvignon Blanc 2006 from South Africa (£7.99) has 12% semillon. Isla Negra Merlot Rosé 2006 from Chile (£6.99) is nothing wholly of the kind being 15% cabernet sauvignon. Morrisons The Best Australian Shiraz 2005 (£7.55) comprises 4% cabernet sauvignon. Morrisons The Best Californian Zinfandel 2005 (£5.99), one of most awful confected gunges I tasted in 2007, has 10% petite syrah, 6% carignan, and 7% rubired (this last being a variety created in a Californian university wine laboratory from a crossing of the port grapes tinto cão and alicante ganzin and is, so I am told, popular in the USA as a red food colouring agent such its richness of hue).

The Co-op, in so many other respects such an honourable and ethically dispositioned retailer, is not above deceiving its customers by misleading single varietal labelling. Its own label Coonwarra Reserve Cabernet Sauvignon 2004 from Australia (£5.99), an extremely fiesty bargain, nevertheless cheats by not disclosing on its front label its affiliation with 6% shiraz and 4% cabernet sauvignon. I love the wine. I hate its deceiving ways. Luis Felipe Edwards Reserve Sauvigon Blanc 2006 from Chile (£5.99) is reserved, frontlabelwise, about its 5% inclusion of viognier and the same producer is also coy about the 10% shiraz in its Reserva Cabernet Sauvignon 2006 (£5.99). Jack Tone Ranch Merlot Reserve 2005 from California (£7.99) is only 76% of this grape, the rest being 13% petite syrah and 11% petit verdot. A merlot? Don't make me laugh. However, at least the Co-op stocks the wine with the most honest label I saw in all of 2007, Bellingham Merlot With A Dash of Malbec 2005 (£7.99, and from the Cape).

Waitrose is a dab hand at disguising blends. Graham Beck Waterside Chardonnay 2006 from South Africa (£4.99) is 14% colombard. Wente Chardonnay 2005 from California (£6.99) contains 2% gewürztraminer and 1% semillon. Duckhorn Sauvignon Blanc 2005, also from California (at £17.50 would you credit) is even more outrageous containing as it does 25% semillon! River Route Limited Edition Merlot 2004 from Romania (£4.79) has 15% cabernet sauvignon. Concha y Toro

A

The following additives are allowed in Australian wines

Acacia / Gum arabic.
Activated carbon.
Albumin / Egg white.
Ammonium bisulphite.
Ammonium sulphate.
Ammonium sulphite.
Argon.
Ascorbic acid.
Bentonite.
Betaglucanase.
Calcium alginate.
Calcium carbonate.
Calcium phytate.
Carbon dioxide.
Casein.
Citric acid.
Copper sulphate.
Diammonium phosphate.
Gelatine.
Isinglass.
Kaolin.
Malic acid.
Metatartaric acid.
Nitrogen.
Oxygen.
Pectolytic enzymes.
Potassium alginate.
Potassium bisulphite.
Potassium caseinate.
Potassium disulphite.
Potassium ferrocyanide.
Potassium hydrogen tartrate / Potassium bitartrate (Cream of tartar).
Potassium metabisulphite.
Potassium sorbate.
Potassium tartrate.
Silicon dioxide / Silica gel / Silica.

Sorbic acid.
Sulphur dioxide.
Tannins.
Tartaric acid.
Thiamin hydrochloride.
Yeast cell walls.
Yeasts (selected).

B

Additives that are permissible in the production of American wines sold in the European Economic Community

I. ECOLOGICAL PRACTICES FOR WINE OF SOUND-RIPE GRAPES
A. The U.S. is pleased to acknowledge the EEC's willingness to permit all U.S. wines treated with the following to be imported into and offered for sale for human consumption in the EEC on a permanent basis;

Acacia (Gum Arabic)
*Acidex
Activated Carbon
Agar Agar
Albumen (including Egg White and Egg White Solution)
*AMA Special Gelatin Solution
Ammonium Carbonate
Ammonium Phosphate (mono-and diabasic)
Ascorbic Acid, Isoascorbic Acid (Erythorbic Acid)
Autolyzed Yeast (including *Amber ByF and *Amberex 1003)
Bentonite (Wyoming Clay)
*Bentonite Compound
Bentonite Slurry
Calcium Carbonate
Carbon Dioxide

Casein
Citric Acid
★Cold Mix Sparkolloid
Compressed Air
Copper Sulphate
Diatomaceous Earth
Enzymes Pectolytic
Gelatin
Gelatin Slurry
Granular Cork
Isinglass
★Klerzyme H.T.
★Koldone
Milk Powder
Nitrogen Gas
Oak Chips, Charred
Oak Chips, Uncharred and Untreated
Oak Chips Sawdust, Uncharred and
Untreated
Potassium Bitartrate
Potassium Carbonate
Potassium Caseinate
Potassium Metabisulfite
Potassium Sorbate (provided the finished
wine contains not in excess of 300 mg
Sorbic Acid per liter)
Silica Gel (Colloidal Silicon Dioxide–
30%)
Sorbic Acid (provided the finished wine
contains not in excess of 300 mg/liter)
Silica Gel (Colloidal Silicon Dioxide–
30%)
Sorbic Acid (provided the finished wine
contains not in excess of 300 mg/liter)
★Sparkaloid No. 1
★Sparkaloid No. 2
★Takamine Cellulase 4,000
Tannin
Tartaric Acid
★Uni-Loid Type 43B

B. The U.S. is pleased to acknowledge

the EEC's willingness to implement
regulatory amendments to permit:

(1) all U.S. wines treated with the
following to be imported into and
offered for sale for human consumption
in the EEC on a permanent basis;

Fermcozyme Vin
★Fermcozyme Vin XX
Ferrous Sulphate
Mineral Oil
Oxygen
★Wine Clarifier
★Yeastex 61

(2) all U.S. wines treated with the
following to be imported into and
offered for sale for human consumption
in the EEC for a period of five years
from the date of this letter, the five year
period being for the purpose of
allowing time for further study and
discussion;

Antifoam Agents (such as 'A', AF
Emulsion, 'C',
Atmos 300) and ★Defoaming Agents
Calcium Sulphate (Gypsum)
★Cufex
Fumaric Acid
Ion Exchange
Lactic Acid
Malic Acid
★Metafine
Polyvinylpolypyrrolidone (PVPP)
Polyvinylpyrrolidone (PVP)
★Sulfex

(3) all U.S. wines produced using
Aqueous Sugar Solutions, in States
where this enological practice is allowed

as of September 1, 1982, to be imported into and offered for sale for human consumption in the EEC until March 15, 1984, this period being for the purpose of allowing time for further study and discussion;

(4) all U.S. wines complying with U.S. regulations governing Sulfur Dioxide to be imported into and offered for sale for human consumption in the EEC for a period of one year after the EEC's revised limitations for Sulfur Dioxide enter into force;

(5) all U.S. sparkling wines to which Hydrogen Peroxide has been added to facilitate secondary fermentation to be imported into and offered for sale for human consumption in the EEC for a period of five years from the date of this letter;

(6) all U.S. wines treated with the following to be imported into and offered for sale for human consumption in the EEC for a period of one year from the date of this letter and in this connection, the U.S. announces that it has proposed regulations deleting the following substances from the list of substances approved for the treatment of wines produced in the U.S.;

Acetic Acid
Actiferm (Roviferm)
Afferin
Bone Charcoal
Carbon
Clari-Preme
Combustion Product Gas
Egg Yolks

Ferrix
Freon C-318
Fulgar
Promine D
Protovac PV-7916
Ridex High
Sodium Bisulfite
Sodium Carbonate
Sodium Caseinate
Sodium Isoascorbate (Sodium Erythorbate)
Sodium Metabisulfite
Sodium Sorbate
Tansul Clay No. 7
Tansul Clay No. 710
Tansul Clay No. 711
Veltol (Maltol)
Veltol Plus (Ethyl Maltol)
Wine Clarifier (Clari-Vine B)
Yeastex

C. The U.S. is pleased to announce that it has proposed regulatory revisions delisting the asterisked names referenced in A, B(1), and B(2) above and relisting them by the generic name of their components. Listed below are the components which do not already appear in the listing for A, B(1), and B(2):

(1) We understand that all U.S. wines treated with components listed in A and partially relisted here may continue to be imported into and offered for sale for human consumption in the EEC on a permanent basis;

Calcium Salt of Malic Acid
Calcium Salt of Tartaric Acid
Carageenan
Cellulase

Cellulose

(2) We understand that all U.S. wines treated with components listed in B(1) and partially relisted here may continue to be imported into and offered for sale for human consumption in the EEC on a permanent basis;

Catalase
Glucose Oxidase
Soy Flour

(3) We understand that all U.S. wines treated with components listed in B(2) and partially relisted here may continue to be imported into and offered for sale for human consumption in the EEC for a period of five years from the date of this letter, the five year period being for the purpose of allowing time for further study and discussion;

Dimethyl Polsiloxane
Polyoxyethylene-40-Monostearate
Sodium Carboxymethylcellulose
Sorbitan Monostearate
Ferrocyanide Compounds (sequestered complexes)

D. With respect to the analogical substances authorized for wines produced in the EEC, the U.S. acknowledges the EEC's intention to delete 'Dried Blood Powder' from the list of substances approved for the treatment of wines produced in the EEC.

E. The U.S. and the EEC both recognize the need to enter into scientific collaboration in order to compare the methods which are actually used to reduce the content of undesirable metal ions in wine, to consider the use of allyl isothiocyanate to create a sterile atmosphere on wine and to consider the use of Metatartaric Acid for the treatment of wine.'

C

List of oenological practices and processes authorised for wines originating in the Republic of South Africa with the following prescriptions or, in their absence, under the conditions laid down in South African rules:

(1) Aeration with argon, nitrogen or oxygen
(2) Heat treatment
(3) Use of fresh, sound and undiluted yeast from recently completed fermentation
(4) Centrifuging and filtration with or without filtering agents on condition that no undesirable residue is left in the end product
(5) Use of yeasts for wine production
(6) Use of preparations of yeast cell walls
(7) Addition of polyvinylpolypyrrolidone
(8) Use of lactic acid bacteria
(9) Addition of ammonium phosphate and di-ammonium phosphate
(10) Addition of ammonium sulphate
(11) Addition of ammonium sulphite or ammonium bisulphite
(12) Addition of thiamin hydrochloride
(13) Use of carbon dioxide, argon or nitrogen to create an inert atmosphere

and to protect against oxidation

(14) Addition of potassium bisulphite or potassium meta-bisulphite

(15) Addition of sulphur dioxide

(16) Addition of sodium meta-bisulphite

(17) Addition of potassium sorbate and sorbic acid

(18) Addition of ascorbic acid

(19) Addition of tartaric acid, malic acid and citric acid for acidification purposes, provided that the initial acidity content is not raised by more than 4 grams per litre, expressed as tartaric acid

(20) Addition of potassium tartrate and potassium-bitartrate

(21) Addition of potassium carbonate

(22) Addition of calcium carbonate

(23) Addition of sodium carbonate

(24) Addition of potassium bicarbonate

(25) Clarification by means of one or more of the following substances:

– edible gelatine

– bentonite

– isinglass

– casein and potassium caseinate

– egg albumin, milk albumin

– kaolin

– pectolytic enzymes

– silicon dioxide

– tannin

– enzymatic preparations of betaglu-canase.

(26) Addition of tannin

(27) Treatment with charcoal (activated carbon)

(28) Use of wood shavings

(29) Addition of potassium ferrocyanide provided that after the treatment the wine must be analysed and test free of any cyanides and cyanates

(30) Addition of acacia or arabic gum only after completion of alcoholic fer-mentation

(31) Addition of potassium, sodium and calcium alginate for bottle fermented sparkling wine

(32) Addition of copper sulphate

(33) Addition of caramel only for liqueur wine

(34) Addition of wine or dried grape distillate or of neutral alcohol of vinous origin for the manufacture of liqueur wines

(35) Addition of grape must or rectified concentrated grape must for the sweetening of wine

(36) Addition of calcium hydroxide

(37) Addition of sodium hydroxide

(38) Addition of lysozyme

(39) Electrodialysis to guarantee tartaric stabilisation of the wine

(40) Use of urease to reduce the urea content in the wine

2. List of oenological practices and processes authorised for wines originating in the Community with the following prescriptions or, in their absence, under the conditions laid down in Community rules:

(1) Aeration or bubbling using argon, nitrogen or oxygen

(2) Heat treatment

(3) Use in dry wines of fresh lees which are sound and undiluted and contain yeasts resulting from the recent vinifica-tion of dry wine

(4) Centrifuging and filtration, with or without an inert filtering agent, on condition that no undesirable residue is left in the products so treated

(5) Use of yeasts for wine production

(6) Use of preparations of yeast cell wall

(7) Use of polyvinylpolypyrrolidone

(8) Use of lactic acid bacteria in a vinous suspension

(9) Addition of one or more of the following substances to encourage the growth of yeasts:

(i) addition of:

– diammonium phosphate or ammonium sulphate

– ammonium sulphite or ammonium bisulphite

(ii) addition of thiamin hydrochloride

(10) Use of carbon dioxide, argon or nitrogen, either alone or combined, solely in order to create an inert atmosphere and to handle the product shielded from the air

(11) Addition of carbon dioxide

(12) Use of sulphur dioxide, potassium bisulphite or potassium metabisulphite, which may also be called potassium disulphite or potassium pyrosulphite

(13) Addition of sorbic acid or potassium sorbate

(14) Addition of L–ascorbic acid

(15) Addition of citric acid for wine stabilisation purposes, provided that the final content in the treated wine does not exceed 1 gram per litre

(16) Use of tartaric acid for acidification purposes, provided that the initial acidity content is not raised by more than 2,5 g/l expressed as tartaric acid

(17) Use of one or more of the following substances for deacidification purposes:

– neutral potassium tartrate

– potassium bicarbonate

– calcium carbonate, which may contain small quantities of the double calcium salt of L (+) tartaric and L (–) malic acids

– a homogenous preparation of tartaric acid and calcium carbonate in equivalent proportions and finely pulverised

– calcium tartrate or tartaric acid

(18) Clarification by means of one or more of the following substances for oenological use:

– edible gelatine

– bentonite

– isinglass

– casein and potassium caseinate

– egg albumin, milk albumin

– kaolin

– pectolytic enzymes

– silicon dioxide as a gel or colloidal solution

– tannin

– enzymatic preparations of betaglucanase

(19) Addition of tannin

(20) Treatment with charcoal for oenological use (activated carbon)

(21) Treatment of:

– white wines and rosé wines, with potassium ferrocyanide

– red wines, with potassium ferrocyanide or with calcium phytate, provided that the wine so treated contains residual iron

(22) Addition of metatartaric acid

(23) Use of acacia after completion of fermentation

(24) Use of DL–tartaric acid, also called racemic acid, or of its neutral salt of potassium for precipitating excess calcium

(25) Use for the manufacture of sparkling wines obtained by fermentation in bottle and with the lees separated by disgorging:

– of calcium alginate, or

– of potassium alginate

(26) Use of copper sulphate

(27) Addition of potassium bitartrate to assist the precipitation of tartar

(28) Addition of caramel to reinforce the colour of liqueur wines

(29) Use of calcium sulphate for the production of certain quality liqueur wines p.s.r.

(30) Addition of lysozyme

(31) Addition of wine or dried grape distillate or of neutral alcohol of vinous origin for the manufacture of liqueur wines

(32) Addition of sucrose, concentrated grape must or rectified concentrated grape must to increase the natural alcoholic strength of grapes, grape must or wine

(33) Addition of grape must or rectified concentrated grape must for sweetening of wine

(34) Partial concentration by physical processes, including reverse osmosis, to increase the natural alcoholic strength of grape must or wine

(35) Electrodialysis to guarantee tartaric stabilisation of the wine

(36) Use of urease to reduce the urea content in the wine.

D

Additives cleared for use in Co-op wines

Bentonite. This is a hugely versatile aluminium silicate clay which though it can be used as cat litter is employed by a winemaker mostly to remove protein particles in white wines and also in some reds. It is used in detox diets, so it is tolerated by the human digestive system though no trace of it should remain in any wine once bottled.

Betaglucanase. This is an enzyme, derived from the naturally occurring fungus Trichoderma harzianum, used to improve the filtering potential of a sweet wine made from grapes affected by noble rot or botrytis. In such wines, the liquid can be goo-ily thick at certain stages of its development and filtering may be considered essential to ensure the wine does not re-ferment in bottle.

Calcium alginate. This, as alginic acid, is derived from seaweed and is used in ice cream and cheese as a thickening agent. It is used to clarify sparkling wines made by the champagne method.

Casein. Derived from cow's milk this is used as a fining agent in white wines to remove any dark matter. It should not remain in the wine.

Charcoal. Used like casein, and is a product of wood distillation.

Gelatine. Derived from animals and useful for removing tannins in red wines when these are present in a large molecular concentration. Should not remain in the wine.

Isinglass. This comes from fish bladders and is used to remove tannins the winemaker considers in excess to his/her requirements or contrary to the fresh style of wine aimed for. No isinglass residues should remain but it does make the wine unsuitable for a strict vegetarian.

Kaolin. A silicate, or mineral clay, used to clarify wine and diasappear, having done its job, leaving no impression of its use.

Ovalbumin. Or egg white, is most effective at removing tannins but it also, like other of the clearing agents on the list here, also results in a loss of character. In my view, egg white is the destroyer of the soul of many a red wine. It is a nothing short of a scandal that its use is not indicated on back labels in as large a type as any health warning.

Lactalbumin. Derived from cow's milk and used like casein to remove sediment in a wine.

Pectinolytic enzymes. These pectinases occur naturally in berries but can be added to the must to speed clarification and settling. They can also be used post-ferment to boost the aromas of certain white varietal wines.

Polyvinyl-polypyrrolidone (PVPP). Is used, as a white powder, to extract tannins and generally make any liquid, not just wine, clearer and less cloudy. Brewers use it to ensure a long shelf life for their products. One proprietory brand of this, called Polyclar, is, as I learned when I asked the company which makes it, a polymerized and crosslinked NVP, vinyl-pyrrolidone. NVP is composed of acetylene and methanol/formaldehyde. Acetylene is derived from limestone and coal. Methanol is a colourless alcohol which bonds with water (and in sufficient quantity can be a nerve poison) and its unique production method, from petroleum, is complex. Formaldehyde is one of modern civilisation's more unfriendly chemical concoctions as it pours out of car exhausts and from cigarettes. The horrendous Greek forest fires of the summer of 2007 would have forced formaldehyde levels to rise as pollutions level rose also. Formaldehyde is, then, carcinogenic. I have no hesitation, however, in reassuring any worried reader than she will not get cancer from any wine treated with PVPP. I am not trying here to scaremonger. I am merely pointing out the nature of some of the treatments used in everyday wine manufacture. It is, surely, nice to know these things.

Potassium alginate. Is an extract of seaweed used to remove tartrates which appear, if not removed, as crystals mostly in white wines (which being served chilled enhances tartrate visibility and its formation into clusters). I generally applaud a wine with these crystals in it as their presence demonstrates a caring winemaker who did not wish to remove character from the wine which using potassium alginate can do. Tartrate crystals are harmless anyway. I am quite happy to crunch them between my teeth when the dregs of a bottle are poured out.

Potassium caseinate. As skimmed milk powder it can assist in the rectifying of oxidation in a white wine and reduce tannins in a red.

Potassium ferrocyanide. Also known as blue fining and yellow prussiate of potash this treatment sounds fearsomely colourful whatever it's called, but in fact it clarifies a wine by ridding it of iron and copper residues.

Silicon dioxide. A liquid silicon which work ingeniously simply by intermarrying with proteins thus making them too heavy to stay suspended in the wine. They drop to the bottom of the tank for simple removal and/or filtering.

Tannin. Powered clearing agent, vegetatively sourced (from oak galls and chestnuts), which removes proteins like the substance above. For many wines going on sale not far from vintage, when settling of proteins and other matter (from yeasts and grape residue) cannot take place naturally as would occur in a barrel over many months, proteins left in the wine would spoil it.

NOTES

1   For the record, the wines most prominently involved were Poderadorfer
    Kaisergarten Beerenauslese 1983, Pamhagener 1979, Edelstaler Kaisergarten
    Trockenbeerenauslese 1981, Weidener Kaisergarten Trockenbeerenauslese
    1981, Edelstaler Kupserhohe Eiswein 1980, and Mönchhofer Steingang
    Trockenbeerenauslese 1980. I got these names from scrutinising the archive of
    the laboratory of the Michigan Department of Agriculture. The lab found
    some wines 'had modest amounts, about 100 parts per million, of diethylene
    glycol, which is used in some kinds of antifreeze.' One other guilty German
    was Haus of Franz Liebfraumilch 1984 from the Nahe region.]

2   Gluck, Gluck, Gluck, BBC 1996.

3   If you want to try Albet y Noya wines (the cava is more exciting than scores
    of champagnes) in the UK, contact the company's distributor Vintage Roots
    via http://www.vintageroots.co.uk.

4   But who needs any of these wines? There are, even if one is restricted to the
    shelves of the last named retailer, several terrific wines on sale there which are
    not high in alcohol, are fairly priced, and deliver fruit of charm and concentra-
    tion. They are the wines which writers should be encouraging their readers to
    enjoy rather than the blistering blockbusters which stand out in wine tastings
    and wine competitions by virtue of their aggressive richness. Just leafing
    through my tasting notes for the Tesco tasting in the autumn of 2007 I found
    some excellent specimens which deliver the goods. Three Choirs Aromatic
    White 2006 (11%, £5.49) is a memorable English white. Château Bonnet
    Entre-deux-Mers Bordeaux Blanc 2006 (12%, £5.99) is prim and poised. Les
    Celliers de Céres Pouilly Fumé 2006 (12.5%, £7.99) is lean and elegantly
    fashioned. J.P Dubost Moulin a Vent 2005 (12%, £9.99) reminds me of
    yesteryear's beaujolais glories. Reserve Crois des Bardes Lalande-de-Pomerol
    2005 (12.5%, £12.99) is classy and firm. Tre Castelli Mon Ferrato Dolcetto
    2006 (12%, £4.99) is wonderfully fresh and perky. And I could go but not for
    long. So there are wines at the UK's largest wine merchant, a few, which are
    not sodden with alcohol yet which perform with wit and verve. Why not
    more of them?

5   However, Tesco, Thresher and Waitrose are all partial to hyperbole and flights
    of fancy and Oddbins and Majestic lists, both put together by the people
    whose only interest is to sell the wines, are subjective and biased.

6   2008 Examples are Pelorus Sparkling Wine NV £17.99 (bulk buy at £11.99),
    Dubois Caron Champagne £17.99 (bulk £11.99), Les Foncanelles

Vermentino/Chardonnay 2005 £4.99 (bulk £3.33), Zenato Soave Classico 2005 £7.99 (bulk £5.33), Selva Capuzza Lugana 2005 £7.49 (bulk £4.99), Femar 'People' Frascati Superiore 2005 £8.99 (bulk £5.99), Muso Tratta La Vis Sauvignon Blanc 2005 £9.99 (bulk £6.66) and Dona Dominga Old Vines Sauvignon Blanc 2006 £6.99 (bulk £4.66). These are all decent wines, which I (at the 3-for-the-price-of-2 discounted price), rated highly. The fact remains, however, that the single bottle prices are inflated, fatuous, and phoney.

7 *Guardian* in April 2007.

8 One of the UK's biggest wine importers and retail suppliers with a £100-million turnover), in conversation with the author.

9 Sold in Britain by organic wine merchant Vintage Roots of Berkshire.

10 The 1996 Alsace Klevener (£33), 1998 Walch Pinot Bianco (£25), 1995 Sandalford Verdelho (£25), 1989 Léoville-Las-Cases (£180), 1996 Morey St Denis Dujac (magnum £140), 1988 Richebourg Jean-Gros (£180), 1986 Barbaresco Sori San Lorenzo Gaja (£240), or the 1996 Goldwater Waiheke Cabernet Sauvignon/Merlot (£67). The 1982 Château Pétrus (£8,515 the jeroboam, a mere touch more than its international auction valuation) no reviewer saw fit to point out either.

11 I am especially aggrieved with this restaurant critic's cavalier treatment of the two Vietnamese restaurants in Shoreditch for which I manage the wine lists. Wine lovers admire the lists at both places, short though they are, containing as they do some gorgeous New World wines, and Cây Tre's list is not mentioned at all and as for the Viet Grill's list it is dismissed by Campion with 'Much is made of wine-matching on the menu but it is hard to resist the allure of a cold beer.'

12 Gary Jones, a Raymond Blanc protégé, rejoined forces as Executive Head Chef in August 1999.

13 When, in October 2007, I asked Jancis about this wine and the spat surrounding it regarding herself and Robert Parker she told me: 'I'm a hate figure now to Parker website users. All men of course. I'm sure they don't know who I am.'

ACKNOWLEDGEMENTS

I would like to thank the several editors and publishers who have, though I retained copyright, published some of the material covered in this book (though almost always in a different form than that published here). These include the *Guardian*, The English Speaking Union, Media Discourse, *Malcolm Gluck's Brave New World*, superplonk.com, and *Waitrose Food Illustrated*.